European and American Wind and Percussion Instruments

James M. Borders European and American Wind and Percussion Instruments:
Catalogue of the Stearns Collection of Musical Instruments,
University of Michigan

Ann Arbor The University of Michigan Press

Camera-ready copy for this volume has been provided by the author.

Copyright © by the University of Michigan 1988
All rights reserved
Published in the United States of America by
The University of Michigan Press
Manufactured in the United States of America

Library of Congress Cataloging-in-Publication Data

Borders, James M. (James Matthew), 1953–
    European and American wind and percussion instruments : catalogue of the Stearns collection of musical instruments, University of Michigan / James M. Borders.
       p. cm.
    Bibliography : p.
    Includes index.
    ISBN 0-472-10070-X :
    1. Wind instruments—Catalogs and collections—Michigan—Ann Arbor. 2. Percussion instruments—Catalogs and collections—Michigan—Ann Arbor. 3. Stearns, Frederick, 1831–1907—Musical instrument collections—Catalogs. 4. University of Michigan. School of Music. I. University of Michigan. School of Music. II. Title. III. Title: Stearns collection of musical instruments.
ML462.A5U5 1988
788′.0074′017435—dc19   88-10657
                                                                           CIP
                                                                           MN

Contents

6 **Preface**

8 **Acknowledgments**

Aerophones
- 9 *Fipple Flutes*
- 12 *Flageolets*
- 13 *Whistles*
- 16 *Ocarinas*
- 17 *Transverse Flutes*
- 28 *Panpipes*
- 29 *Fifes*
- 31 *Clarinets*
- 41 *Basset Horns*
- 43 *Tenor and Bass Clarinets*
- 46 *Saxophones*
- 48 *Single Reed Horns*
- 49 *Oboes*
- 53 *Tenor and Baritone Oboes*
- 56 *Bassoons*
- 60 *Contrabassoons*
- 62 *Sarrusophones*
- 64 *Double Reed Pipes*
- 66 *Bagpipes*
- 72 *Free Reed Instruments*
- 75 *Cornetti*
- 77 *Serpents, Ophimonocleides, Russian Bassoon, Ophicleides*
- 80 *Signal Horns*
- 84 *Horns*
- 90 *Bugles*
- 96 *Reproductions of Roman Instruments*
- 98 *Trumpets*
- 110 *Trombones*
- 120 *Cornets*
- 129 *Alto Horns*
- 132 *Baritones*
- 135 *Euphoniums*
- 138 *Tubas*
- 141 *Trombe*
- 149 *Systems of Valves*

Membranophones
- 150 *Timpani*
- 151 *Tubular Drums*
- 153 *Frame Drums*
- 155 *Friction Drums*
- 156 *Singing Membranes*

Idiophones
- 157 *Concussion Sticks, Castinets, Cymbals*
- 158 *Musical Coins, Tuning Fork, Xylophones, Glockenspiels*
- 160 *Bells*
- 164 *Crescents, Rattles*
- 166 *Nail Violin, Jew's Harp, Blown Plaques*

167 **Bibliography**

168 **Index 1**

170 **Index 2**

Preface

The University of Michigan Stearns Collection is one of the largest collections of musical instruments in the United States. Comprising more than two thousand items from all over the world, it is an extraordinary research and teaching asset of the School of Music. The Collection is named in honor of Frederick Stearns (1831-1907), a manufacturer of pharmaceuticals who donated 904 instruments to the University in 1899. Since then, thanks to four generations of donors and enthusiastic patrons, the Collection has grown in size and scope, making necessary the publication of a third catalogue. (The first *Catalogue of Stearns Collection of Musical Instruments* was compiled by Professor Albert A. Stanley of the School of Music and published in 1918; a second, revised edition was issued three years later.) This volume is devoted to Western European and American wind and percussion instruments.

The catalogue is organized into three sections following the typology of the Sachs-Hornbostel system: aerophones, wind instruments in which the vibrating element is a column of air enclosed in a tube or receptacle; membranophones, instruments in which the vibrator is a stretched membrane; and idiophones, instruments in which the substance of the body is the sound-producing agent. Under these headings, instruments with like attributes are grouped together, then further distinguished according to mechanical features, size, or shape, instruments of the most common size or shape being described first. Similar instruments are listed in order of accession number and, in the case of keyed woodwinds and brass, from the fewest to the most keys. (Index 2 is arranged according to accession number.)

Each instrument is separately identified and described. The identification is made in a series of line items, as follows:

Line 1: Accession number.
Line 2: Name, alternate name, remarks concerning authenticity in parentheses; Pitch, transposing instruments, for example, clarinets in A, are so designated (lowest-sounding note intended by the maker in parentheses).
Line 3: Provenance and approximate date of manufacture.
Line 4: Maker's name, shop, or dealer.

The description of each instrument is made in a short prose paragraph. The first sentence relates: (a) the number of sections which comprise the fully assembled instrument irrespective of alternate, substitute, or missing sections—remarks pertaining to the sections appear in parentheses (sections are numbered sequentially from the top, i.e. the section nearest the player's mouth not counting the mouthpiece, bocal, or staple, to the bottom); (b) the material of which the body is made; (c) whether the body is decoratively turned, carved, or otherwise decorated. Ferrules or other mounts are described in the first sentence following a semicolon; sections of an instrument made of material different from that of the main corpus, such as the brass gooseneck and bell section of a bass clarinet in maple, are described in a separate sentence.

The following sentence relates the number and type of keys, valves (three assumed), or other mechanical pitch-changing devices; key metal; shape of key flaps (with references to drawings in other catalogues see Bibliography, p. 167) and how the keys are attached to the body. Other noteworthy features of the pitch-changing devices—such as unusual key mechanisms or arrangements of keys, ornate key touches, types of tuning slides, etc.—or the instrument as a whole—for example, the presence and number of tuning holes in the bell section of an oboe, or the location of twinned tone holes—are described in a separate sentence. (Tone holes and keys are identified according to standard fingerings. Thus the abbreviation "R1" designates the tone hole, and "R1 key" the key, controlled by the right hand, index finger.) The descriptions conclude with information about the playing pitch of an instrument, whether high, low, or measured in Hertz (a' = 440 Hz.) when such information can be ascertained. Remarks pertaining to accessories and the condition of an instrument are found at the end of the paragraph.

Each entry concludes with measurements which are intended to furnish the reader with a general impression of the size and shape of the object. Overall length in centimeters is generally provided (the sounding length of transverse flutes, i.e. from the center of the embouchure hole to the end of the instrument, appears in parentheses); other measurements, such as width (W), height (H), diameter (∅) in centimeters, and bore diameter in millimeters (∅, I∅, O∅), depend on the type of instrument being described. (Bore measurements of cornets, trumpets, and other brass instruments were taken inside tuning slides unless otherwise specified; measurements of clarinet bores were taken between L_2 and L_3 of the upper body section.) Photographs of complete instruments, along with certain details, accompany many of the descriptions.

Pitch designations used in the descriptions are made in accordance with the following system:

c'''	two octaves above c'
c''	one octave above c'
c'	middle c
c	one octave below c'
C	two octaves below c'
CC	three octaves below c'.

Following each description, any inscription on the instrument is transcribed exactly as it appears on the object. The location of the inscription or inscriptions is also specified. Inscriptions are printed in upper and lower case Roman type; engravings in cursive script are not differentiated typographically. The division of an inscription into lines is indicated by slashes; conjectural additions appear in square brackets. Textual descriptions of makers' marks appear in square brackets, other information in parentheses.

Acknowledgments

This catalogue could not have been completed without the help of a number of people. Thomas MacCracken, Richard Rephann of the Yale Collection of Musical Instruments, Laurence Libin of the New York Metropolitan Museum of Art, and Robert Eliason, former Curator of Musical Instruments at the Henry Ford Museum, offered sound advice at an early stage. Bob's observations concerning lower brass instruments were particularly valuable. William Waterhouse, Phillip Young, Lloyd Farrar, and Grant Moore also made useful suggestions.

Robert Vernon, whose insights as an instrument builder were invaluable, and Samuel Wiersma assisted me in making the descriptions. Bob also created or adapted the measuring devices used in the project. The students of the University of Michigan School of Music who participated in classes and seminars on the history of musical instruments, particularly John Hancock, Arturo Gonzales, and Stephen Davison, have each contributed something to this book. The late Robert Warner, Professor Emeritus of the School of Music and former Director of the Stearns Collection, in many ways set the stage for this volume.

A number of people helped transform my descriptions into a catalogue. William Greene took all the photographs; Carol Hinote assisted him. Catherine Schwab oversaw the photographic work and, along with my wife, Ann Marie Borders, proofread the typescript. The design of the catalogue is the work of Prof. Dwayne Overmyer of the University of Michigan School of Art.

I owe a special debt of gratitude to my colleague, William P. Malm, Director of the Stearns Collection and Professor of Ethnomusicology, who first encouraged me to explore the treasures of the Stearns Collection.

This project has had the generous support of the National Endowment for the Arts and the Horace H. Rackham Graduate School of the University of Michigan. In addition, I wish to thank Dean Paul Boylan of the School of Music, who made available funds and research facilities for this project.

Aerophones　　　*Fipple Flutes*

503
Treble Recorder in A
Paris, 19th century
Prosper Colas

Three boxwood sections; rosewood beak mouthpiece and terminal mount; horn ferrules. Undercut tone holes. (a' 450)

2: PROSPER COLAS / A / PARIS

39.2 (34.8) cm.

504
Alto Recorder in F
Paris? 19th century
No inscription (Prosper Colas?)

Three boxwood sections; beak mouthpiece, terminal mount, and ferrules in horn. Undercut tone holes. Not playable. Very similar to 503.

46.8 (41.8) cm.

505
Alto Recorder in F
Leipzig, 18th century, second quarter
Johann Cornelius Sattler (fl. ca. 1718-1745)

Three dark stained boxwood sections with decorative turnings. Curved windway. Mouthpiece and windway restored (see Warner 1970: 74-76). (a' 415)

1, 2: [three-pointed crown mark] / I.C.E.
　　　SATTLER / S
3: [three-pointed crown]
(see ibid., p. 75)

49.3 (44) cm.

504　　505

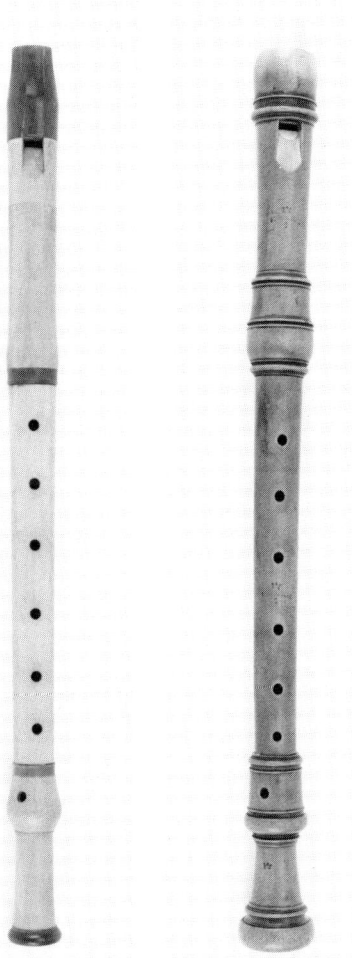

506

Alto Recorder in F
Nürnberg, late 17th / early 18th century
Jacob Denner (1681-1735)

Composite instrument (18th-century [?] replacement head section). Three boxwood sections with decorative turnings; horn ferrule. Restored (see Warner 1968: 88-96); replica of original head section (506 A). (a' 430 with replacement head section; a' 415 with modern replica)

2, 3: (within unfurled banner)
  I. DENNER / (below banner)
  I [tree mark] D
(see ibid., p. 91)

50.1 (44) cm. (either head section)

507
Alto Recorder in G
Germany (Nürnberg?), late 17th / early 18th century
N. I. (?) Fische

Three dark stained plum or pearwood sections with decorative turnings; horn ferrule (replacement). Repaired crack in foot section (see Warner 1970: 73-74). (a' 415)

1: (within unfurled banner) N.I. FISCHE
(see ibid., p. 69)

45 (39) cm.

576
Bass Recorder in F, 1 key
France? late 17th / early 18th century
Souvé

Four dark stained maple sections with decorative turnings; brass crook; ivory nozzle mouthpiece. One brass key (ornate touch), flat, round flap, mounted in bulbous ring. Restored (see Warner 1970: 70-72). (a′ 415)

1-3: SOUVE / [five-pointed star]
(see ibid., p. 71)

99 (88.2) cm.

508
Treble Beaked Flute in A, 4 keys
Erfurt, mid-19th century
Franz Carl Kruspe (fl. 1829-1885)

Three dark stained boxwood sections; German silver ferrules. Four nickel-plated keys, modern cup type, mounted on pillars. Small thumbhole with German silver bushing; single tuning hole. Restored. (a′ 455)

1-3: [lyre] / KRUSPE / ERFURT / [wheel with six spokes mark]

48.9 (43.6) cm.

502
Alto Beaked Flute in F, 1 key
Milan, 1883
No inscription (Giuseppe Pelitti)

Three painted (simulating ivory) pearwood sections. One brass key, modern cup type, mounted on pillars.

49.1 (46.4) cm.

513
Walking-Stick Fipple Flute in D, 1 key
England? mid-19th century
No inscription

Five stained cocus sections; ivory cap; nickel-plated ferrules (one missing) and terminal mount (missing). One nickel-plated key, shallow cup type, mounted in bulbous ring. Fingerholes of various sizes; two tuning holes. Nickel-plated pillars on either side of head section intended for decorative cord.

87.6 (25.4) cm.

1591 (formerly 513 A)
Walking-Stick Fipple Flute in A, 7 keys
Pest, Hungary, 19th century, second
 quarter
Au. Bleszner

Four sections: boxwood head section and one-piece body, maple mouthpiece/handle and terminal section; horn ferrules; brass terminal mount with steel tip. Seven silver keys, shallow cup type, shell-shaped flaps, mounted in knobs or in channels cut directly into the tube. Ivory-bushed thumbhole; tone holes with keys brass-bushed; two tuning holes.

2, 3: [coat of arms] / AU. BLESZNER / IN PEST

89.9 (37) cm.

493
Galoubet (B♭)
France? early 19th century
No inscription

Pearwood with decorative turnings; brass band below beak mouthpiece. Two fingerholes and thumbhole of nearly equal size.

38.4 (31.9) cm.

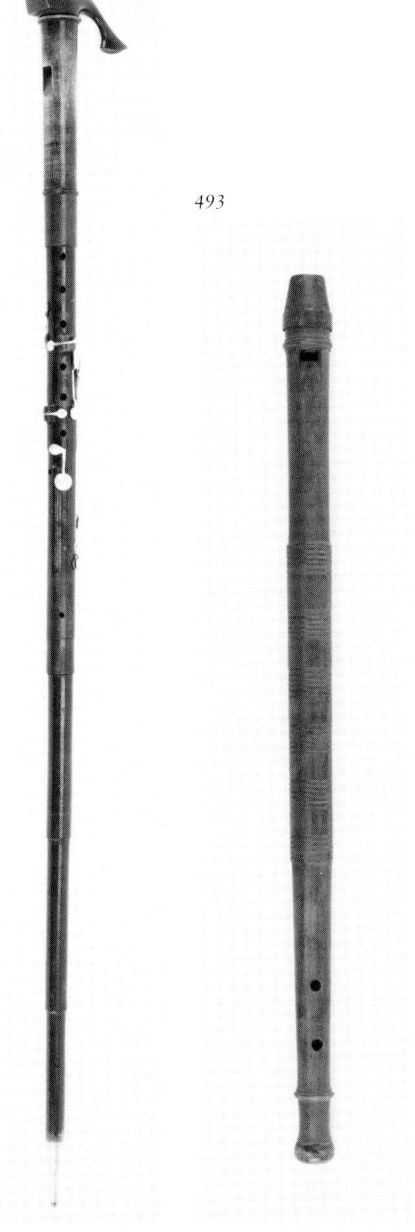

Flageolets

**509
French Flageolet (C)**, 1 key
Lyon, 19th century, first quarter
F. Tabard (fl. ca. 1820-1848)

Four boxwood sections with decorative turnings; horn nozzle mouthpiece, ferrules, and terminal mount. One brass key, flat, square flap, mounted on pillars attached to an elliptical brass plate.

4: [mark] / F. TABARD / [mark]

48.6 (30.3) cm.

**511
Flûte d'Accord,** 7 keys
Germany? mid-19th century
No inscription

Two rosewood sections; nickel-plated ferrules. Seven nickel-plated keys, contoured to the body, round flaps, mounted on pillars. Corpus with two parallel conical tubes sounding a major third apart; seven pairs of tone holes, twinned thumbhole; tuning hole, left side.

42.5 (31.5) cm.

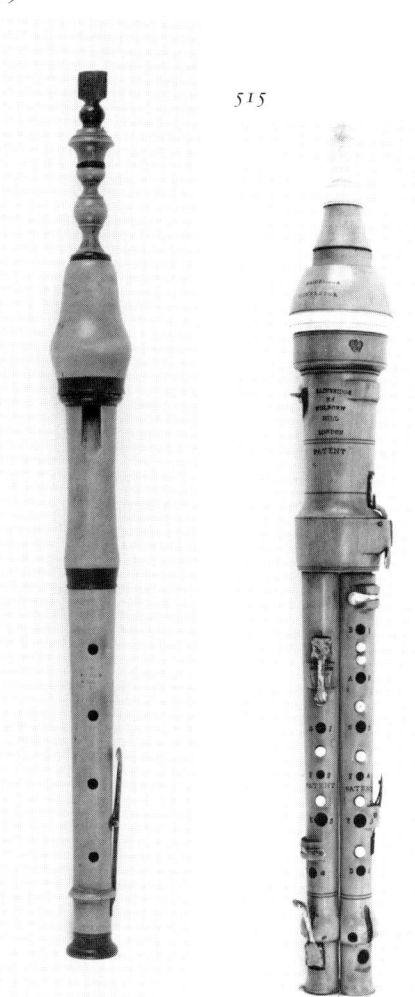

509

515

515
Double Flageolet (C), 9 keys
London, 19th century, first decade
William Bainbridge (fl. 1802-1835)

Four boxwood sections (including two body sections of equal length) with decorative turnings; ivory ferrules, nozzle mouthpiece, spacing studs, and terminal mounts. Nine silver keys (one missing), flat flaps (Young, Design F), mounted in knobs and rings. Sections 2, 3, and 4 stamped: PATENT; fingerings and pitches stamped on both body sections. Shutter (controlled by R th. key) diverts the flow of air from the right tube.

2: [crown mark] / BAINBRIDGE / 35 / HOLBORN / HILL / LONDON
1: BAINBRIDGE / INVENTOR

39.8 (31.6) cm.

516
Double Flageolet, 14 keys
London, ca. 1850
D'Almaine & Co. (fl. 1836-1866)

Six cocus sections; ivory nozzle mouthpiece; silver-plated ferrules (one missing) and terminal mounts (missing). Fourteen silver-plated keys, early cup type, mounted in knobs and partial rings. Fingerings and resultant pitches stamped on body sections. Shutter (controlled by R th. key) diverts the flow of air from the right tube.

2: (on cartouche) D'ALMAINE & CO / LATE / GOULDING & D'ALMAINE / SOHO SQUARE / LONDON
3-6: [mark] / D'ALMAINE & CO

67.5 (56.3) cm.

Whistles

486
Whistle Flute (Tin Whistle) (D), Side-blown
Germany? early 20th century
No inscription

Nickel-plated tin. Six fingerholes of various sizes.

33.6 cm.

1471 (formerly 486 A)
Whistle Flute (C), Side-blown
U.S.A.? early 20th century
No inscription

Two nickel-plated brass sections. Six fingerholes of various sizes. Body section stamped: C.

42.3 cm.

487
Whistle Flute (Tin Whistle) (D), End-blown
Germany? early 20th century
No inscription

Nickel-plated tin body; turned oak mouthpiece. Fingerholes of various sizes.

35.7 cm.

486

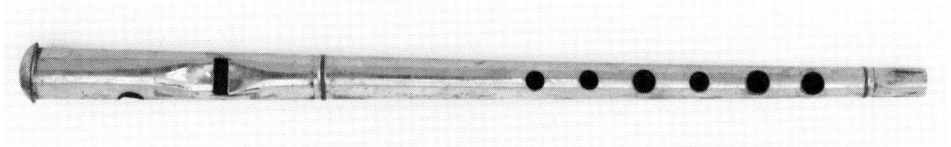

1507
Whistle Flute, End-blown
Maker and provenance unknown

Two steel sections (mouthpiece missing). Six fingerholes and thumbhole. Crude.

28.3 cm. (extant section)

1648
Whistle Flute (C), End-blown
Maker and provenance unknown

Brass. Six fingerholes. Crude.

32.2 cm.

489
Omnitonic Whistle Flute, End-blown
Germany? late 19th century
Maker unknown

Six nickel-plated tin tubes in a circular arrangement, plated tin band at the top, soldered at the base; separate mouthpipe. Fundamentals,stamped: C, D, E♭, E, F, F♯. Fingerholes of various sizes.

33.9 cm.

512
Walking-Stick Whistle Flute (D), Side-blown; **Ocarina**
Paris, late 19th century
Ch. Mathieu (fl. ca. 1890)

Two sections: painted (dark brown, simulating wood grain) tin with metal ocarina handle molded in the shape of a small bird, painted (dark brown) bamboo terminal section with German silver tip. Six fingerholes; two tuning holes. Ocarina with ten tone holes, solmization syllable cast next to each.

1: CH. MATHIEU / MQUE DEPOSÉE / (within lyre) [monogram:] C M / MÉDAILLES D'OR / BREVETÉ / S.G.D.G.

91.2 (26.3) cm.
Ocarina: 11 cm.

575
Walking-Stick Whistle Flute (D), End-blown
Paris, late 19th century
Ch. Mathieu (fl. ca. 1890)

Two sections: painted (dark brown, simulating wood grain) tin with nickel-plated tin cap, painted (dark brown) cane terminal section with German silver tip. Six fingerholes; two tuning holes.

Cap: CH. MATHIEU [mark]

91.3 (26.4) cm.

452
Whistle
Spain? 19th century
Maker unknown

Earthenware; in the shape of a water pot.

H: 103 mm.   ⌀: 70 mm.

466
Dog Whistle
Germany? 19th century
Maker unknown

Glazed earthenware, grey with blue and green spots; in the shape of a dog.

L: 64 mm.   H: 54 mm.

467 to 471
Dog Whistles
Germany? 19th century
Maker unknown

Glazed earthenware, grey with blue and/or brown spots; in the shape of dogs. These whistles were apparently produced in the same shop.

L: apprx. 75 mm.   H: apprx. 67 mm.

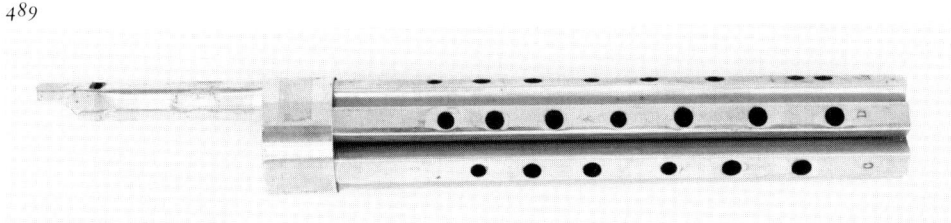

489

452

466

473
Cuckoo Call
Germany? 19th century
Maker unknown

Painted (grey, blue, black) and glazed earthenware; in the shape of a peasant boy holding a cuckoo in his right hand and an alphorn in his left, sitting on a tree stump. One fingerhole.

H: 102 mm.   ⌀ (base): 38.5 mm.

474
Bird Call
Switzerland? 19th century
Maker unknown

Cylindrical body in pine; pine piston (raises fundamental a semitone) at the end of the tube. Piston turns a painted wooden bird.

L: 170 mm.   ⌀: 28 mm.

587
"Flûte Harmonique"
Paris, late 19th century
Maurice Baduel (fl. ca. 1876)

Painted (black) metal wind chest and mouthpiece; thirty painted (black) brass flue pipes; threaded couplers of nickel-plated brass; white and black ivory buttons. Pipes activated by pistons arranged in keyboard sequence; compass: g to c′′′. Painted (black) wooden pedestal (587 A), lyre motif, brass rods with blue silk insets. Oval medallion at either end, cast (left): FLUTE HARMONIQUE BADUEL & LOUVRIER / (within unfurled banner) BREVETES S.G.D.G. / (below banner) PARIS; (right): M [lyre] B.

L: 54.5 cm.
Pedestal, L: 46.6 cm.   H: 17 cm.

481
"Magic Flute"
U.S.A., ca. 1900
Maker unknown

Tin. Upper portion of instrument held between teeth and lips, whistle sounds one tone as performer hums.

L: 6.6 cm.

587

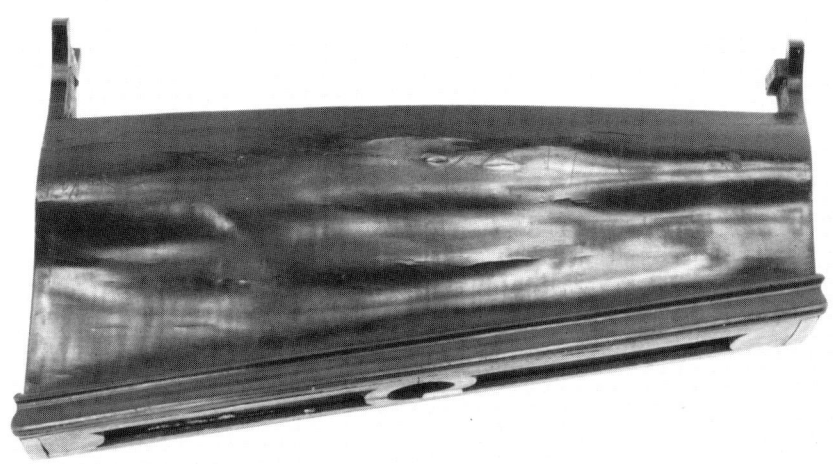

1822
"Humantone"
U.S.A., mid-20th century
Gretch Co. (founded 1883)

Molded brown plastic. Same principle of activation as 481.

L: 11.1 cm.

Ocarinas

482
Ocarina (A)
Germany? late 19th century
R. Teschner

Painted (black, gold) and glazed clay. Eight fingerholes, two thumbholes. Numbers 1 through 10 painted next to tone holes.

12.8 cm.

483
Ocarina (D)
Vienna, late 19th century
H. Fiehn (fl. 1877-1914)

Painted (black, gold) and glazed clay. Eight fingerholes, two thumbholes. Numbers and resultant pitches painted next to tone holes. Handle stamped: D / 5. Two embossed gold seals, one with maker's insignia plus: H. FIEHN / VIENNA / MADE IN AUSTRIA; the other featuring a medallion from an exhibition in Sydney, Australia, 1879.

15.6 cm.

484
Ocarina (F)
Paris, ca. 1890
A. E. Mazzetti

Painted (brown, black) clay; nickel-plated brass piston; cork stopper. Eight fingerholes, one thumbhole. Fully extended, the piston lowers the fundamental a semitone.

(On cartouche) FABRICAN / A. E. MEZZETTI
 à Paris

20.2 cm. (28 cm., piston fully extended)

485
Ocarina (F)
Paris, late 19th century
Cie Gle. de L'Ocarina

Painted (reddish brown) clay. Seven fingerholes, no thumbholes.

CIE GLE DE L'OCARINA / BREVETÉE S.G.D.G.
 PARIS

30 cm.

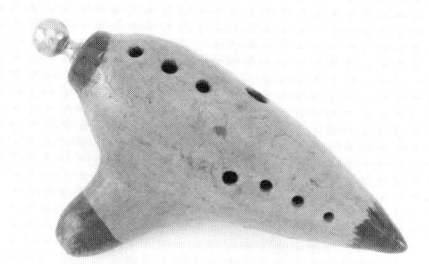
484

Transverse Flutes

558
Transverse Flute (D), 1 key
Milan, 18th century, third quarter
Carlo Palanca (fl. ca. 1775)

Originally four boxwood sections (head and upper body sections extant). Ivory ferrule (fine turnings) and cap.

1, 2: CARLO / PALANCA

40.8 cm. overall (31.7 cm., center of embouchure hole to center of the third tone hole)

560
Transverse Flute (D), 1 key
London, mid-18th century
Thomas Cahusac (fl. ca. 1755-1795)

Four dark stained boxwood sections; ivory ferrules (fine turnings) and cap. One silver key, contoured to the body, square flap, mounted in bulbous ring. Tenon of head section restored in 1985.

1-4: CAHUSAC / LONDON

61.7 (53.5) cm.

561
Transverse Flute (D), 1 key
London, 18th century, last quarter
Proser (fl. 1777-1795)

Composite instrument. Four boxwood sections; ivory ferrules and cap (modern replacements). One brass key, flat flap (Young, Design E), mounted in bulbous ring. Lower body and foot sections are 19th-century replacements, stamped: LAWSON / LONDON.

1, 2: PROSER

60.8 (54.1) cm.

1592
Transverse Flute (D), 1 key
New York, mid-19th century
Maker unknown

Four rosewood sections; nickel-plated ferrules; wooden cap without screw cork. One nickel-plated key, modern cup type, mounted in bulbous ring. Restored prior to acquisition in 1964. Stamped (1, 2): N. YORK.

61.2 (53.4) cm.

558

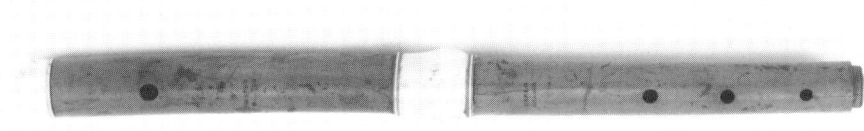

560

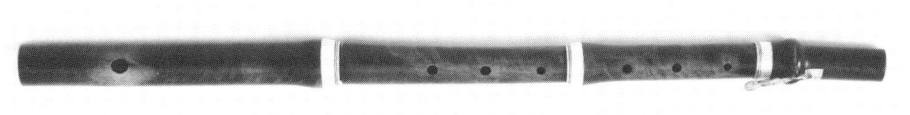

558 detail

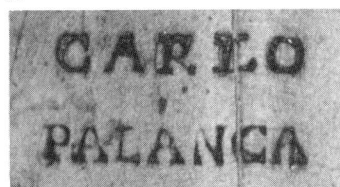

560 detail

1908
Transverse Flute (D), 1 key
New York, ca. 1863
Firth, Pond & Co.

Four rosewood sections; ivory ferrules (one missing) and cap without screw cork. One German silver key, flat, round flap, mounted in bulbous ring.

2: FIRTH POND & CO. / FRANKLIN SQE / N-YORK / GERMAN SILVER
1, 3, 4: FIRTH POND & CO. / N-YORK

60.7 (53) cm.

1909
Transverse Flute in F, 1 key
Germany? mid-19th century
No inscription

Four cocus sections; German silver ferrules. One key (missing), mounted in bulbous ring. Cork stopper.

50.1 (43.5) cm.

1910
Transverse Flute (D), 1 key
Germany? early 20th century
Maker unknown (Lyon and Healy, dealer [founded 1864])

Four rosewood sections; German silver ferrules (one missing); wooden cap. One German silver key, modern cup type, mounted on pillars.

1: Lyon and Healy / Chicago.

61.2 (52.9) cm.

1911
Transverse Flute (D), 1 key
U.S.A., mid-19th century
Maker unknown (Klemm & Bro., dealer [1840-1880])

Four stained boxwood sections; horn ferrules; brass band on foot section (replacement). Cork stopper. One brass key, flat, round flap, mounted in bulbous ring. Poor condition.

1: KL[EMM & B]RO. / PHIL[ADELPHIA]

60 (53.5) cm.

571
Transverse Flute (D), 4 keys
Paris, 1809
Claude Laurent (fl. 1806-1857)

Four glass sections with finely ground interior surface; silver ferrules with metal tenons; rose-cut rock crystal cap. Four silver keys, contoured to the body, circular flaps, mounted on pillars attached to elliptical plates. Cemented glass disk instead of cork. Alternate upper body section. Mahogany case with brass fittings (571 A).

Ferrule, head section: Laurent / à Paris / 1809

62.5(55.3); 62.1 (54.8) cm.

1473 (formerly 561 A)
Transverse Flute (D), 4 keys
Germany? late 19th century
No inscription

Four rosewood sections (head, tuning barrel, upper, lower body sections); German silver ferrules and bands (two missing). Four German silver keys, modern cup type, mounted on pillars. Brass-lined head section, tuning barrel.

60.5 (52.6) cm.

1498
Transverse Flute (D), 4 keys
New York, 19th century, second quarter
Firth, Hall & Pond (fl. 1832-1848)

Five rosewood sections; ivory ferrules, cap, and screw cork. Four silver keys, early cup (saltspoon) type, mounted in knobs. Brass-lined head section, tuning barrel. Serial number: 3230.

3: FIRTH HALL & POND / FRANKLIN SQE / N-YORK
1, 2, 4, 5: FIRTH HALL & POND / N-YORK

60.4 (52.8) cm.

571

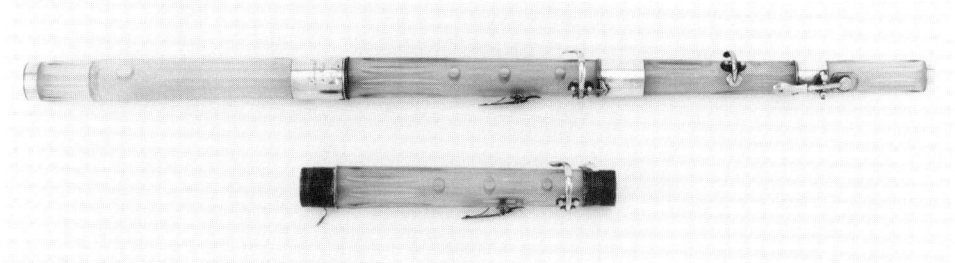

1616
Transverse Flute (D), 4 keys
Germany? late 19th century
No inscription

Four cocus sections (head, tuning barrel, upper, lower body); German silver ferrules. Four German silver keys, modern cup type, mounted on pillars. Brass-lined head section, tuning barrel.

60.8 (52) cm.

1721
Transverse Flute (D), 4 keys
U.S.A.? mid-19th century
No inscription

Four boxwood sections, cap. Four brass keys, early cup (saltspoon) type, mounted in knobs and bulbous ring. Wooden sockets. Crudely repaired.

61.4 (54.2) cm.

1928
Transverse Flute (D), 4 keys
Nürnberg, mid-18th century
J. A. Löhner (fl. ca. 1740)

Four boxwood sections with two alternate upper body sections *(corps de rechange)*; ivory ferrules (fine turnings), cap, and screw cork. Four silver keys (brushed), mounted in knobs and bulbous ring; alternate body sections with brass keys. Wooden case (1928 A).

1, 4: [mark] / JA LÖHNER / A / NÜRNBERG
2A: [mark] / JA. LÖHNER / 5
2B: [mark] / JA. LÖHNER / 6
2C: [mark] / JA. LÖHNER / 7
3: [mark] / JA. LÖHNER

61.8 (54.2); 61.1 (53.5); 60.4 (52.8) cm.

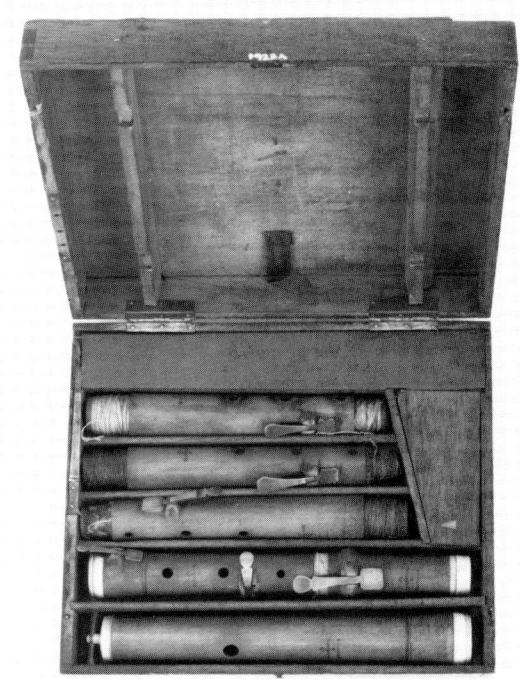

1928 detail

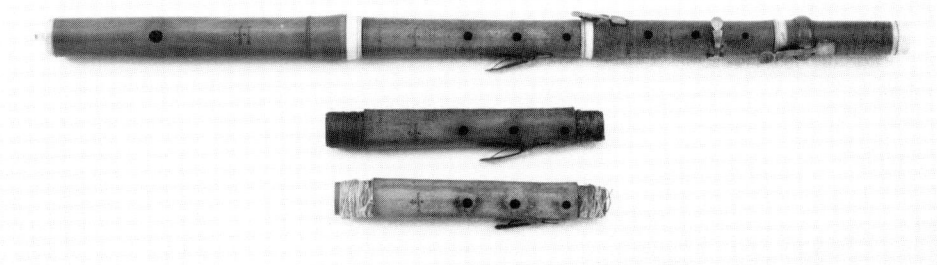

1928

562
Transverse Flute in Bb, 5 keys
London, 19th century, first quarter
Tebaldo Monzani (1762-1839)

Four cocus sections; engraved silver ferrules; cocus cap with silver band. Silver-lined sockets. Five silver keys (one modern replacement) flat, square flaps with crown engravings, mounted in knobs and bulbous ring. Upper and lower body sections stamped: PATENT. Serial number: 1116.

2: [crown mark] / MONZANI & CO. /
   24 DOVER ST. / LONDON / 1116 / B
1, 3, 4: [crown] / MONZANI & CO. / B

76.3 (67) cm.

563
Transverse Flute in F, 6 keys
London, 19th century, first quarter
Tebaldo Monzani (1762-1839)

Three cocus sections; engraved silver ferrules; cocus cap with silver band. Silver-lined sockets. Six silver keys, flat, square flaps with crown engravings, mounted in knobs. Upper and lower body sections stamped: PATENT. Serial number: 1117.

2: [crown mark] / MONZANI & CO. /
   24 DOVER St. / LONDON / 1117 / F
1, 3: [crown] / MONZANI & CO. / F

53.3 (46.8) cm.

562 detail

1500
Transverse Flute (D), 7 keys
New York, 19th century, second quarter
Firth, Hall & Pond (fl. 1832-1848)

Five rosewood sections; vulcanized rubber tuning barrel (replacement); ivory ferrules (fine turnings), cap, and screw cork. Seven silver keys, early cup (saltspoon) type, four knob or ring mounted, three on pillars (recessed seating of pads suggest these keys were later additions). Brass-lined head section, tuning barrel. Serial number: 3159.

3: FIRTH HALL & POND / FRANKLIN SQE /
   N-YORK
5: FIRTH HALL & POND / N-YORK

60.6 (53.5) cm.

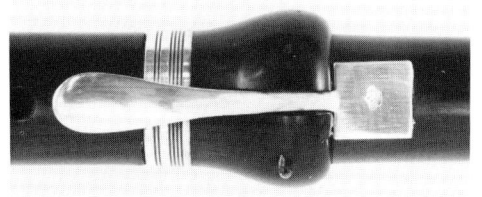

562 detail

562

563

564
Transverse Flute (C), 7 keys
London, late 18th century
Richard Potter (1728-1806)

Five boxwood sections; ivory ferrules (fine turnings), cap, and screw cork. Seven silver keys, pewter plugs, one mounted in a brass saddle, six knob mounted, channels lined with brass shims. Three numbered ring gradations (6 mm. apart) on tuning barrel; calibrated screw cork. Brass-lined head section, tuning barrel. Ferrules on head and foot sections stamped: PATENT.

2: POTTER / JOHNSON'S COURT / FLEET STREET / LONDON
3, 4, 5: POTTER / LONDON

67.3 (59.5) cm.

1499
Transverse Flute in F, 7 keys
Paris, late 19th century
Buffet, Crampon & Cie (founded 1836)

Five grenadilla sections; German silver ferrules. German silver-lined sockets and reinforced tenons. Seven German silver keys, modern cup type, mounted on pillars. Metal-lined tuning barrel. Serial number: M 685.

1,3,5: [lyre] / BUFFET / Crampon & Cie / A PARIS / [monogram:] B C / MADE IN FRANCE / LP
2: [monogram:] B C / MADE IN FRANCE / LP

52.2 (45.4) cm.

565
Transverse Flute (C), 8 keys
London, 19th century, last quarter
John Henry Ebblewhite (fl. 1840-1901)

Five cocus sections; engraved nickel-plated ferrules; cocus cap. Eight nickel-plated brass keys, five early cup (saltspoon) type (two missing), three R4 soft metal plugs (c′, c♯′, e′♭; one missing), countersunk metal plate seating, knob mounted. Large tone holes.

1, 2, 3: J. H. EBBLEWHITE / MAKER / 4 & 5 HIGH ST. / ALDGATE LONDON

65.8 (57.1) cm.

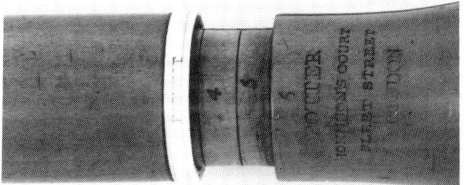

564 detail

564

565

573
Transverse Flute (C), 8 keys
New York, 19th century, second quarter
C. Peloubet (fl. ca. 1829-1835)

Five ivory sections; silver ferrules (one missing), cap, and screw cork. Silver band over embouchure hole (W: 6.2 cm.). Eight silver keys, five flat, round flaps with soldered key shanks (Heyde 1978: 145, Design 29), three R4 soft metal plugs (c', c'♯, e'♭) countersunk metal plate seating, mounted in knobs and partial square ring. Serial number: 252.

3: P. H. TAYLOR'S / 252 / APPROVED / PATTERN / C. PELOUBET / NEW-YORK / TWILL'S / MUSIC SALOON / N-YORK
1: P. H. TAYLOR'S / APPROVED / PATTERN
4, 5: C. PELOUBET / NEW-YORK

66.7 (59.5) cm.

1651
Transverse Flute (C), 8 keys
U.S.A.? early 20th century
No inscription

Three German silver sections. Eight German silver keys, modern cup type, axle-mounted on pillars. Simple system; cylindrical bore. Fabric covered case (1651 A).

68.9 (61) cm.

1906
Transverse Flute (C), 8 keys
Austria or Germany? mid-19th century
No inscription

Five stained cocus sections; German silver ferrules and cap. Eight German silver keys, modern cup type, mounted on pillars. Brass-lined head section, tuning barrel.

64.8 (56.8) cm.

1912
Transverse Flute (C), 8 keys
London, ca. 1838
William Camp (fl. ca. 1837-1879)

Five cocus sections; nickel-plated ferrules; cocus cap. Eight nickel-plated brass keys, six early cup (saltspoon) type, two R4 soft metal plugs, countersunk metal plate seating, mounted in knobs and partial ring. Walnut case with two metal clasps (1912 A).

3: CAMP / FROM / RUDAL & ROSE / 81 TOTTENHAM CT RD / LONDON
2: CAMP / 81 TOTTENHAM CT RD / LONDON
4, 5: CAMP / LONDON

67.2 (59.4) cm.

1907
Transverse Flute (C), 8 keys
Germany or Austria? mid-19th century
No inscription

Five cocus sections; German silver bands and cap. Eight German silver keys, mounted on pillars. Brass-lined head section, tuning barrel.

69 (59.5) cm.

1913
Transverse Flute (C), 8 keys
Germany, mid-19th century
Maker unknown

Four sections: three cocus, nickel-plated brass head section; nickel-plated ferrules, cap, and band on bottom of tuning barrel. Eight nickel-plated keys, modern cup type, mounted on pillars. Brass-lined head section, tuning barrel.

MADE IN GERMANY / C / LP / [lyre]

69 (60.2) cm.

1912

566
Transverse Flute (C), 9 keys
London, ca. 1809-1817
William Henry Potter (1760-1848)

Five boxwood sections; ivory ferrules (fine turnings), cap, and screw cork. Nine silver keys, pewter plugs, one mounted in a brass saddle, eight in wooden knobs. Three numbered ring gradations (6 mm. apart) on tuning barrel; calibrated screw cork. Brass-lined head section, tuning barrel.

2: WILLM HENY POTTER / JOHNSON'S
   COURT / FLEET STREET / LONDON
3, 4, 5: WILLM HENY / POTTER

67.1 (59.2) cm.

567
Transverse Flute (B), 9 keys
London, mid-19th century
G. C. Payne (fl. 1808-1835)

Five cocus sections; silver ferrules. Nine silver keys, early cup (saltspoon) type (one missing), mounted in knobs and partial ring.

2, 3: PAYNE / No. 13 Lt.NEWPORT
   St. / LONDON
4: PAYNE / LONDON

69.9 (60.9) cm.

569
Transverse Flute (B), 9 keys
Hannover, mid-19th century
Heinrich Friedrich Meyer (1814-1897)

Two sections: nickel-plated brass body, ivory head section. Nine nickel-plated brass keys, modern cup type, mounted on pillars. B key repaired.

1: [crown] / MEYER / HANNOVER

70 (62.3) cm.

1650
Transverse Flute (C), 9 keys
Graslitz, mid-19th century
Vincent Kohlert Söhne (founded in 1840)

Four ebony sections (head, tuning barrel, upper, lower body); German silver ferrules. Nine German silver keys, modern cup type, mounted on pillars. Alternate $b^\flat$ touch (R1). Brass-lined head section, tuning barrel. Low pitch. Serial number: 8507.

3: V. KOHLERT SONS / MAKERS / GRASLITZ /
   AUSTRIA / [seven medallions from world expositions, three stamped:] CHICAGO,
   PARIS, LONDON

68.8 (60.8) cm.

566 detail

566

569

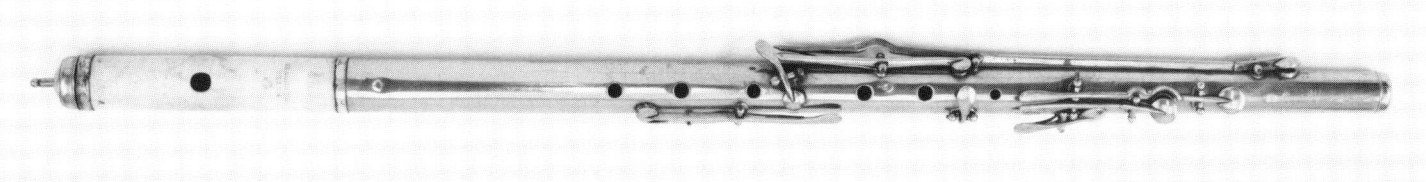

1627
Transverse Flute (C), 10 keys
Paris, early 20th century
Buffet, Crampon & Cie (founded 1836)

Five vulcanized rubber sections; German silver ferrules; German silver cap and screw cork. Ten German silver keys, modern cup type, mounted on pillars (c′, c′♯ keys on clutch). Low pitch.

[lyre] / BUFFET / Crampon & Cie / A PARIS / MADE IN FRANCE / LP

62.6 (55.5) cm.

1914
Transverse Flute (B), 10 keys
Austria? late 19th century
No inscription

Four sections: three cocus, nickel-plated metal head section; nickel-plated ferrules. Ten nickel-plated keys, modern cup type, mounted on pillars. Metal-lined head section, tuning barrel.

69 (62) cm.

1628
Transverse Flute (B), 11 keys
Germany or Austria? mid-19th century
No inscription

Four rosewood sections; nickel-plated ferrules, fittings, cap, and screw cork. Eleven nickel-plated keys, modern cup type, mounted in knobs, channels with metal shims. Variety of touches; raised R3 tone hole. Ferrules fastened with metal pins.

70 (61.7) cm.

1652
Transverse Flute (C), 11 keys, Improved Siccama Diatonic System
London, late 19th century
William Henry Hawkes & Son (fl. 1860-1930)

Four vulcanized rubber sections. Two ring keys (L1, 2: Brille mechanism venting c′♯), plus eleven German silver keys, modern cup type, mounted on pillars. Leather covered case (1652 A).

EXCELSIOR / CLASS / HAWKES & SON / DENMAN STREET / PICADILLY CIRCUS / LONDON

65.7 (57.3) cm.

1628

1652

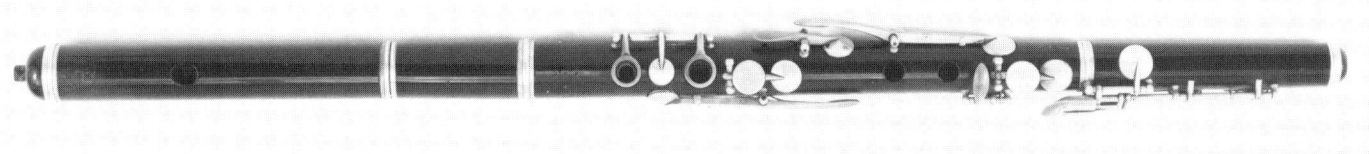

1626
Transverse Flute (B♭), 12 keys
Germany or Austria? mid-19th century
No inscription

Four cocus sections (head, tuning barrel, upper, lower body sections); German silver ferrules and engraved cap. Twelve German silver keys, eight modern cup type, four loose riveted keys (the latter with metal-bushed tone holes), mounted on pillars attached to metal plates. Rollers for b, c′, c′♯ (R4) keys. Brass-lined head section, tuning barrel. Monogram, tuning barrel: M N.

74.6 (65.9) cm.

568
Transverse Flute (A), 13 keys
Bremen, 19th century, second quarter
Johann Josef Roedel (fl. 1810-1840)

Three dark stained boxwood sections; nickel-plated ferrules and cap. Thirteen nickel-plated brass keys, later cup type, mounted in knobs and partial ring, channels with brass shims. Brass rollers for b, c′, c′♯ (R4) keys. Shanks for low b♭ and a keys missing. Tone holes with keys metal-bushed.

[mark] / J. ROEDEL / [mark]

82 (69.2) cm.

570
Transverse Flute (C), Boehm System
Paris, 19th century, third quarter
Thibouville-Buffet (fl. ca. 1868-1873)

Three nickle-plated sections. Sixteen nickel-plated keys, modern cup type (five perforated), axle-mounted on pillars. Boehm (1847) system. Briccialdi B♭ thumb lever; closed g′♯ key.

THIBOUVILLE / BUFFET / A / PARIS

69.1 (60.4) cm.

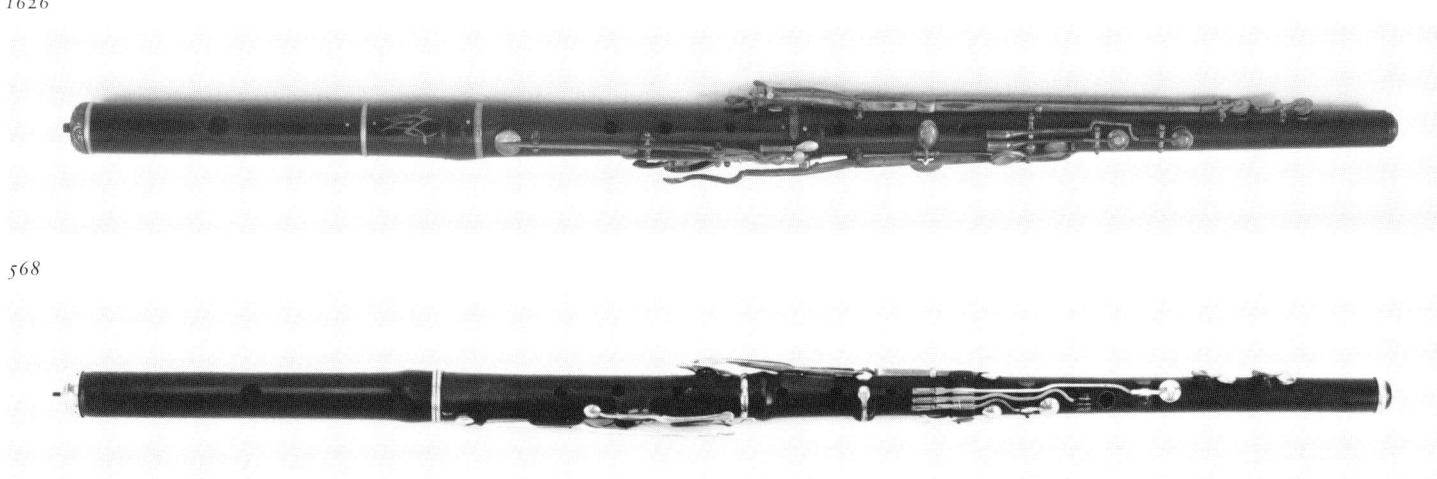

1626

568

1653
Transverse Flute (C), Boehm System
Denver, early 20th century
Jean Mignolet (fl. ca. 1920)

Two sections: nickel-plated body, cocus head section. Ten nickel-plated keys and hole covers, modern cup type, axle-mounted on pillars. Modified Boehm (1847) system. Closed g'♯ key. Fabric-covered case (1653 A).

1: J. MIGNOLET / PARIS-DENVER / FRANCE-COLO[RADO]
2: J. MIGNOLET / DENVER COLO[RADO] / PARIS FRANCE

62.4 (54) cm.

559
Alto Flute in A, 1 key
Germany, mid-18th century
No inscription

Four maple sections; wooden sockets; wooden cap without screw cork. One brass key, flat flap (Young, Design H) mounted in bulbous ring.

76 (67) cm.

583
Piccolo (D), 1 key
England? mid-19th century
No inscription

Two heavily varnished dark wood sections; ivory ferrule. Single German silver key, modern cup type, mounted on pillars. Chamfered tone holes.

29.9 (25.7) cm.

1475
Piccolo (D), 1 key
England? mid-19th century
No inscription

Two rosewood sections with decorative turnings. One nickel-plated key, early cup (saltspoon) type, mounted in bulbous ring. Alternate recorder head section in rosewood.

30.1 (25.1) cm.; 28.1 cm. (as recorder)

585
Piccolo (D), 4 keys
England? mid-19th century
No inscription

Three rosewood sections (head, tuning barrel, body section); German silver ferrules and cap. Four German silver keys, modern cup type, mounted on pillars. Brass-lined head section, tuning barrel.

30.1 (25.7) cm.

559 detail

559

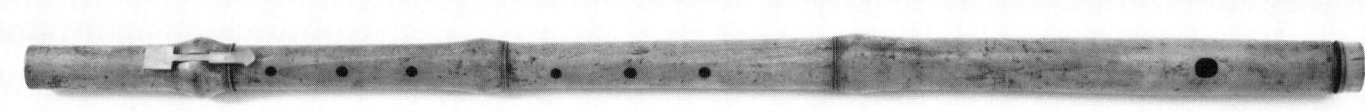

585

1472 (formerly 510 A)
Piccolo (D), 5 keys
England? late 19th century
No inscription

Two boxwood sections, cap; nickel-plated ferrules. Five nickel-plated keys, modern cup type, mounted in knobs. Alternate English flageolet head in two boxwood sections, ivory nozzle mouthpiece; nickel-plated ferrules.

30 (24.7) cm.; 43.35 cm. (as flageolet)

1554
Piccolo (D), 5 keys
England? late 19th century
No inscription

Two boxwood sections, cap; nickel-plated ferrules. Five nickel-plated keys, modern cup type, mounted in knobs. Alternate English flageolet head in two boxwood sections, ivory nozzle mouthpiece; nickel-plated ferrules. Practically identical to 1472.

30.2 (24.75) cm.; 43.5 cm. (as flageolet)

586
Piccolo (D), 6 keys
England? late 19th century
No inscription

Three rosewood sections, cap; German silver ferrules. Six German silver keys, modern cup type, mounted on pillars. Brass-lined head section, tuning barrel.

29.8 (25.1) cm.

574
Walking-Stick Flute (D), 1 key
France? early 19th century
No inscription

Maple, carved to resemble bamboo cane; threaded boxwood cap; brass terminal mount. One wooden key, contoured to the body, round flap, mounted in a channel cut into the tube. Two holes above embouchure hole intended for decorative cord.

72.5 (55.8) cm.

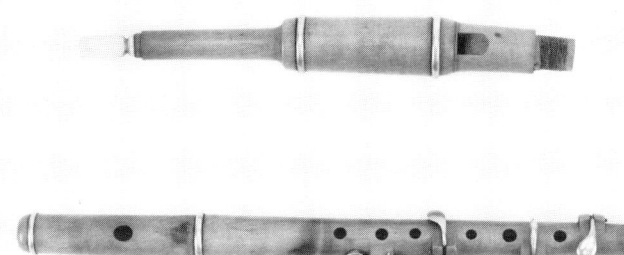

1472

574

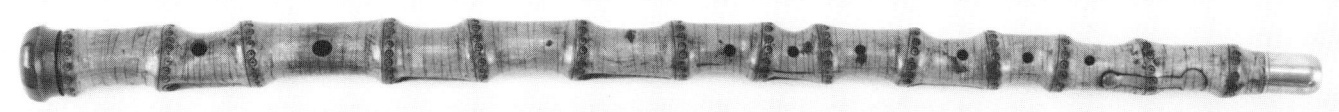

578
Walking-Stick Flute (D), 1 key
Germany? 19th century
No inscription

Four boxwood sections (including terminal section); maple cap; brass ferrules (engraved) and terminal mount with steel tip. One brass key, flat, rectangular flap, mounted in a channel cut into the tube. Two ivory-bushed holes above embouchure hole intended for decorative cord.

83.3 (52.4) cm.

579
Walking-Stick Flute
Italy? 19th century
No inscription

Painted (black, gold) sheet metal with metal bands simulating ferrules. Not playable.

112.7 (101.3) cm.

Panpipes

446
Panpipes
Italy, 19th century
Maker unknown

Single row of five stopped brass pipes, painted (red, green). Raft form. Compass: e'-b'.

IN MI MAGGIORE / PRIMO LAVORO

L: 12.2   W: 6.9 cm.

578

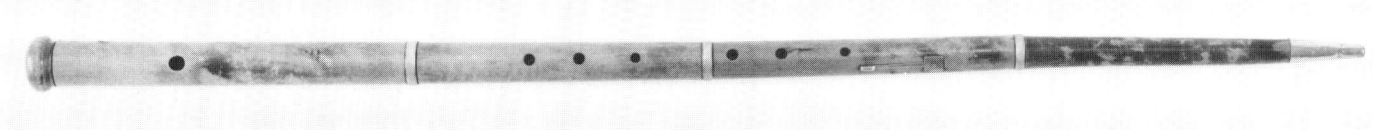

Fifes

580
Fife (A)
U.S.A.? early 20th century
No inscription

Brass-plated steel. Crude.

39.8 (34) cm.

581
Fife (B♭)
Berchtesgaden, mid-19th century
Paul Walch (1810-1873)

Two boxwood sections with decorative turnings; horn ferrules and cap. (a′ 450)

C / PAUL WALCH / BERCHTESGADEN / [mark]

37.6 (30.3) cm.

1552
Fife (B♭)
Maker and provenance unknown

Three rosewood sections, cap; nickel-plated ferrules. One nickel-plated key, cup type, knob mounted. Large tone holes. Brass-lined head section, tuning barrel.

38 (32) cm.

1915
Fife (B♭)
Maker and provenance unknown

Two nickel-plated brass sections. (a′ 420)

43.1 (24.6) cm.

1917
Fife (B♭)
Maker and provenance unknown

Ebony; two German silver ferrules. (a′ 450)

41.6 (34) cm.

581

1552

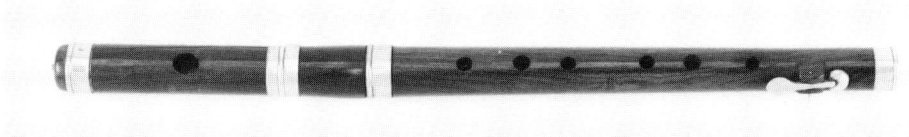

1921
Fife (B♭)
New York, late 19th century
George Cloos (fl. 1860's)

Two nickel-plated brass sections. Vulcanized rubber band over embouchure hole. (a' 440)

GEO. CLOOS / [monogram:] G C

41.3 (33.3) cm.

1922
Fife (B♭)
Maker and provenance unknown

Boxwood; two brass ferrules. Band over embouchure hole missing. (a' 435)

43.4 (34.1) cm.

582
Fife (C)
Maker and provenance unknown

Boxwood; two engraved brass ferrules. Band over embouchure hole missing. Stamped: C.

37.3 (30) cm.

1916
Fife (C)
Maker and provenance unknown

Rosewood; two engraved German silver ferrules and band over embouchure hole. Chamfered tone holes. (a' 415)

37.6 (30.9) cm.

1918
Fife (C)
U.S.A.? 19th century
Maker unknown

Rock maple; two engraved brass ferrules. Band over embouchure hole missing.

36.4 (29.3) cm.

1919
Fife
Maker and provenance unknown

Rosewood; two engraved brass ferrules. (a' 425)

37.7 (31.2) cm.

1920
Fife (C)
Maker and provenance unknown

Ebony; two engraved German silver ferrules. Severe crack.

39.1 (30.5) cm.

1923
Fife (C)
U.S.A.? 19th century
Maker unknown

Rock maple; two engraved brass ferrules. (a' 445)

36.6 (30.3) cm.

1921

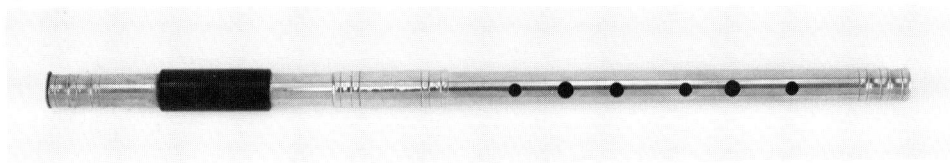

1918

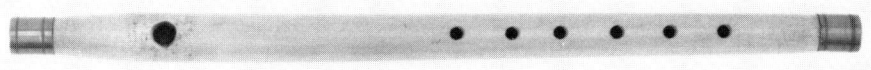

Clarinets

614
Clarinet in E♭, 5 keys
Adorf, late 18th century
J. G. Zencker (fl. ca. 1800)

Five stained boxwood sections; horn ferrules. Five brass keys, flat flaps (Young, Design H), mounted in knobs, square and bulbous rings; one channel lined with brass shims. Rosewood mouthpiece.

2: [crown mark] / G. ZENCKER / IUN: / S
3: S / IN ADORF

42.5 cm.
⌀: 12.6 mm.

614

616
Clarinet in C, 5 keys
London, early 19th century
Valentin Metzler (fl. 1788-1833)

Five boxwood sections with decorative turnings (1, 3); ivory ferrules (fine turnings) and bell mount. Five brass keys, flat, plain square flaps, mounted in square and bulbous rings. One-piece barrel and mouthpiece.

1-4: (within unfurled banner) V. METZLER
    LONDON

59.8 cm. (including mouthpiece)
⌀: 13.5 mm. (top, upper body section)

616

1993
Clarinet in C, 5 keys
England? early 19th century
No inscription

Composite instrument. Five boxwood sections with decorative turnings (3); ivory ferrules (fine turnings) and bell mount; barrel with horn ferrules. Five brass keys, flat flaps (Young, Designs H, S), mounted in square and bulbous rings. Repaired g♯/d″♯ (R4) key.

53.4 cm.
⌀: 14 mm.

616 detail

615
Clarinet in B♭, 6 keys
Dresden, ca. 1810
(Johann) Heinrich Grenser (1764-1813)

Five boxwood sections; ivory ferrules. Six brass keys, flat flaps (Young, Designs C, J), mounted in knobs, square and bulbous rings. Rosewood mouthpiece.

1, 2: [crown of Saxony mark] / H. GRENSER / B / [lambda]
3: B / H. GRENSER / [lambda]
4: [crown of Saxony] / H. GRENSER / DRESDEN / [lambda]

58.6 cm.
⌀: 14.2 mm.

1493 (formerly 616 A)
Clarinet in C, 6 keys
Paris, ca. 1840
Martin Frères (founded 1840)

Five boxwood sections; ivory ferrules (fine turnings) and bell mount (missing). Six brass keys, flat, round flaps, mounted in knob and rings; c′♯/g′′♯ (L4) key mounted on pillars attached to a rectangular brass plate.

1, 2, 4, 5: [fly mark] / MARTIN / [five-pointed star] FRERES [five-pointed star] / A PARIS / [monogram:] M F
3: [monogram:] M F

51.3 cm.
⌀: 14 mm.

1555
Clarinet in C, 7 keys
New York, early 19th century
Edward Riley (fl. 1814-1831)

Five boxwood sections with decorative turnings (2, 3); finely turned ivory ferrules. Seven brass keys, flat flaps (Young, Design C), mounted in knobs and bulbous ring. Lower body section with expanding bore. No mouthpiece.

2, 4: E. RILEY / 29 CHATHAM ST / N-YORK
3: E. RILEY

52.1 cm.
⌀: 13 mm.

618
Clarinet in C, 10 keys
Paris, mid-19th century
Henry Gunckel

Four boxwood sections; ivory ferrules and bell mount. Ten brass keys (straight speaker key in German silver, replacement), shallow cup type, mounted on pillars. Flap f/c′′(R4) key with mopstick-yoke mechanism; crossover g′♯ and a′ keys. Ebony mouthpiece.

1-4: [cornet mark] / (within oval) HENRY GUNCKEL / PARIS / (below oval) [monogram:] H G / C

48.6 cm.
⌀: 14 mm.

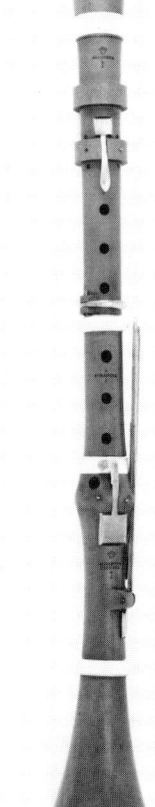

615

615 detail

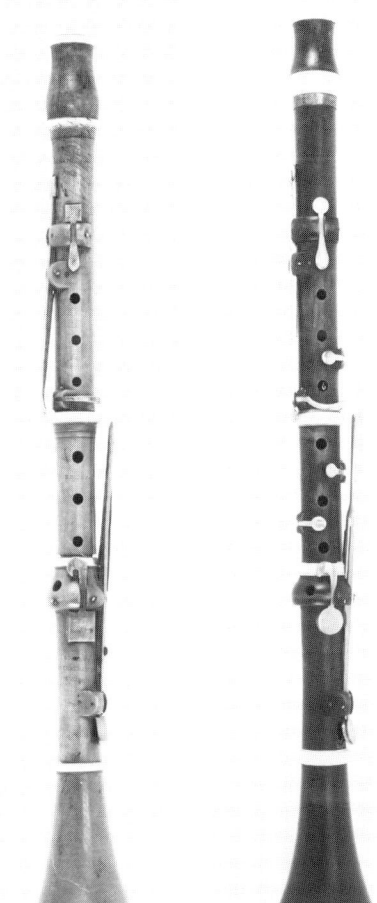

1555   621

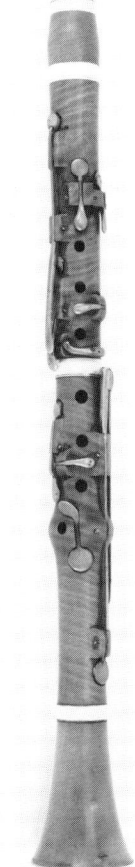

1847

621
Clarinet in A, 10 keys
New York, mid-19th century
C. G. Christman (fl. 1828-1857)

Five dark stained boxwood sections; ivory ferrules (fine turnings) and bell mount; metal band extending and reinforcing tenon on top of upper body section. Ten nickel-plated keys, flat, round flaps, mounted in knobs and bulbous ring. Rosewood mouthpiece.

2, 4, 5: C. G. CHRISTMAN / 404 / PEARL ST / NEW-YORK
1, 3: C. G. CHRISTMAN

61.9 cm.
⌀: 14 mm.

626
Clarinet in B♭, 10 keys
Austria? ca. 1830
No inscription

Three brass sections (threaded joints). Ten brass keys, shallow cup type, mounted in brass saddles soldered to tube. No mouthpiece.

56.1 cm.
⌀: 13.5 mm.

1847
Clarinet in C, 12 keys
U.S.A.? mid-19th century
No inscription

Four flame boxwood sections; ivory ferrules (fine turnings) and bell mount. Twelve brass keys, flat, round flaps (three soldered to key shanks), mounted in knobs and bulbous ring (half recessed into long key shanks); two L4 rollers. Grenadilla mouthpiece.

51.5 cm.
⌀: 14.2 cm.

617   622

617
Clarinet in B♭, 13 keys
London, ca. 1835
Thomas Key (fl. ca. 1804-1858)

Four grenadilla sections; ivory ferrules (fine turnings) and bell mount (missing). Thirteen silver-plated keys (one missing; six engraved, including initials: T K), round flaps (five soldered to key shanks), contoured to the body, mounted in knobs, square (partial) and bulbous rings, three silver-plated saddles; leaf springs resting on brass plates; two L4 rollers. Unusual construction: 1 >--> 2 <---->. Tone holes with keys metal-bushed. Steel reinforcing pins. Rosewood mouthpiece.

2, 3: KEY / LONDON / [unicorn mark]
4: KEY / LONDON / [unicorn] / CHARING CROSS

60.3 cm.
⌀: 14.5 mm.

620
Clarinet in C, 13 keys
Mons, ca. 1835
Willame

Four boxwood sections; finely turned ivory ferrules. Thirteen brass keys (one missing; touch for e' [L4] key missing), modern cup type, mounted on pillars; leaf springs resting on metal slides. Flap f/c'' (R4) key; crossover g♯ and a' keys.

1, 2, 4: [mark] / WILLAME / C
3: [mark] / WILLAME / A MONS / C

52.2 cm.
⌀: 15 mm.

622
Clarinet in C, 13 keys
Fulda, ca. 1830
Johann Mollenhauer (fl. 1822-1830)

Four boxwood sections; ivory ferrules (fine turnings) and bell mount. Thirteen brass keys (one missing), flat, round flaps, mounted in knobs and bulbous ring. Alternate touches, c'♯/g''♯ (L4/R1), d'♯/a''♯ (L3/R1 kn.), f'♯/c'''♯ (L2/L3 kn.) keys; flap f/c'' key; mechanical linkage allowing placement of speaker tone hole on top of the tube. Steel reinforcing pins. No mouthpiece.

2: MOLLENHAUER / FULDA / C / [mark]
3, 4: [mark] / MOLLENHAUER / FULDA / C

51.7 cm.
⌀: 13.5 mm.

623
Clarinet in A, 13 keys
England? mid-19th century
Maker unknown

Four ebony sections sheathed in nickel-plated brass. Thirteen nickel-plated brass keys, modern cup type, mounted on pillars. Flap f/c'' (R4) key; speaker tone hole on left side of the tube.

Bell mount: 13// / T.B. / NO. 29.

61.9 cm.
⌀: 14.2 mm.

1557 (formerly 629 A)
Clarinet in A, 13 keys
Paris, 1882?
(Louis-Emile) Jerôme Thibouville-Lamy
(founded ca. 1864)

Four boxwood sections (barrel missing); ivory ferrules and bell mount (missing). Thirteen German silver keys, modern cup type, mounted on pillars; leaf springs on metal slides. Flap f/c'' (R4) key; crossover g'♯ and a' keys. German silver thumb rest, stamped: J.T.L.

Bell: [lyre with rays mark] / J.T.L. / JERÔME THIBOUVILLE-LAMY / PARIS / 82

55.4 cm. (without barrel)
⌀: 15 mm.

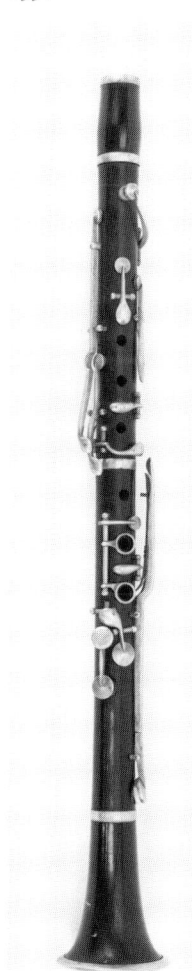

1556

1556
Clarinet (Simple system) in A, 2/13 keys
Paris, mid-19th century
Martin Frères (fl. 1840–present)

Four ebony sections; German silver ferrules and bell mount. Two ring keys (R2, 3: Brille mechanism venting b/f''♯) plus thirteen German silver keys, modern cup type, mounted on pillars; no rollers. Flap f/c'' (R4) key; wraparound speaker key.

2, 3, 4: [fly mark] / (within oval) MARTIN FRE.S / [mark] / A PARIS / (below oval) [monogram:] M F / A

60.8 cm.
⌀: 15.3 mm.

1665
Clarinet (Simple system) in C, 2/13 keys
Paris? late 19th century
No inscription

Four ebony sections; German silver ferrules and bell mount. Two ring keys (R2, 3) plus thirteen German silver keys, modern cup type, mounted on pillars; no rollers. Flap f/c'' key (R4); crossover g'♯ and a' keys; wraparound speaker key. High pitch (all sections stamped: HP / C).

50.2 cm.
⌀: 14.5 mm.

1738
Clarinet (Simple system) in E♭, 2/13 keys
Paris? late 19th century
No inscription

Four ebony sections; German silver ferrules and bell mount. Two ring keys (R2, 3) plus thirteen German silver keys, modern cup type, mounted on pillars; no rollers. Flap f/c'' key (R4); crossover g'♯ and a' keys; wraparound speaker key.

41.9 cm.
⌀: 13 mm.

1739
Clarinet (Simple system) in A, 2/14 keys
Paris? late 19th century
Maker unknown (Carl Fischer, dealer [founded ca. 1872])

Four grenadilla sections; German silver ferrules and bell mount. Two ring keys (R2, 3) plus fourteen German silver keys, modern cup type, mounted on pillars; no rollers. Patent C♯ articulation (e/b' [L4] key closes f♯/c''♯); crossover g'♯ and a' keys.

4: C. FISCHER / SUPERIOR / RELIABLE

60.2 cm.
⌀: 15 mm.

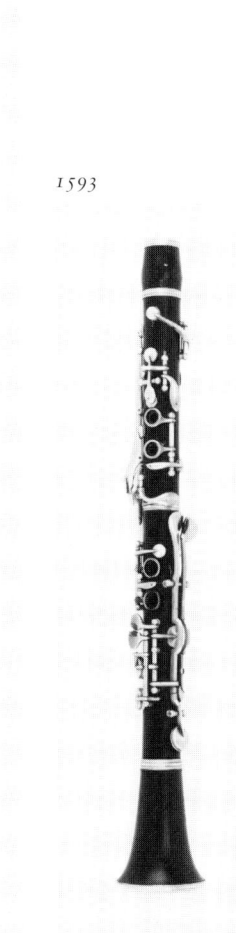

624
Clarinet (Simple system) in B♭, 2/15 keys
Paris? late 19th century
No inscription

Four grenadilla sections; nickel-plated ferrules and bell mount. Two ring keys (R2, 3) plus fifteen nickel-plated keys, modern cup type, mounted on pillars; no rollers. Patent C♯ articulation; crossover g'♯ and a' keys; wraparound speaker key; b♭ key (R3) placed on right side of the tube.

57.7 cm.
⌀: 15 mm.

1794
Clarinet (Simple system) in B♭, 4/15 keys
Paris, early 20th century
Guy Humphrey (fl. ca. 1900-1925)

Four stained grenadilla sections; German silver ferrules and bell mount. Four rings (L1, 2 and R2, 3: Brille mechanisms venting g', g'♯, a', and b/f''♯ respectively) plus fifteen German silver keys, modern cup type, mounted on pillars; four L4 and R4 rollers. Patent C♯ articulation; crossover g'♯ and a' keys; straight speaker key on back side of the tube. Low pitch.

2-4: (within oval) GUY / HUMPHREY / PARIS / (below oval) [two five-pointed stars]
4: (above oval; within unfurled banner) QTE SUPERIEURE / (below banner) LP / B

59.3 cm.
⌀: 15 mm.

1593
Clarinet (Simple system) in E♭, 4/16 keys
Graslitz, early 20th century
Vincent Kohlert Söhne (founded 1840)

Four ebony sections; German silver ferrules and bell mount. Four ring keys (L1, 2 and R2, 3) plus sixteen German silver keys, modern cup type, mounted on pillars; four L4 and R4 rollers. Patent C♯ articulation; crossover g'♯ and a' keys; wraparound speaker key; b♭ key (R3) placed on right side of the tube. Low pitch. Serial number (bell section): 3550.

4: V. KOHLERT SONS / MAKERS / GRASLITZ / CZECHO-SLOVAKIA / [seven exposition medalion, three marked:] CHICAGO, PARIS, LONDON / E♭

43.6 cm.
⌀: 13 mm.

1793
Clarinet (Simple system) in B♭, 4/16 keys
Paris, late 19th century
Pierre Dumont (fl. ca. 1889)

Two nickel-plated brass sections. Four ring keys (L1, 2 and R2, 3) plus sixteen nickel-plated keys, modern cup type, mounted on pillars; four L4 and R4 rollers. Patent C♯ articulation; crossover g'♯ and a' keys; straight speaker key on back side of the tube. Serial number: 1856.

Bell: PIERRE DUMONT

59.1 cm.
⌀: 14.9 mm.

625

Clarinet (Simple system) in B♭, 4/17 keys
Magdeburg, early 20th century
H. Sauerhering (fl. 1877-1909)

Four dark stained boxwood sections; brass ferrules. Four ring keys (L1, 2 and R2, 3) plus seventeen brass keys, modern cup type, mounted on pillars; four L4 and R4 rollers. Hole for speaker key on left side of the tube; thumbhole with brass bushing.

1-4: B / SAUERHERING / MAGDEBURG

59.4 cm.
⌀: 15 mm.

1798

Clarinet (Simple system) in E♭, 5/16 keys
Elkhart, Ind., ca. 1920
C. G. Conn Ltd. (founded 1915)

Four vulcanized rubber sections; German silver ferrules and bell mount. Five ring keys (L1-3; R2, 3) plus sixteen German silver keys, modern cup type, mounted on pillars; four L4 and R4 rollers. Patent C♯ articulation; crossover g'♯ and a' keys; wraparound speaker key; c'♯/g''♯ key with alternate R1 touch. Metal-bushed thumbhole. Low pitch. Serial number (2, 3): E66475L. Conn square case (1798 A).

2, 3: (within oval) C. G. CONN / ELKHART, / INDIANA
1, 4: TRADE [lyre with perching eagle mark] MARK

42.7 cm.
⌀: 13.5 mm.

1737

Clarinet (Simple system) in A, 6/17 keys
Paris, early 20th century
Henri Selmer & Cie (founded 1885)

Four ebony sections; German silver ferrules and bell mount. Six ring keys plus seventeen German silver keys, modern cup type, mounted on pillars; four L4 and R4 rollers. Patent C♯ articulation; articulated c'♯/g''♯ key resited on lower body section; alternate g♯/d'♯ (L4) key; crossover g'♯ and a' keys (with adjustment screw); straight speaker key. Serial number (3): K 4545. Hard rubber mouthpiece. Alligator fabric-covered case (1739 A).

1-4: (on cartouche) HENRI / SELMER / PARIS
2: (below cartouche) BREVETÉ / S.G.D.G.
4: (below cartouche) SOLE AGENTS / U.S. & CAN. / (within unfurled banner) SELMER / ELKHART [mark: man standing within triangle] INDIANA / REG. U.S. PAT. OFF. / MADE IN FRANCE

59.9 cm.
⌀: 15.3 mm.

1789   1848

1788
Clarinet (Simple system) in B♭, 6/17 keys
New York, ca. 1910
Penzel & Müller (founded 1880)

Four black stained grenadilla sections; German silver ferrules and bell mount. Six ring keys plus seventeen German silver keys, modern cup type, mounted on pillars; four L4 and R4 rollers. Patent C♯ articulation (e/b′ lever with adjustment screw); articulated c′♯/g′♯ key (with adjustment screw); improved B♭ mechanism with mechanical linkage between the speaker key and L1 ring (improves quality of g′, g′♯, and a′); alternate g♯ / d′♯ (L4) key; crossover G′♯ and a′ keys; wraparound speaker key. Thumbhole with metal bushing. Hard rubber mouthpiece; extra barrel. Leather-covered case (1788 A).

1-4: B / [mark: eagle with wings poised downward] / (within oval) G. L. PENZEL / & MÜLLER / NEW YORK
4: (below oval) PAT'D APR. 18, 1899

57.4 cm.
⌀: 15 mm.

1789
Clarinet (Simple system) in B♭, 6/17 keys
New York, ca. 1910
Penzel & Müller (founded 1880)

Mechanically identical to 1788. Lower body section stamped: LP. Hard rubber mouthpiece.

59.3 cm.
⌀: 15.2 mm.

1790
Clarinet (Simple system) in A, 6/17 keys
New York, ca. 1910
Penzel & Müller (founded 1880)

See description of 1788. Lower body section stamped: LP. Glass mouthpiece.

63.3 cm.
⌀: 15.2 mm.

1848
Clarinet (Boehm system) in A, 5/17 keys
Boston, early 20th century
The William S. Haynes Co. (fl. 1900-1934)

Three silver sections (barrel and bell missing). Five ring keys plus seventeen silver keys, mounted on pillars. Full Boehm system. Double-wall metal clarinet (patented by C. G. Conn, Aug. 27, 1889) with screw valve at top and sliding band at bottom of single body section. Serial number: 157. Leather-covered wooden case (1848/9 A).

THE / HAYNES CLARINET / MADE BY / WM. S. HAYNES CO. / BOSTON, MASS. / 157

49.4 cm.
⌀: 15.1 mm.

1849
Clarinet (Boehm system) in B♭, 5/17 keys
Boston, early 20th century
The William S. Haynes Co. (fl. 1900-1934)

Three silver sections (barrel and bell missing). Serial number: 152. See description of 1848.

46.5 cm.
⌀: 15.25 mm.

1783
Clarinet, Upper Body Section
U.S.A., ca. 1920
No inscription

Grenadilla. Keywork in German silver and brass. Incorporates numerous mechanical improvements including plateau keys with adjustable mechanisms, articulated c'♯ / g''♯ key.

24.15 cm.

628
Alto Clarinet in F, no keys (Fraud)
Florence, late 19th century
Leopoldo Franciolini shop

Composite instrument (see Ripin: 40, illus. 13). Four sections: two leather-covered maple body sections (six fingerholes plus thumbhole) with ivory ferrule, boxwood (bass clarinet?) barrel with ivory ferrules, boxwood bell (oboe?) with decorative turnings and ivory mount. Grenadilla mouthpiece (bass clarinet?).

81.1 cm.
⌀: 19 mm.

629
Alto Clarinet, 15 keys
Mainz, mid-19th century
Joseph Seidel (1820-1862)

Four boxwood sections including curved barrel; ivory ferrules (fine turnings) bell mount, and thumb rest. Fifteen brass keys, modern cup type, mounted on pillars. Flap f/c'' key. Grenadilla mouthpiece.

2-4: SEIDEL / MAINZ / (within oval) C. E.

76.4 cm.
⌀: 16 mm.

629

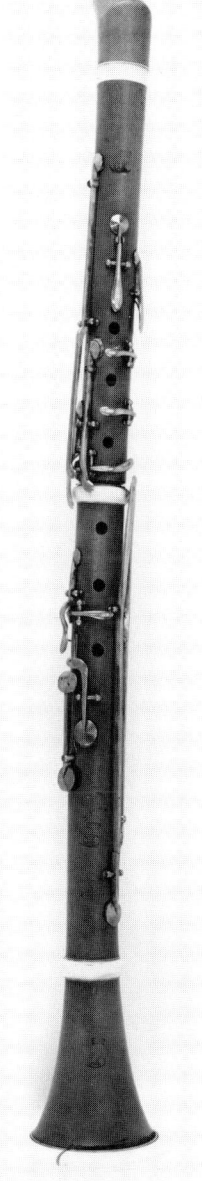

1783

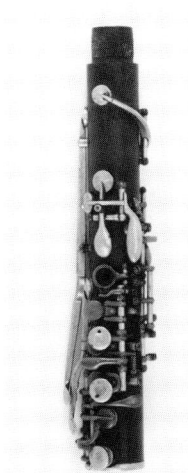

643
Walking-Stick Clarinet
Paris, late 19th century
Ch. Mathieu (fl. ca. 1890)

Two sections: one-piece painted (dark brown simulating wood grain) metal body with nickel-plated mouthpiece, painted (dark brown) bamboo terminal section with steel tip (missing). Threaded nickel-plated protective cap for mouthpiece. No keys; nine fingerholes, plus two tuning holes. Similar to 512 and 575, walking-stick duct flutes.

Cap: CH. MATHIEU / B.TE S.G.D.G. / MQUE DEPOSÉE / [on lyre, initials:] C M / MÉDAILLES D'OR / [floral vinestems]

91 (33.6) cm.

642
Walking-Stick Clarinet in C, 5 keys
Alt St. Johann in Toggenburg, early 19th
  century
Ulrich Ammann (1766-1842)

Four stained boxwood sections (two body sections, mouthpiece cap with threaded brass ring, non-functional terminal section), ingeniously carved to simulate natural knobs in the stock; brass fittings; head cap with horn fitting, mother-of-pearl inlay. Five wooden keys carved to simulate texture of unfinished wood, cup type, mounted in knobs. Tenons with brass reinforcing rings; brass reinforcing pins, both body sections. Ebony mouthpiece.

1-3: [five-pointed star] / AMMANN [five-pointed star] / C

83.3 (48.5) cm.
⌀: 13.8 mm.

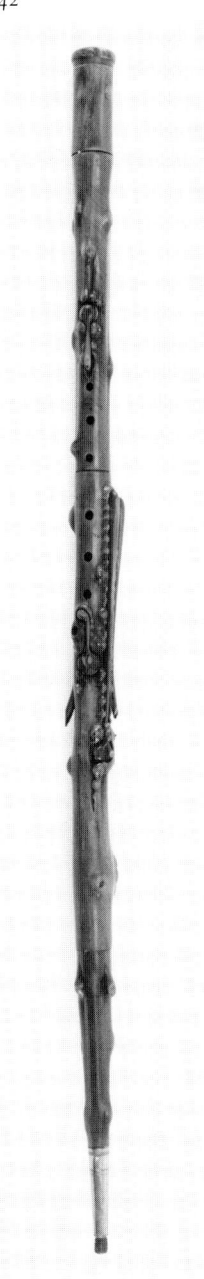

Basset Horns

634
Basset horn, 8 keys
Brunswick, 1789
Wilhelm Hesse (1760-1795)

Five boxwood sections including curved barrel; finely turned ivory ferrules; brass fittings. Brass bell. Eight brass keys (two missing), flat, rectangular flaps, mounted in square rings (rings for extended keys half recessed into shanks).

2: W. HESSE / CAMMERMUSICUS
4: W. HESSE
5: W. HESSE / BRUNSWICK / 1789

85.5 (115.4) cm.
⌀: 14.5 mm.

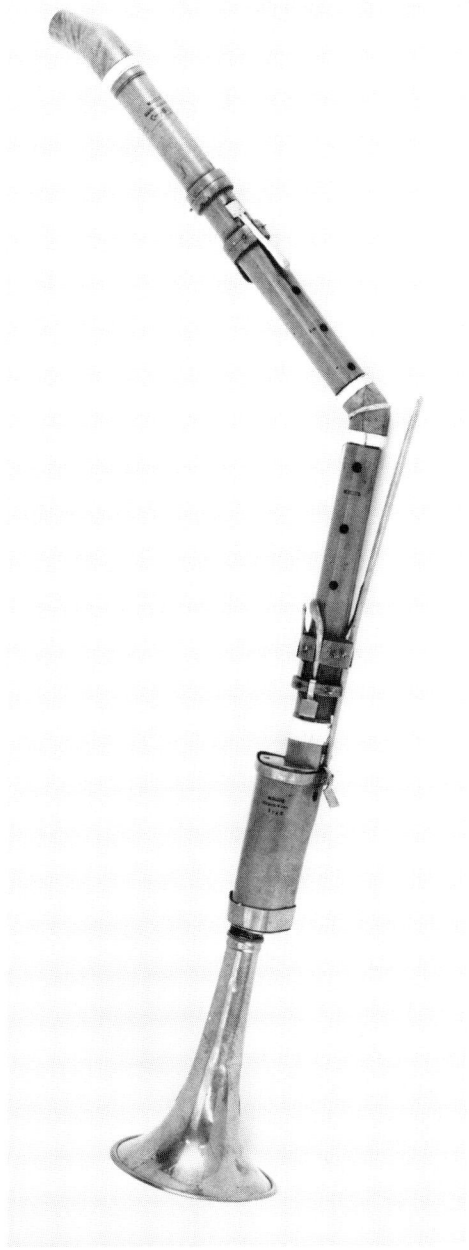

634

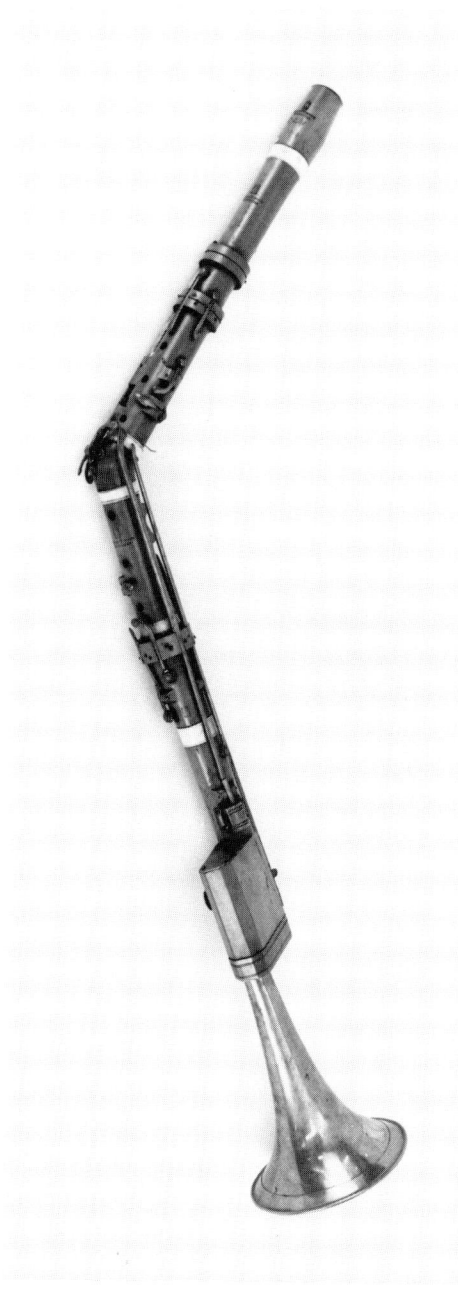

633
Basset horn, 14 keys
Dresden, ca. 1810
(Johann) Heinrich Grenser (1764-1813)

Five boxwood sections; finely turned ivory ferrules; brass fittings. Brass bell, oval, with leg rest. Fourteen brass keys (one missing; two key shanks missing), flat flaps, twelve rectangular (Young, Design C; three with soldered key shanks), one oval (Young, Design V), mounted in square and bulbous rings, and brass saddles. Steel reinforcing pins.

2, 4: [crown of Saxony mark] / H. GRENSER / DRESDEN
1: [crown of Saxony] / 2

93 (95.2) cm.
⌀: 15.1 mm.

632
Basset horn, 16 keys
Presburg, mid-19th century
F. Schoelnast (fl. ca. 1820-1840)

Six boxwood sections; finely turned ivory ferrules; brass fittings. Brass bell. Sixteen brass keys, soft metal plugs, mounted in knobs or square rings (rings for extended keys half recessed into shanks) and brass saddles.

1, 2, 4, 6: [Hungarian coat of arms] / F. SCHÖLNAST / PRESBURG
5: [Hungarian coat of arms]

89.1(97.1) cm.
⌀: 15.4 mm.

Tenor and Bass Clarinets

631

630

631
Tenor Clarinet in E♭, 3/17 keys
Paris, late 19th century
Buffet, Crampon & Cie (founded 1836)

Two dark stained maple sections; silver-plated brass ferrules. Silver-plated goose neck and upturned bell. Three ring keys (R1, 2, L2; tone holes with brass bushings), plus seventeen silver-plated keys, modern cup type, mounted on pillars. Crossover g'♯ and a' keys (a' key opens g'♯ key, closes e' vent hole); L2 ring closes small vent key below a/e'' tone hole; g♯/d''♯ flap key. Brass reinforcing pins.

1, 2: [lyre] / (within oval) BUFFET / Crampon & Cie / A PARIS / (below oval) [monogram:] B C
1 : (below monogram) BREVETÉS/ S.G.D.G.

73.3 (90) cm.
⌀: 17 mm. (top, upper body section)

630
Tenor Clarinet (Simple system) in E♭, 4/13 keys
Paris, 19th century, third quarter
Halary shop (founded 1768) /
  Jules-Léon Antoine (fl. 1855-1873)

Three brass sections. Four ring keys (L1, 2, R2, 3) plus thirteen brass keys (one missing), shallow cup type, mounted on pillars. R2 and 3 rings close open-standing key venting b nat. tone hole (with adjusting screw). Silver-plated brass mouthpiece. Serial number, upturned bell: 462.

Bell: [mark: eagle with wings poised downward, crown overhead] / HALARI / FOURNSEUR DE L'EMPEREUR / A PARIS
Side of bell: L / (upside down) A S

77.8 (93) cm.
⌀: 22 mm.

639
Bass Clarinet (Simple system) in B♭, 18 keys
Paris, late 19th century
Buffet, Crampon & Cie (founded 1836)

Two dark stained maple sections; silver-plated brass ferrules. Silver-plated goose neck and upturned bell. Eighteen silver-plated keys (two uncovered tone holes), modern cup type, mounted on pillars. Two speaker keys; crossover g′♯ and a′ keys (a′ key opens g′♯ tone hole); g♯/d′′♯ flap key.

1, 2: [lyre] / (within oval) BUFFET / Crampon & Cie / A PARIS / (below oval) [monogram:] B C
1: (below monogram) BREVETÉS S.G.D.G.

84.8 (125.6) cm.
⌀: 22.9 mm.

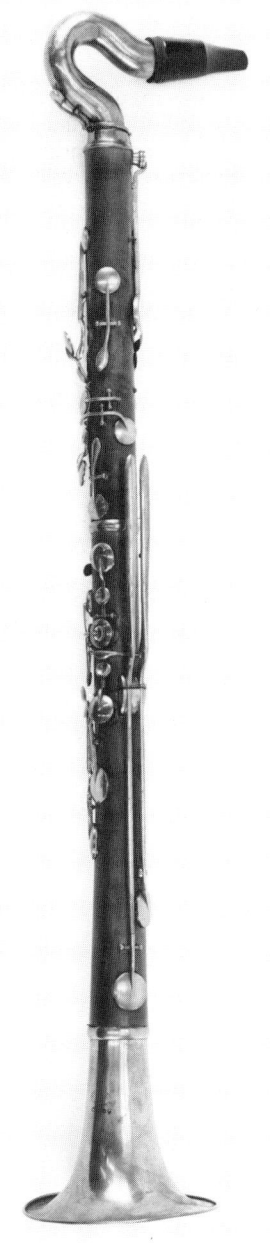

635
Bass Clarinet (Simple system) in B♭, 20 keys
Paris, mid-19th century
Auger Buffet, jeune (1831-1885)

Two maple sections, doubled over; brass fittings and U-bend. Brass goose neck and bell. Twenty brass keys, modern cup type, mounted on pillars. Two speaker keys (these tone holes with brass bushings).

1: A. BUFFET / JNE / PARIS / BREVETÉS
2: A. BUFFET / JNE / PARIS

66.5 (124) cm.
⌀: 30.1 mm. (top, upper body section)

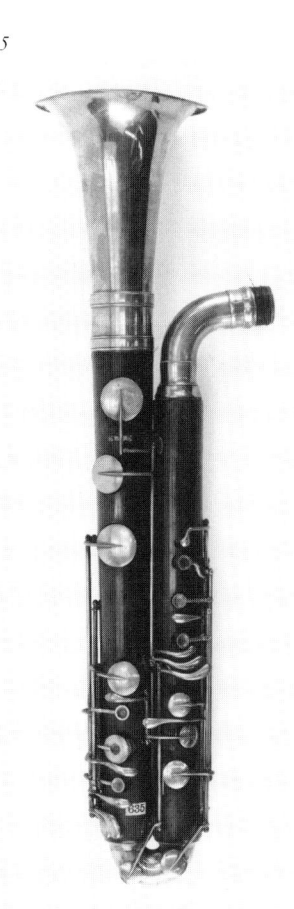

637
Bass Clarinet in B♭ (Simple system), 20 keys
Brussels, ca. 1840
Adolphe (Antoine Joseph) Sax (1814-1894)

Two stained maple sections; brass ferrules. Brass goose neck and bell (replacement; stamped: [within oval] CH. ROTH / A / STRASBOURG / BREVETE / S.G.D. GI). Twenty brass keys, shallow cup type, mounted on pillars. Two speaker keys; tone holes with brass bushings.

1, 2: * / SAX / A BRUXELLES / *

106 (117.6) cm.
⌀: 28.5 mm.

638
Bass Clarinet (Simple system) in B♭, 21 keys
Paris, mid-19th century
Buffet, Crampon & Cie (founded 1836)

One-piece dark stained maple body. Brass goose neck and upturned bell. Twenty-one brass keys, modern cup type, mounted on pillars attached to elliptical brass plates; one key mounted in brass saddle. Two speaker keys; pillars for L4 and R4 keys soldered to extended arm of rod and axle mechanism. Brass reinforcing pins. Ebony mouthpiece with brass ferrule.

[lyre] / (within oval) BUFFET / Crampon & Cie / A PARIS / (below oval) [monogram:] B C

76.7 (130) cm.
⌀: 30 mm. (top, body)

636
Bass Clarinet in B♭ (Simple system), 24 keys
Erfurt, late 19th century
Carl Kruspe (fl. ca. 1897)

Four varnished rosewood sections, doubled over (two parallel tubes permanently joined to boot section); brass ferrules and fittings. Brass goose neck and bell; nickel-plated bell garland. Twenty-four brass keys (three uncovered tone holes), modern cup type, mounted on pillars. Compass extended to E♮. Grenadilla mouthpiece with brass ferrule.

1, 2, 4: [lyre] / [wheel with six spokes mark] / KRUSPE / ERFURT /
On bell garland: C. Kruspe / Erfurt

89.1 (177) cm.
⌀: 23 mm.

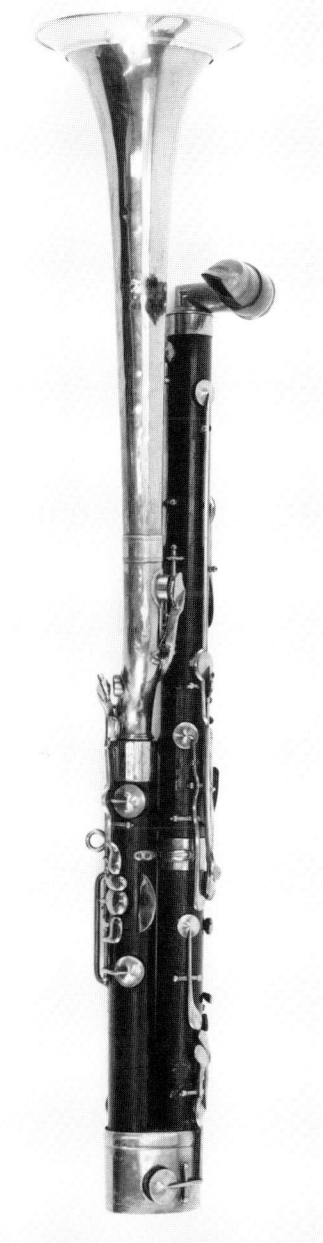

636

Saxophones

1797
Sopranino Saxophone in E♭, Straight
Elkhart, Ind., 20th century, second quarter
Buescher Band Instrument Co.

Nickel-plated brass (brushed), engraved bell (floral motif); mother-of-pearl buttons. Twenty-two nickel-plated keys. Serial number: 189815; "TRUE TONE" trade mark. Low pitch.

THE / Buescher / ELKHART / IND.

46.4 cm.

640
Soprano Saxophone in B♭, Straight
Brussels, late 19th century
Charles Mahillon & Cie (fl. 1836-1937)

Brass. Eighteen brass keys. Serial number: 2361.

C. Mahillon / FOURNISSEUR BREVETE / DE L'ARMEE / ET DES / CONSERVATOIRES / BRUXELLES

62.8 cm.

1787
Soprano Saxophone in B♭, Curved
Elkhart, Ind., 20th century, second quarter
Buescher Band Instrument Co.

Nickel-plated brass (brushed), engraved bell (floral motif); mother-of-pearl buttons. Twenty-two nickel-plated keys. Serial number: 24333; "TRUE TONE" trade mark. Low pitch.

THE / Buescher / ELKHART / IND.

44.6 cm.

1792
Soprano Saxophone in C, Straight
New York, 20th century
Selmer Co. (fl. ca. 1904-1927)

Brass, engraved bell (floral motif); mother-of-pearl buttons. Twenty-two brass keys. Serial number: P 22981. Low pitch.

Selmer / NEW YORK

56.7 cm.

1795
Soprano Saxophone in B♭, Straight
Elkhorn, Wis., 20th century
Frank Holton & Co.

Nickel-plated brass (brushed), engraved bell (floral motif); mother-of-pearl buttons. Twenty-five brass keys. Serial number: 31587. Low pitch.

MADE BY / Frank Holton & Co. / ELKHORN / WIS.

65.4 cm.

1799
Alto Saxophone in E♭, Curved
Elkhorn, Wis., 20th century
Frank Holton & Co.

Nickel-plated brass (brushed), engraved bell (floral motif); mother-of-pearl buttons and rollers. Twenty-six brass keys. Serial number: 29752. Low pitch. Original metal-lined mouthpiece.

MADE BY / Frank Holton & Co. / ELKHORN / WIS.

62 cm.

640

1596
Alto Saxophone in E♭, Curved
Toledo, Ohio, ca. 1920
Allen Loomis

Brass; silver-plated touches and rollers. Twenty-six brass keys including third octave key, low A extension (L4 roller). Instrument incorporates numerous mechanical and acoustical improvements; relatively small diameter tone holes; many keys resited. Serial number: 6.

[logo:] LOOMIS / 6 / ALLEN LOOMIS / 3101 MONROE ST. / TOLEDO, OHIO, U.S.A. / PATENTED APRIL 6, 1920 / OTHER PATENTS PENDING

64 cm.

1596 detail

641
Tenor Saxophone in C
Paris, mid-19th century
Adolphe (Antoine Joseph) Sax (1814-1894)

Silver-plated brass. Twenty silver-plated brass keys. Extremely lightweight. Serial number: 20669.

No 20669 Saxophone tenor en ut breveté / Adolphe Sax á Paris / F.teur De la M.son Mil.re de l'Empereur / [monogram:] A S / (in cross-stroke of letter S:) PARIS

67.6 cm.

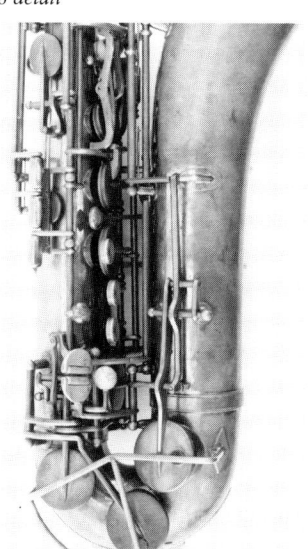

1596 detail

1596

641

1791
Tenor Saxophone in B♭
Elkhorn, Wis., 20th century, second quarter
Frank Holton & Co.

Nickel-plated brass (brushed), engraved bell (floral motif); mother-of-pearl buttons and rollers. Twenty-six brass keys. Serial number: 24274. Low pitch. Original metal-lined mouthpiece.

MADE BY / Frank Holton & Co. /
ELKHORN / WIS.

82 cm.

1796
Baritone Saxophone in E♭
Elkhart, Ind., modern
C. G. Conn Ltd. (founded 1915)

Brass; mother-of-pearl buttons and rollers. Twenty-three brass keys. Serial number: 78996. Low pitch.

MADE BY / C. G. CONN LTD. / ..... / .....

102 cm.

Single Reed Horns

594
Single Reed Horn, Curved
Switzerland? late 19th century

Goat horn; threaded animal horn mouthpiece; brass reed. Cord.

37.4 cm.

595
Single Reed Horn, Curved
Italy? late 19th century

Painted (black) brass, two ornamental pommels; metal reed. Two brass rings for cord.

64.8 cm.

596
Single Reed Horn, Curved
Germany? late 19th century

Conical tube and bell of soldered sheet tin; perforated brass cap. Two metal rings for cloth strap.

44.4 cm.

597
Single Reed Horn, Straight (**Pedlar's Horn**)
U.S.A.? early 20th century

Conical tube, mouthpiece, and bell of soldered nickel-plated sheet tin; tin reed.

51.7 cm.

598
Single Reed Horn, Straight **(Pedlar's Horn)**
U.S.A.? early 20th century

Conical tube, mouthpiece, and bell of soldered nickel-plated sheet tin; tin reed. Similar to 597.

53.9 cm.

712
Single Reed Horn, Curved
Argentina? 19th century

Two sections: brass tube, horn mouthpiece; brass reed. Two brass rings for cord.

21.4 cm.

Oboes

665
Oboe (C), 2 keys
London, late 18th century
William Maurice Cahusac (fl. 1794-1816)

Three dark stained boxwood sections; finely turned ivory ferrules and bell mount, plain straight finial; single brass band on upper body section (not original). Two silver keys, flat, round flaps, mounted in partial square ring and block; c′ key with "swallow-tail" touch. Twinned L3 tone hole; two tuning holes in bell.

1-3: CAHUSAC / LONDON

57.9 cm.
Reedwell depth: n.a. (tapered)
Min. ⌀: 5.65 mm.

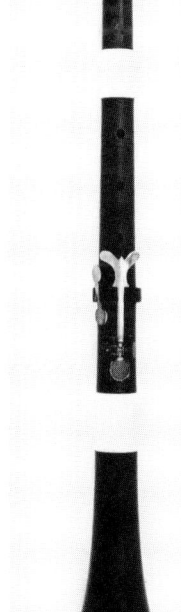

665 detail

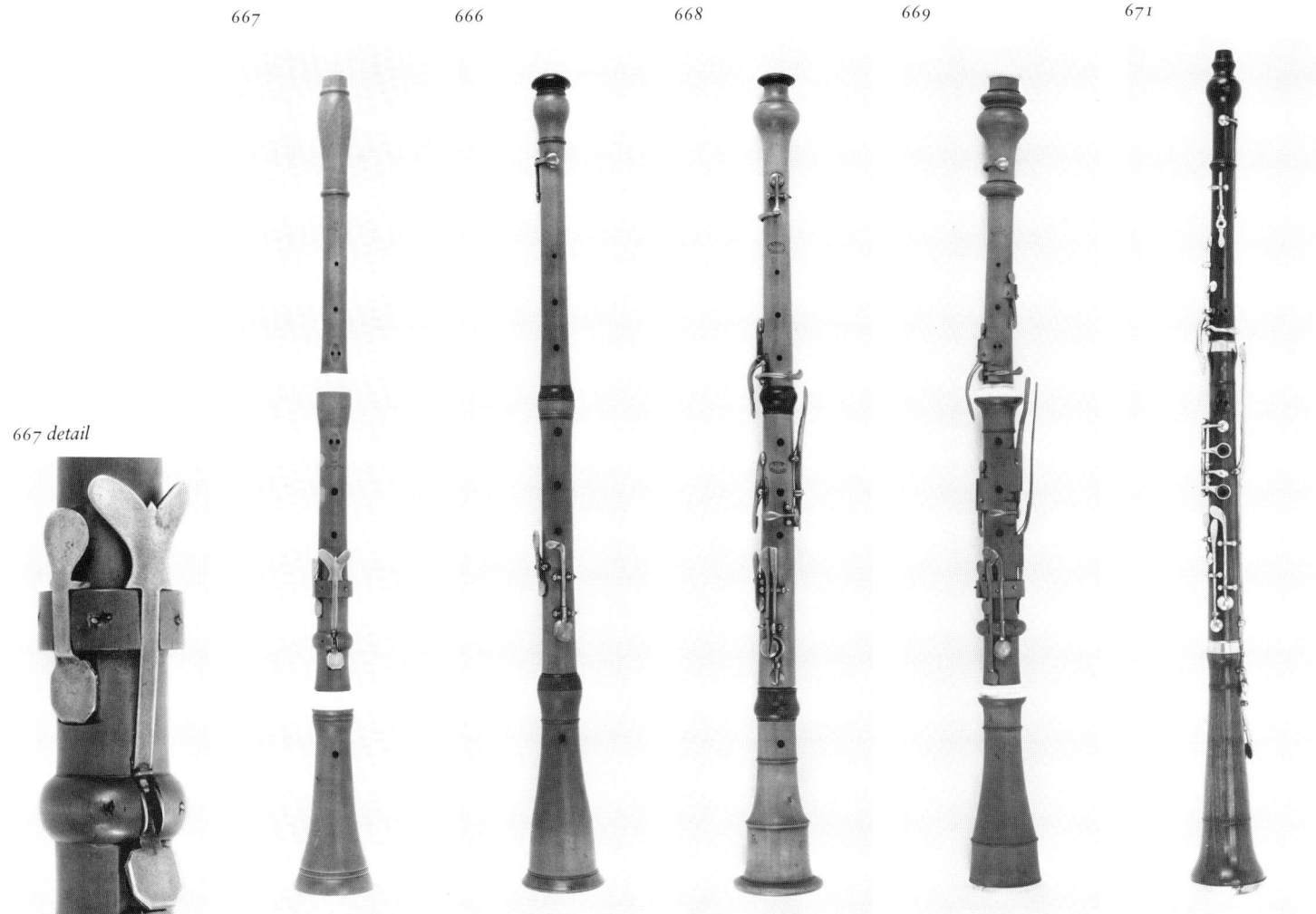

667
Oboe (C), 2 keys
Brussels, ca. 1750
Jean-Hyacinth-Joseph Rottenburgh
  (1672-1765)

Three boxwood sections with decorative turnings; finely turned ivory finial (modern replacement in plastic), ferrules, and bell mount. Two brass keys, flat, octagonal flaps (Young, Design N), mounted in rings; c′ key with "swallow-tail" touch. Twinned L3 and R1 tone holes; two tuning holes in bell. Restored.

1-3: I. H. / ROTTENBURGH / *
  (see Langwill: 221)

58.2 cm.
Reedwell depth: n.a. (tapered)
Min. ⌀: 5.0 mm.

666
Oboe (C), 3 keys
Germany? mid-19th century
No inscription

Three boxwood sections with decorative turnings; horn finial and ferrules; separate bell rim in boxwood. Three brass keys (c′, d′♯ register), contoured to the body, round flaps, mounted on pillars screwed directly into tube. Two tuning holes in bell. Octave tone hole with brass bushing.

55.5 cm.
Reedwell depth: 15.2 mm.
Min. ⌀: 4.5 mm.

668
Oboe (C), 8 keys
Persiceto, Italy, ca. 1820
Giacinto Riva

Three boxwood sections with decorative turnings (3); horn finial and ferrules; bell rim in boxwood. Eight brass keys, shallow cup type, mounted on pillars, two pair attached to elliptical brass plates. Alternate f′ touch (L4/R3). Octave tone hole with brass bushing.

1-3: (within oval) G. RIVA / [mark] /
  PERSICETO

55.1 cm.
Reedwell depth: 18.7 mm.
Min. ⌀: 4.85 mm.

669
Oboe (B), 12 keys
Vienna, ca. 1817
Stephen Koch (1772-1828)

Three boxwood sections with decorative turnings; finely turned ivory finial, ferrules, and plain bell mount. Twelve brass keys (two open), flat, round flaps, mounted in wooden saddles and rings. Twinned L3 tone hole. Sellner pattern keywork less low b♭ key, with alternate f′ touch (L4/R3; see Heyde 1978: 148, Design 20) and extra d′♯ key. Crossover c′ and c′♯ touches (linkages, see ibid., Design 11). Seven tone holes covered by keys with brass bushings.

1-3: [crest] / S: KOCH / WIEN

56.4 cm.
Reedwell depth: 13 mm.
Min. ⌀: 4.5 mm.

671
Oboe (B♭), 2/12 keys
New York, ca. 1840
Edward Baack (1839-1872)

Three grenadilla sections; engraved nickel-plated ferrules, plain bell mount. Two ring keys (R2, 3: Brille mechanism venting f′♯) plus twelve nickel-plated keys (including vented B′ [L1] key), early cup (saltspoon) type, mounted on pillars. Key shanks decorated with cross-hatch engravings. Twinned L3 and R1 tone holes. Octave tone hole with metal bushing. Low b♭, b tone holes on long, gradually flaring bell section.

2, 3: E. BAACK / N-YORK

58.5 cm.
Reedwell depth: 20.7 mm.
Min. ⌀: 4.8 mm.

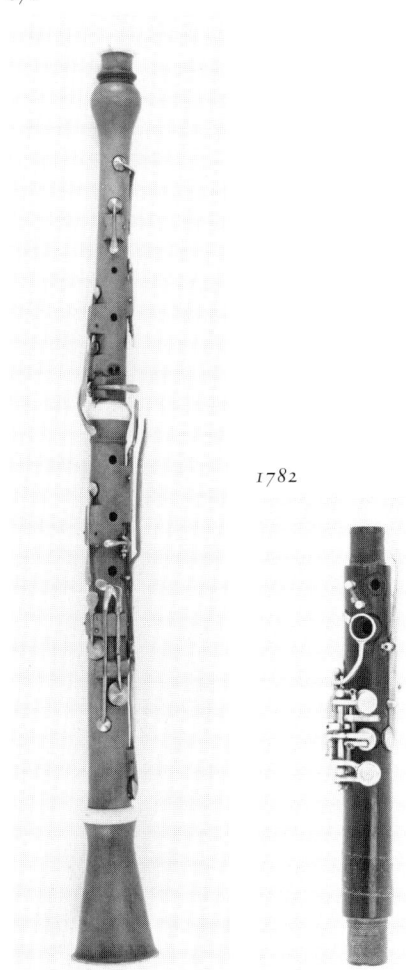

670

1782

670
Oboe (B), 13 keys
Austria? ca. 1830
No inscription

Four boxwood sections including tuning section with decorative turnings; finely turned finial, ivory ferrules, and bell mount. Thirteen brass keys, modern cup type, mounted in wooden saddles and brass pillars. Twinned L3 tone hole; oval tone holes. Sellner pattern keywork less low b♭ key, with alternate f' touch (L4/R3); extra d'♯ key. Crossover c' and c'♯ touches. Note c'', c''♯ keys on upper body section. Octave and L1 tone holes with metal bushings.

54.5 cm.
Reedwell depth: n.a. (tapered)
Min. ⌀: 4.8 mm.

1654
Oboe (B), 2/12 keys
Biebrich, late 19th century
Wilhelm H. Heckel (1856-1909)

Four grenadilla sections including tuning section; German silver ferrules. Two ring keys (R2, 3) plus thirteen German silver keys, modern cup type, mounted on pillars. Sellner pattern keywork less low b♭, with f'♯ Brille (rings open articulated c' key; with adjusting screw); alternate b'♭ touch (L th.). Bulbous baluster and suddenly flared bell chararacteristic of Austrian instruments. Leather-covered wooden case (1654 A).

1, 3, 4: HECKEL / [crown mark] BIEBRICH [crown mark]

54.5 cm.
Reedwell depth: 17.8 mm.
Min. ⌀: 4.9 mm.

1780
Oboe (B), 4/13 keys
Paris, ca. 1875
Buffet, Crampon & Cie (founded 1836)

Three grenadilla sections (ebonite graft: top 10.4 cm. of upper body section); German silver ferrules and bell mount. Four ring keys (L2, 3, R2, 3) plus thirteen German silver keys including perforated plate for b' key (L1), modern cup type, mounted on pillars. Military-style instrument with two octave keys; Triébert thumb-plate action (closes b'♭ and c'' keys on the top of the tube); high d'' trill key; rod and axle linking b' plate, g' ring, and g'♯ key (ring or key closes plate); e'♭ / b "butterfly" touch (missing). No lip on flared bell. Low pitch. Imported by Carl Fischer Co., New York. Leather-covered wooden case, stamped: U.S. (1780 A).

2, 3: (within oval) [lyre] / BUFFET / Crampon & Cie / A PARIS / (below oval) [monogram:] BC

56.9 cm.
Reedwell depth: 19.5 mm.
Min. ⌀: 4.45 mm.

1782
Oboe, Upper Body Section
U.S.A., ca. 1924
No inscription

Ebony. Keywork in German silver. Incorporates a number of mechanical improvements including semi-automatic octave mechanism (Pat. No. 1,336,359), sliding arm permitting easy access to octave vent holes for cleaning (Pat. No. 1,505,359).

21.7 cm.

*Tenor and
Baritone Oboes*

672

Tenor Oboe (Cor Anglais), 10 keys
Vienna, ca. 1825
Stephan Koch (1772-1828)

Four dark stained maple sections with decorative turnings, bulb bell; horn ferrules. Ten brass keys including extra D♯ (nominal) key (R4, L4), flat flaps of various shapes, seven octagonal (Young, Design N), two round, one trapezoidal (Young, Design H), mounted in brass saddles and wooden rings (low B linkage [R3], see Heyde 1978: 148, Design 2); register key mounted in particularly wide bulbous rings. Twinned L3 tone hole. Alternate F touch (L4/R3); ornate touches (R4 in partic.). Octave tone hole with metal bushing.

1, 3, 4: S: KOCH / WIEN

74 (77.7) cm.
Reedwell depth: 17.7 mm.
Min. ⌀: 5.4 mm.

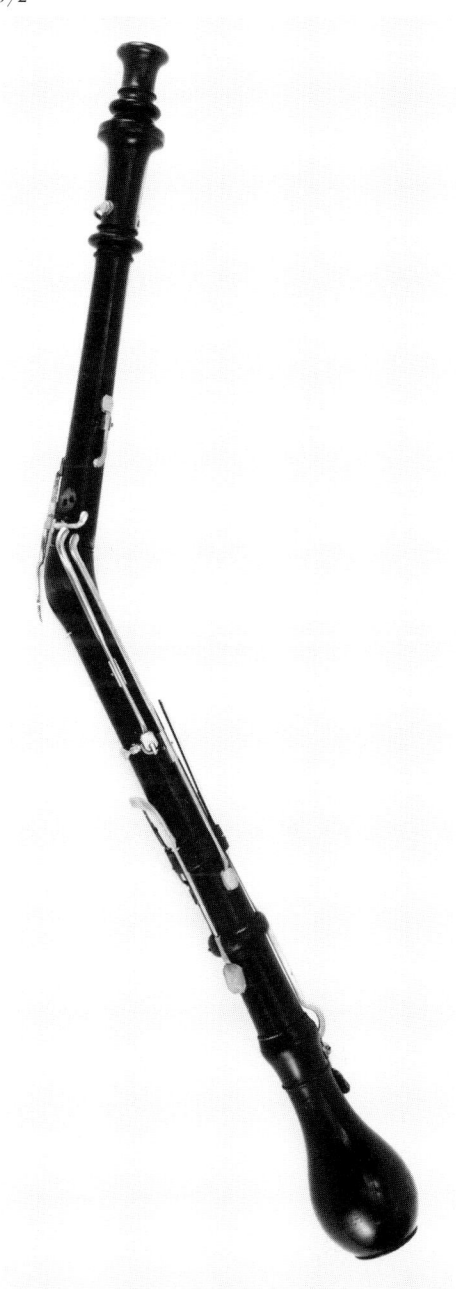

672

674

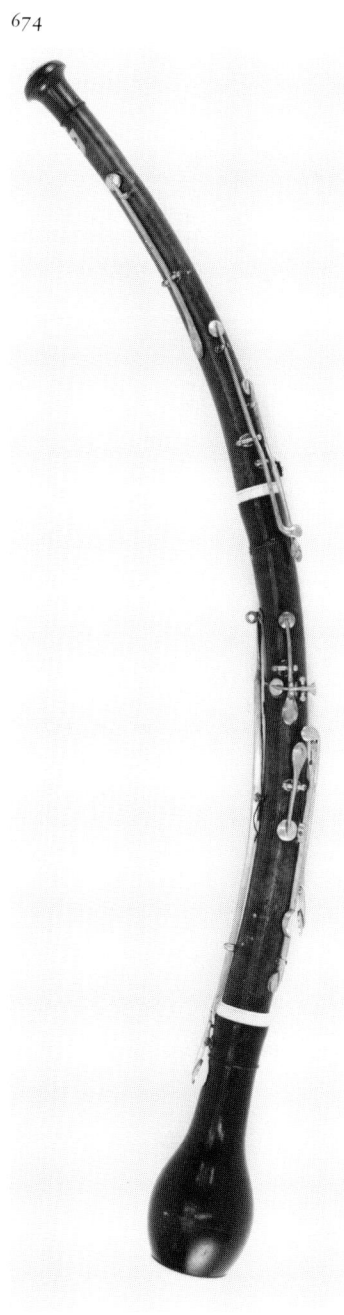

674
Tenor Oboe (Cor Anglais), 10 keys
Paris, ca. 1840
Guillaume Triébert, père (1770-1848)

Three pearwood sections: two leather-covered, dark stained bulb bell; horn and ivory ferrules and mounts; ivory band encircling metal-lined inlet tube. Funnel-shaped finial in horn; reinforcing German silver bands on tenons. Ten German silver keys, shallow cup type, mounted on pillars attached to elliptical plates; C (nominal) key (R4) mounted in metal saddle. Twinned L3 tone hole.

1-3: [tower mark] / TRIEBERT / A PARIS

74.4 (78.5) cm.
Reedwell depth: 22 mm.
Min. ⌀: 5.65 mm.

673
Tenor Oboe (Cor Anglais), 14 keys
Germany or Austria? mid-19th century
No inscription

Six sections: five in boxwood including tuning section (construction: 1 |---> 2 <---->) and bulb bell with decorative turnings, ivory elbow; ivory ferrules; inlet of tuning section lined with mother-of-pearl butted to a slightly expanding conical brass tube. Fourteen brass keys including extra D♯ (nominal) key (R4, L4), flat, round flaps, welded key shanks (Heyde 1978: 145, Design 29), knob mounted. Twinned R3 tone hole. Alternate B♭ touchpiece (L th./R1 kn.).

77.3 (79.9) cm.
Reedwell depth: 29 mm.
Min. ⌀: 5.7 mm.

675
Tenor Oboe, 3/17 keys
Paris, mid-19th century
Mangeant (fl. ca. 1842-1862)

Three dark stained fruitwood sections including bulb bell; nickel-plated ferrules and sockets. Three ring keys (L2, R2, 3) plus seventeen nickel-plated keys (including L1 perforated plate), modern cup type (except C [nominal] key with soft metal plug), mounted on pillars. Two octave keys; high D trill key; E♭ / B "butterfly" touch. Twinned L3 tone hole.

MANGEANT / BREVETÉ / PARIS

78.8 cm.
Reedwell depth: 21.6 mm.
Min. ⌀: 5.35 mm. (first tenon: 11.6 mm.)

676
Baritone Oboe in C, 12 keys
Paris, mid-19th century
Guillaume Triébert, père (1770-1848)

Five sections: three in rosewood, with maple boot and upturned bulb bell; finely turned ivory ferrules; brass fittings. Twelve brass keys (one ring key), flat, round flaps, mounted in brass saddles or pillars; two keys in channels cut into the wall of the instrument. Alternate B♭ touch (R3/L1). Vented B key (replacement in copper). Note altered position of G♯ tone hole, angle-drilled low B (tone hole redrilled); plugged tone hole at top of boot joint. Bassoon shape and manufacturing techniques, such as angle-drilled tone holes.

4, 5: [tower mark] / TRIEBERT / A PARIS

72.5 (102.2) cm.
Reedwell depth: 20 mm.
Min. ⌀: 5.7 mm.

675   676

676 *detail*

Bassoons

677
Bassoon, 5 keys
Late 18th century?
Maker and provenance unknown
  (Leopoldo Franciolini, dealer)

Composite instrument. Three painted (black) maple sections extant (boot, wing, long sections), bell section replaced with painted brass dragon's head; brass fittings. Five brass keys mounted in saddles (all except one bracket missing). Inscription on boot and body sections obliterated. Red paper stamp of the Florentine dealer Leopoldo Franciolini on boot section, marked in blue crayon: 16 MO RO (see Ripin: 40, illus. 14).

Boot and body sections: 98 cm.
With dragon's head bell: 144.7 cm.

678
Bassoon, 6 keys
Liverpool, early 19th century
J. & H. Banks (fl. ca. 1811)

Four dark stained maple sections; brass ferrules. Six brass keys, flat flaps, three shell-shaped (Young, Design Y), three elongated figure-eight keys, mounted in brass saddles. Flared bell. Damaged (worm holes).

1-3: J & H / BANKS

124.6 cm.

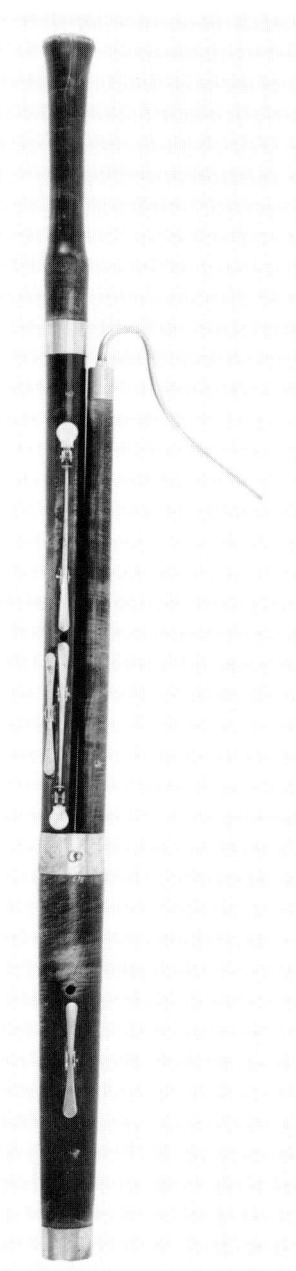

678

1743
Bassoon, 8 keys
Paris, 19th century, second quarter
Jean-Nicolas Savary, jeune (1786-1853)

Four dark stained maple sections, bell with decorative turnings; brass ferrules. Eight brass keys, contoured to the body, round flaps soldered to key shanks (Heyde 1978: 145, Design 29), mounted in brass saddles. Two R4 (F, G♯) keys with rollers. Flared bell.

All sections: [mark] / Savary / Jeune / A
    PARIS / [mark]

127 cm.

679
Bassoon, 10 keys
London, 19th century, second quarter
Thomas Key (fl. ca. 1804-1858)

Four dark stained maple sections; brass ferrules. Ten brass keys, countoured to the body, five shell-shaped flaps (Young, Design Y), three round flaps soldered to key shanks, two elongated figure-eight keys, mounted in brass saddles (saddles for extended R th. and R1 side keys attached to brass plates). Two R4 (F, G♯) keys with rollers. L thumbhole ivory-bushed; six tone holes (four covered by keys) with metal bushings. Bell with reverse conical bore. Original crook, stamped: G 4.

1, 3, 4: KEY / LONDON / [unicorn mark]
2: KEY / LONDON / [unicorn] /
    CHARING CROSS

122.7 cm.

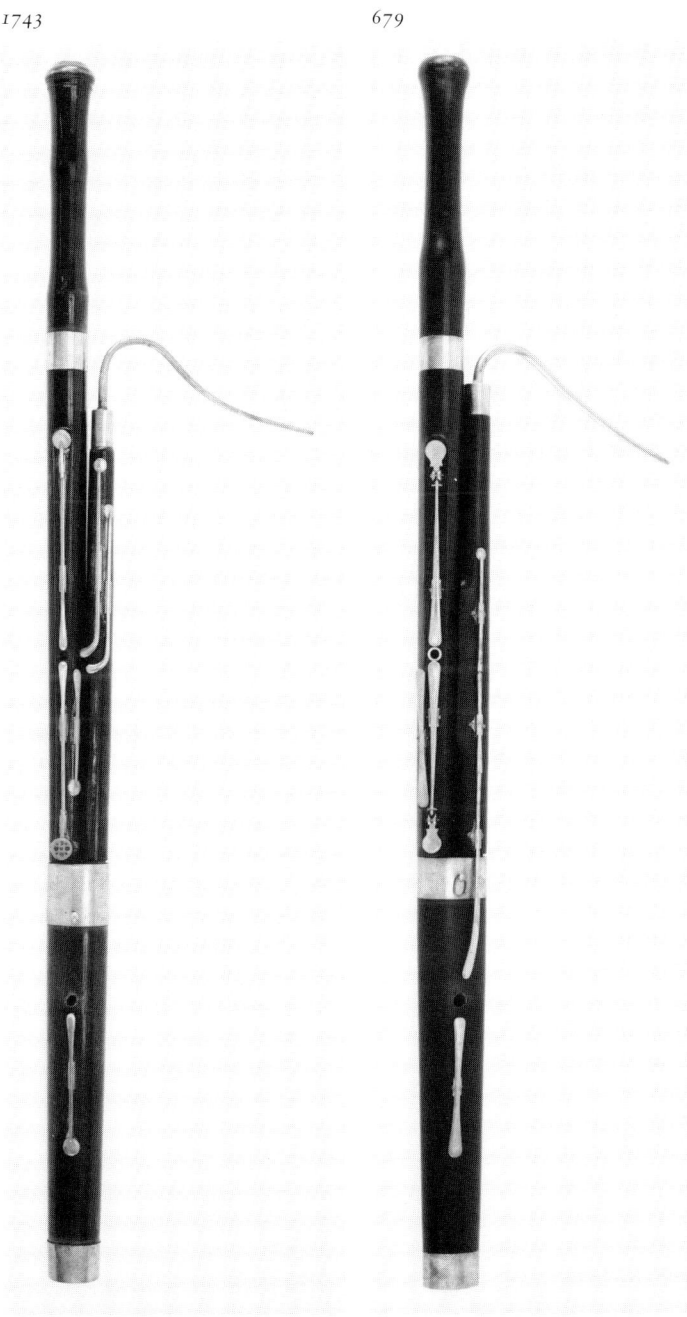

680

680
Bassoon, 13 keys
Bamberg, mid-19th century,
Adler shop (fl. 1819-1923)

Four dark stained maple sections; brass ferrules. Thirteen brass keys, contoured to the body, round flaps, nine mounted in brass saddles (half recessed into key shanks), four axle-mounted keys on hinges attached to brass plates. Heckel-Almenraeder key system (ca. 1820). L4 (C♯) key with R thumb alternate fingering. Flared bell. Original crook.

I-3[mark] / ADLER / BAMBERG / [three clovers]

131.5 cm.

1742
Bassoon, 14 keys
Dresden, mid-19th century
Franz Schadenberg

Four stained maple sections; German silver ferrules. Fourteen German silver keys, shallow cup type, mounted on pillars.

All sections: [lyre] / F. SCHADENBERG / DRESDEN / [five-pointed star]

127.3 cm.

681
Bassoon, 16 keys
London, ca. 1875
Boosey & Co. (fl. ca. 1850-1900)

Four painted (black) rosewood sections, bell with decorative turnings; silver-plated ferrules and bell mount. Sixteen silver-plated keys, modern cup type, mounted on pillars. French system (mechanism for high a register key missing). Serial number (all except long section): 5511; long section: 5384. Boot section stamped: R.A.B. [Royal Army Band?] / [18]78. Hinged metal cover over U-bend. Silver-plated crook.

Body and boot sections: BOOSEY [& C]O / 295 REGENT STREET / LONDON

125 cm.

682
Bassoon, 16 keys
Paris, ca. 1889
Arsène-Zoé Lecomte & Cie (1818-1892)

Two nickel-plated brass sections. Sixteen nickel-plated keys, modern cup type, mounted on pillars. Original crook.

Bell: A. LECOMTE & CIE / rue ST GILLES, 12 / PARIS

134.3 cm.

1558

1558
Bassoon, 20 keys
Adorf, late 19th century
Julius Jehring (1824-1905)

Three dark stained maple sections; nickel-plated ferrules and fittings. One-piece long and bell section doubled over in a second U-bend (range extended to low A) covered with a false bell, end of tube with perforated cap. Twenty nickel-plated keys, modern cup type, mounted on pillars. Two R4 (F, G♯) keys on rollers.

1, 3: (within oval) GESETZLICH / J. JEHRING / GESCHÜTZT

110.3 cm.

1558 detail

Contrabassoons

683
Contrabassoon, 11 keys
Biebrich, mid-19th century
Heckel shop (founded 1831)

Five dark stained maple sections; nickel-plated ferrules. Eleven nickel-plated keys, modern cup type, mounted on pillars. Two-piece crook. Embossed coat of arms: griffin on shield; crown above shield, initials K.T.W. below.

HECKEL / BIEBRICH

175.8 cm.

1744
Contrabassoon, 12 keys
Biebrich, mid-19th century
Heckel shop (founded 1831)

Four dark stained maple sections; nickel-plated ferrules. Twelve nickel-plated keys (all missing), mounted on pillars. Two-piece crook (missing). Damaged in fire. Compared with 683: (1.) boot section, two lowest keys (R th.) axle-mounted, (2.) long section with two keys, (3.) one-piece wing section, three holes covered by keys.

HECKEL / BIEBRICH

172.2 cm.

683

684
Contrabassoon, 17 keys
Breslau, mid-19th century
Christoph Geipel

Dark stained maple; brass ferrules and fittings. Wide bore and large tone holes. Seventeen brass keys, shallow cup type, mounted on pillars. German silver bell mount.

On shield: Verfertigt / Von Chrp. Geipel / in Breslau

138 cm.

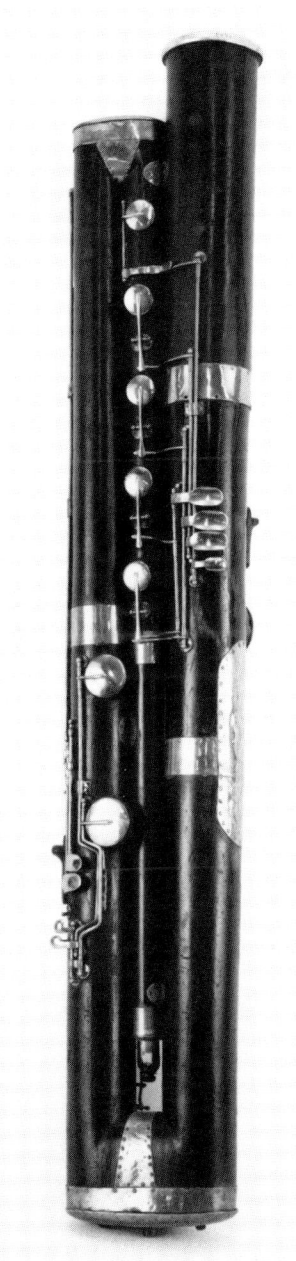

684

Sarrusophones

686
Soprano Sarrusophone in B♭
Paris, late 19th century
Pierre Louis Gautrot, aîné (fl. 1845-1884)

Brass. Nineteen brass keys (L1 vented), modern cup type, mounted on pillars.

Gautrot Marquet / breveté s.g.d.g. à Paris

47.1 cm.

687
Tenor Sarrusophone in B♭
Paris, late 19th century
Henri Sax

Brass. Nineteen brass keys, modern cup type, mounted on pillars.

No 504 / Henri Sax / 5. rue Lallier / Paris

71.9 cm.

685
Contrabass Sarrusophone
London, late 19th century
Charles Mahillon & Cie (fl. 1836-1935)

Brass. Seventeen brass keys, modern cup type, mounted on pillars with rods and axles. Leather bands.

[coat of arms] / GOLD METAL / PARIS 1878 / [star of David] / C. MAHILLON / LONDON / & / BRUSSELS

104 cm.

Double Reed Pipes

652
Double Reed Pipe, Straight
Germany? late 19th century
No inscription

Three ebony sections, finely turned finial; German silver ferrules. Twinned L3 tone hole; chamfered tone holes. Flared bell.

44.4 cm.

652

656
Double Reed Pipe, Straight
Milan, late 19th century
Giuseppe Pelitti (fl. ca. 1835-1893)

Two sections: painted (black) hardwood, nickel-plated brass bell. Eight tone holes, including L thumb and R4.

2: [seal of commune of Milan] /
G. PELITTI. MILANO. / (surrounded by three seven-pointed stars)

50.8 cm.

653
Double Reed Pipe, Straight, 1 key
England? late 19th century
No inscription

Two cocus sections; German silver ferrules (one missing). One German silver key, modern cup type, mounted on pillars. Two tuning holes in pear-shaped bell.

34.9 cm.

655
Double Reed Pipe, Straight, 1 key
Brittany, mid-19th century
No inscription

Two sections: ebony body, dark stained cherrywood bell with decorative turnings; ivory ferrules (fine turnings) and bell mount; serrated pewter bands. One brass key with "swallow-tail" touch, flap countoured to the body, round, mounted in a brass saddle.

31.5 cm.

654
Double Reed Pipe, Straight, 2 keys
Germany? late 19th century
No inscription

Two pearwood sections; brass ferrule. Two brass keys, modern cup type, mounted on pillars. Two tuning holes in bulb bell.

35.9 cm.

599
Double Reed Pipes, 2 keys
Milan, 1883
No inscription (Giuseppe Pelitti)

Five painted (simulating ivory) maple sections; tin plate with two channels for double reeds. Two conical tubes, right side with three fingerholes, two brass keys, modern cup type, mounted on pillars; left side with four fingerholes and thumbhole. Two flared bells. Similar style to 502, beaked flute.

60.3 cm.

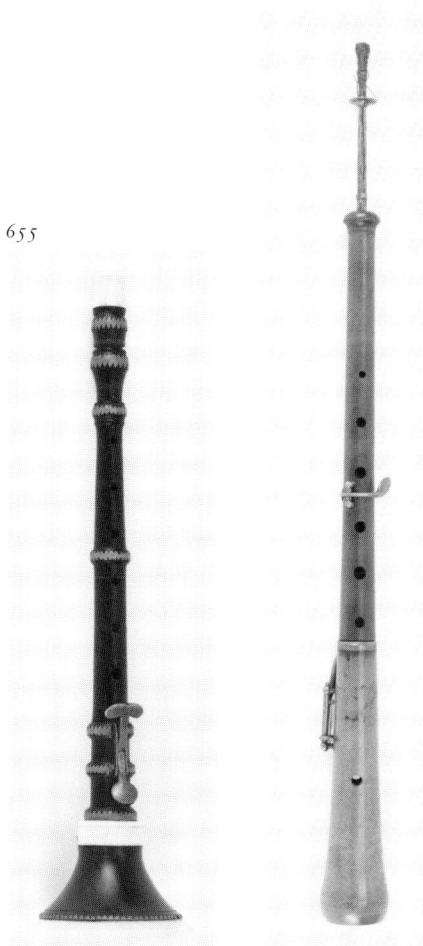

654

655

657
Double Reed Pipe, Curved
Italy? late 19th century
No inscription

Painted (black) brass conical tube with soldered bell. Six small fingerholes.

61.8 cm.

658
Double Reed Pipe, Curved
Italy? late 19th century
No inscription

Painted (black) brass conical tube with soldered bell. Six small fingerholes. Similar to 657.

84.4 cm.

659
Double Reed Pipe, S-shaped
Italy? late 19th century
No inscription

Patinated bronze conical tube. Six fingerholes of various sizes.

58.3 cm.

660
Double Reed Pipe, Straight
Italy? late 19th century
No inscription

Brass conical tube. No fingerholes.

43.3 cm.

661
Crumhorn (Fraud), J-shaped
Florence, late 19th century
Leopoldo Franciolini shop

Leather-covered pine; hard rubber threaded cap. Seven fingerholes; two tuning holes. (See Ripin: 43, illus. 22.)

61 cm.

Bagpipes

688
Bagpipe, "Zampogna"
Italy
Maker unknown (Leopoldo Franciolini, dealer)

Boxwood pipes; horn ferrules fastened with boxwood pegs. Goatskin bag. Round boxwood stock holds four pipes. Two chanters, each with four crudely cut fingerholes. Twinned R4 and L4 tone holes. Threaded joints. Two drone pipes. Red paper stamp of the Florentine dealer Leopoldo Franciolini on the stock (see Ripin: 40, illus. 4).

L, chanters: 29.4, 45 cm.

691
Bagpipe, "Cornemuse"
France

Boxwood pipes; ivory and horn ferrules; pewter bands and inlay. Bag with velvet cover, undecorated. Wooden stock for chanter and tenor drone inset with mirrors and pewter bands. Small pewter whistle (L: 38 mm.) in stock between passages, accessible through hinged wooden door with perforated brass plate; whistle activated by simple rotary switching mechanism. Conical chanter with six fingerholes, thumbhole, plus R4 "swallow-tail" key (open) in German silver, ivory fontanelle. Two tuning holes in flared horn bell. Two drone pipes, tenor in two sections.

L, chanter: 24.9 cm.

691

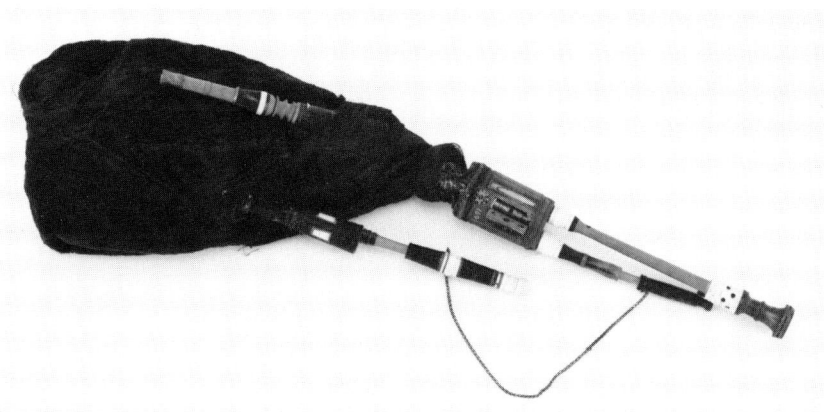

692
Bagpipe, "Cornemuse"
France

Ivory pipes, one-piece stock decorated (top) with carved fleur-de-lys, (bottom) with woman's portrait (Marie Antionette?). Bag with brown velvet cover, embroidered flower; green silk ribbons. Bellows (692 A) covered in brown velvet, borders embroidered with gold thread. Conical chanter with seven fingerholes and thumbhole. Twinned R4 tone hole. Two tuning holes. Single drone pipe in two sections.

L, chanter: 26.4 cm.

693
Bagpipe, "Biniou de Berry"
Effiat, Puy-de-Dôme, 19th century
Bechonnet

Ebony pipes; ivory ferrules and disks; dark stained wooden stock with mother-of-pearl and ebony inlay, decorated with an engraving of a bagpipe player on mother of pearl (top) and (back) geometrical design in red paint on wood veneer. Bag with dark green velvet cover, embroidered with red, white, gold, and green threads; three white buttons. Maple bellows (963 A) with decal of bourgeois lady holding a fan; red painted borders. Conical chanter with seven fingerholes (alternate R4/L4 fingerhole) and thumbhole. Two tuning holes. Two drone pipes, tenor in two sections, bass in three sections.

Stock, bellows, and chanter: BECHONNET / A-EFFIAT / PUY-DE-DÔME.

L, chanter: 42.4 cm.

694
Bagpipe, "Union pipe"
Ireland, mid-19th century

Composite instrument. Dark stained boxwood, rosewood, maple pipes; ivory ferrules; brass and German silver fittings. Round stock holds three drone pipes. Dark stained maple bellows (698); ivory ferrule. Bag missing. Chanter (replacement) with seven fingerholes (R3 brass-bushed) and thumbhole. Three regulators, treble with four brass keys (one missing; one replacement in German silver), tenor with two keys, bass with four keys (one missing), flat, square flaps, mounted in knobs. Three drone pipes, bass with metal coil.

L, chanter: 38.4 cm.

693

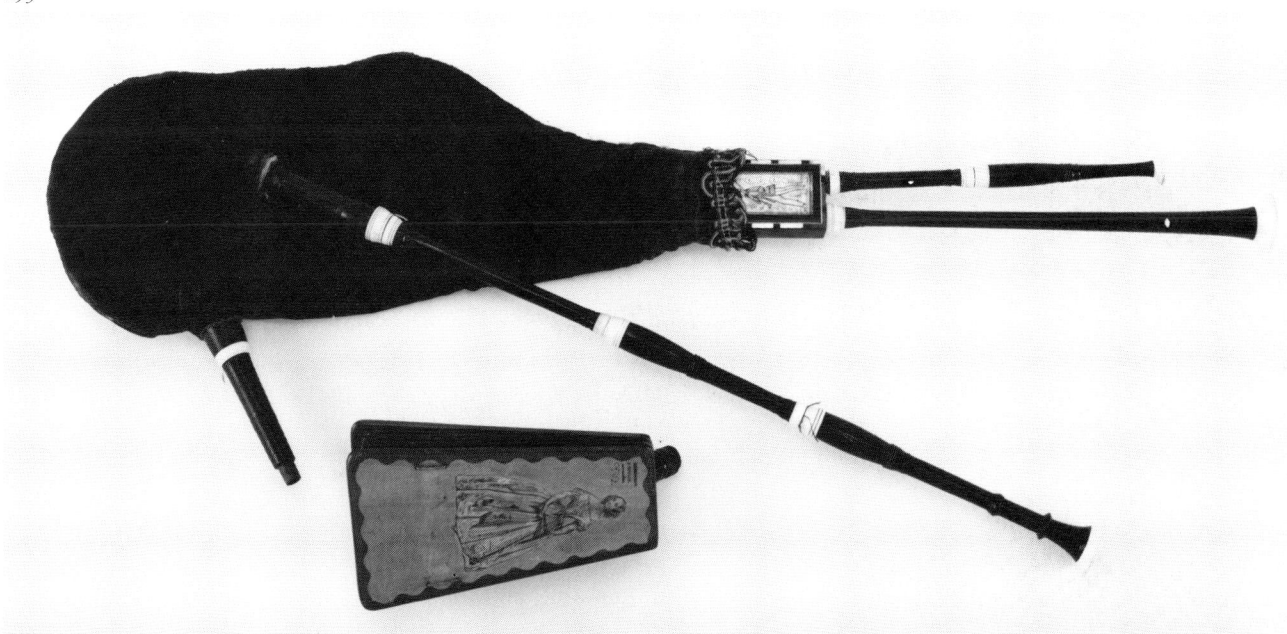

695
Bagpipe, "Cornemuse"
France, Bourbonnais

Maple pipes decorated with pewter lattice work; pewter ferrules. Oval stock holds chanter and drone pipes. Leather bag. Conical chanter with seven fingerholes (alternate R4/L4 fingerhole) and thumbhole. Two tuning holes. Two drone pipes, tenor in two sections, bass in three sections.

L, chanter: 64.9 cm.

696
Bagpipe chanter
Glasgow, early 20th century
Peter Henderson

Two ebony sections; ivory ferrule and disk. Seven fingerholes and thumbhole.

P. HENDERSON / GLASGOW

L: 27.8 cm.

697
Bagpipe
Spain

Boxwood pipes; horn ferrules. Bag with blue and red velvet cover, gold embroidered borders; brass buttons. Conical chanter with seven fingerholes and thumbhole. Three tuning holes. Two drone pipes, bass in three sections. Stoppers.

L, chanter: 31.1 cm.

695

697

699
Bagpipe, "Highland pipe"
Scotland

Dark stained wood of various types; single ivory ferrule, two-piece ivory disk on chanter; brass and tin fittings. Bag with plaid cotton cover, embroidered with purple and gold thread. Conical chanter with seven fingerholes and thumbhole. Two tuning holes. Two long pewter stays on chanter fastened with cotton twine. Two drone pipes (each in two sections); one false drone pipe.

L, chanter: 36.8 cm.

699

700
Bagpipe, "Cornemuse"
France

Dark stained maple pipes; ivory ferrules. Stock pegged and banded (metal tube connects passages); ivory and ebony inlay. Bag with red velvet cover (replacement). Conical chanter with seven fingerholes and thumbhole. Two tuning holes. Single drone pipe in two sections.

L, chanter: 39.3 cm.

613
Single Reed pipe
Italy? 19th century
No inscription

Two sections: cylindrical boxwood body with decoratively carved and painted gourd bell, gourd reedcap with carving of a peasant couple, farming tools, and vinestems; ivory ferrules and bell mount. Four fingerholes; compass: c′ to g′. Upcut cane reed.

42.2 cm.

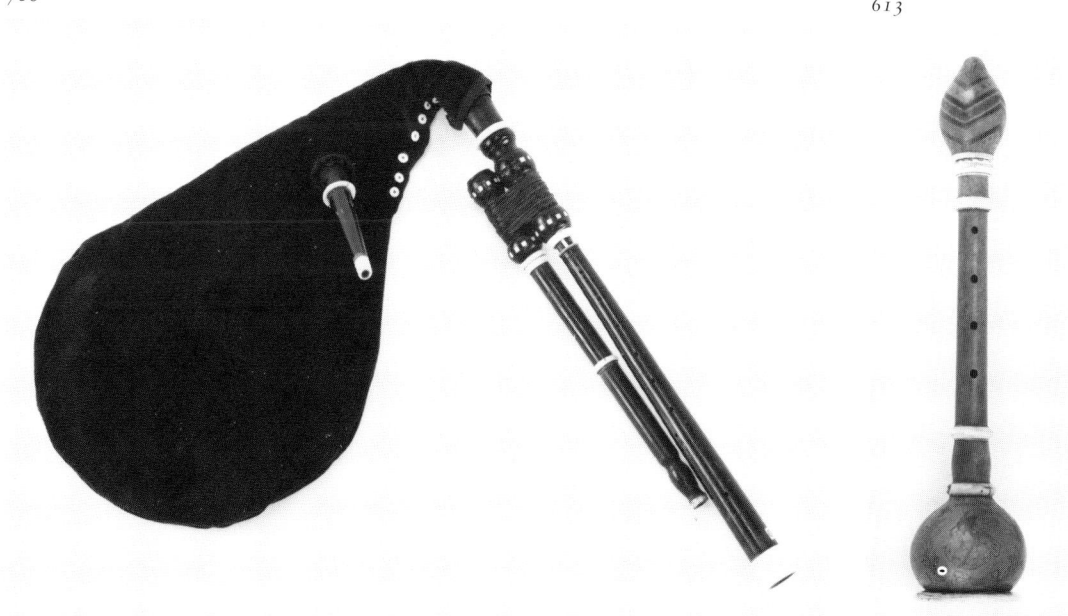

700

613

Free Reed Instruments

726
Harmonica
Germany? 19th century
No inscription

Brass body, two handles; shallow circular bone mouthpiece on the back of the instrument attached to a flat, fruitwood base. Thirty-three reeds; twenty-six front and seven rear brass keys. Front keys arranged in keyboard sequence, all etched with pitch names.

L: 21 cm.   W: 12.5 cm.

727
Harmonica
Brunndobra, late 19th century
G. A. Doerfel (fl. ca. 1897/8)

Wooden body; nickel-plated tin covers; perforated cylindrical housing. Twenty reeds with ten holes. Stamped: DOERFEL'S / Turret Dustproof.

L: 9.9 cm.   ⌀: 32 mm.

728
Harmonica
Austria, late 19th century
Müster

Gumwood body; nickel-plated tin covers. Twenty-four reeds with twelve doubled holes (octaves). Nickel-plated metal bell attached to top of the instrument, activated by a spring-loaded wire lever. Stamped, top: GESETZLICH GESCHÜTZT [two exposition seals].

L: 12.75 cm.   W: 5.6 cm.

729
Harmonica
Germany? late 19th century
No inscription

Cylindrical pine body; nickel-plated tin perforated strips. Thirty-three reeds; three rows of eleven holes. Re-entrant tuning (not fully playable).

L: 37.3 cm.   ⌀: 24 cm.

726

728

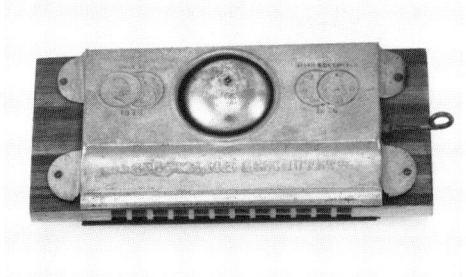

730
Harmonica
Germany, late 19th century
Ch. Messner & Cie (founded 1830)

Gumwood body; nickel-plated tin covers. Thirty-two reeds with eighteen doubled holes (unisons). Stamped, top: CH. MESSNER / FOUNDER OF THE TROSSINGEN / HARMONICA-INDUSTRY / FACTORY FOUNDED IN 1830 / MADE / IN / GERMANY; (back): DAVID'S HARP / TRADE MARK / REGISTERED / CH. MESSNER & CIE [four exhibition seals].

L: 19.8 cm.   W: 3.3 cm.

731
Harmonica
Germany, late 19th century
Gebr. Meinhold

Gumwood body; nickel-plated tin covers. Forty reeds with twenty doubled holes (octaves). Stamped, top: ORGAN NIGHTINGALE / WARRANTEED[monogram:] M / GENUINE / MADE IN GERMANY; back: [four exhibition seals] / GESETZLICH GESCHÜTZT / GEBR. MEINHOLD.

L: 19.7 cm.   W: 3.3 cm.

732
Harmonica
Germany, late 19th century

Painted (black) wood; brass-plated tin covers. Forty reeds with twenty doubled holes (unisons). Stamped, top: WILH [crest] THIE.

L: 14.3 cm.   W: 2.6 cm.

735
Harmonica ("Gunters Mund-Harmonica-Trompete")
Germany, late 19th century
Güntner

Two sections: pine body in triangular nickel-plated tin housing set on a hollow tube, nickel-plated bell section. Twenty reeds with ten holes.

L: 10.4 cm.   W: 2.6 cm.
L: (with bell): 37.7 cm.

713
Pocket Signal Horn
England? 19th century
No inscription

Nickel-plated brass mouthpipe and valve casing; brass bell with nickel-plated lip. Braided tassel (gold). Two free reeds; one piston valve with restraining screw. Instrument sounds two tones (a and d'). Valve casing stamped: 21.

17.3 cm.

735

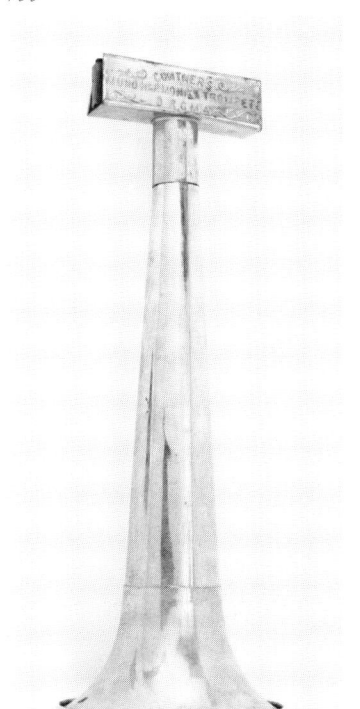

713

719
Pitch pipe
U.S.A., late 19th century
No inscription

Brass reed; steel fittings; nickel-plated tin housing. Sliding mechanism changes the length of free reed. Top with calibrated scale; compass: f to f'.

6.2 cm.

733
Vertical Mouth Organ, Trumpet Shape (Toy)
Italy? late 19th century
Maker unknown

Tin. Eight reeds in cylinders activated by tin keys with flat, round flaps.

32.4 cm.

734
Vertical Mouth Organ, Clarinet Shape
Italy? late 19th century
No inscription

Brass. Thirteen brass keys, shallow cup type, twelve key shanks and touches mounted on two transverse rods with adjusting screws, L th. key mounted in brass saddle. Reeds in cylinders.

56.4 cm.

736
Vertical Mouth Organ, Recorder Shape
    (**Harmonicor**)
France? late 19th century
No inscription

Cylindrical mahogany body; nickel-plated metal pipes; white and black ivory buttons. Twenty-five reeds activated by pistons, arranged in keyboard sequence (one hand plays the diatonic, the other chromatic tones); compass: c'-c'''. Curved nickel-plated brass crook.

48.4 cm.

Cornetti

831
Cornetto (A)
Germany? late 17th / early 18th century
No inscription

Parchment-covered pear or apple wood; iron reinforcing band at receiver. Slightly curved; octagonal tube. Six fingerholes and thumb-hole (worn). Decorative scoring along corpus.

56.5 cm.
Receiver ⌀: 10.6 mm.

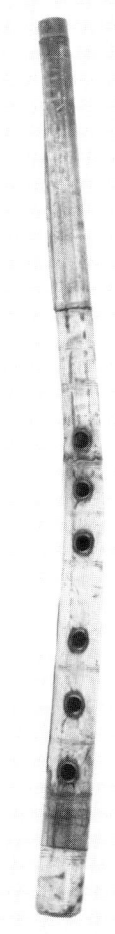

831

829
Cornetto (G) (Fraud)
Florence, late 19th century
Leopoldo Franciolini shop

Leather-covered pine; boxwood and ivory ferrule. S-shaped; round tube. Six fingerholes. (See Ripin: 43, illus. 23.)

44.6 cm.

830
Cornetto (G) (Fraud)
Florence, late 19th century
Leopoldo Franciolini shop

Leather-covered pine; ivory ferrule; brass bands. S-shaped; round tube. Six fingerholes.

52 cm.

832
Cornetto (C) (Fraud)
Florence, late 19th century
Leopoldo Franciolini shop

Leather-covered pine; ivory ferrule. Curved; round tube. Six fingerholes.

43 cm.

833
Cornettino (Fraud)
Germany? 19th century
No inscription

Leather. Curved; round tube. Six crudely bored fingerholes, arbitrarily spaced. Acquired in 1868, Hamburg (Stanley 1921: 124).

34.9 cm.

834
Corno torto (Tenor Cornetto) (Fraud)
Florence, late 19th century
Leopoldo Franciolini shop

Leather-covered pine; ivory ferrule. S-shaped; round tube. Six fingerholes arbitrarily spaced. Single brass key, flat flap (Young, Design O), brass saddle half recessed into key shank, steel leaf spring. (See Ripin: 42, illus. 15.)

72 cm.

835
Cornetto (D) (Fraud)
Florence, late 19th century
Leopoldo Franciolini shop

Leather-covered pine; ivory ferrule. Curved; octagonal tube. Six fingerholes arbitrarily spaced. Single brass key, flat flap (Young, Design N), mounted in brass saddle, sheet metal spring. Red paper stamp of Florentine dealer, Leopoldo Franciolini. (See Ripin: 42, illus. 12.)

87.5 cm.

836
Corno curvo (Fraud)
Florence, late 19th century
Leopoldo Franciolini shop

Leather-covered pine; ivory ferrule; two brass bands with brass rings for cord. No fingerholes. (See Ripin: 42, illus. 4.)

74.5 cm.

Serpents,
Ophimonocleides,
Russian Bassoon,
Ophicleides

935
Serpent
France? early 19th century
No inscription

Leather-covered fruitwood body; brass crook and fitting. Crook with brass ring and retaining wing nut.

84.2 cm.
Receiver ⌀: 11.5 mm.

903
Serpent Militaire (Fraud)
Florence, late 19th century
No inscription (Leopoldo Franciolini shop)

Leather-covered pine body; brass crook. Figure-eight shape. Six fingerholes arbitrarily spaced. (See Ripin: 38, illus. 8.)

74 cm.
Receiver ⌀: 15 mm.

935

923
Serpent Militaire (Fraud)
Florence, late 19th century
No inscription (Leopoldo Franciolini shop)

Leather-covered pine body; brass crook and bell. Coiled. Six small fingerholes arbitrarily spaced.

94 cm.
Bell ⌀: 28.5 cm.
Receiver ⌀: 14.7 mm.

899
Ophimonocleide (Serpent Coeffet)
France, 19th century, second quarter
Jean-Baptiste Coeffet? (fl. 1828-1845)

Leather-covered wood body sections; six fingerholes with ivory bushings (three missing); brass crook, ferrules, U-bend guard (missing), and bell. One brass key, round flap, contoured to the bell section, mounted in brass saddles. Crook with inner/outer U-slide.

96.6 cm.
Bell ⌀: 18.3 cm.
Receiver ⌀: 11.55 mm.

934
Ophimonocleide (in B♭)
Paris, mid-19th century
Darche (fl. 1830-1855)

Veneered wood lower body section; brass crook, upper body section, fittings, and bell rim. Three brass keys, modern cup type, two mounted on pillars attached to plates (Heyde 1982: 233, Design 27), one in brass saddle, steel leaf springs. Water key.

Inside bell: DARCHE / Rue de Rivoli / BREVETÉ / à Paris

96 cm.
Bell ⌀: 16.3 cm.
Receiver ⌀: 11 mm.

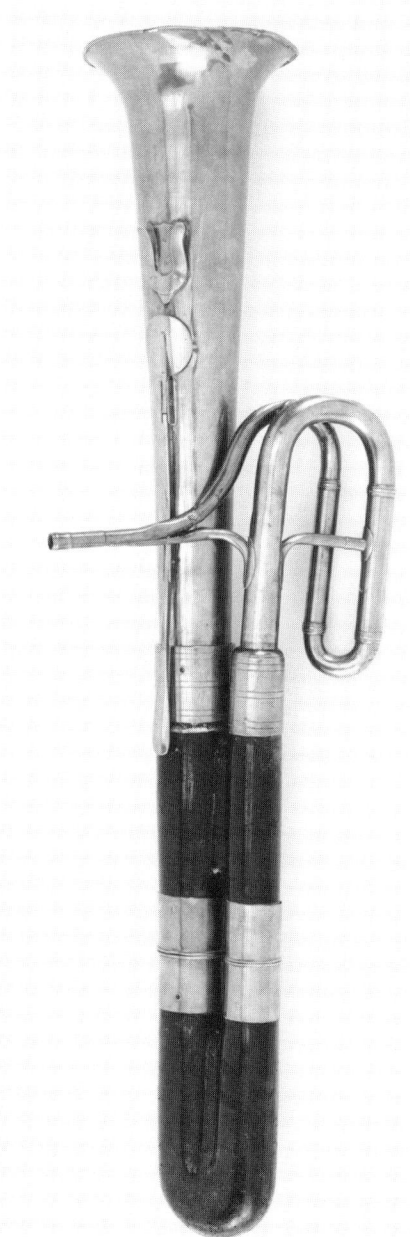

899

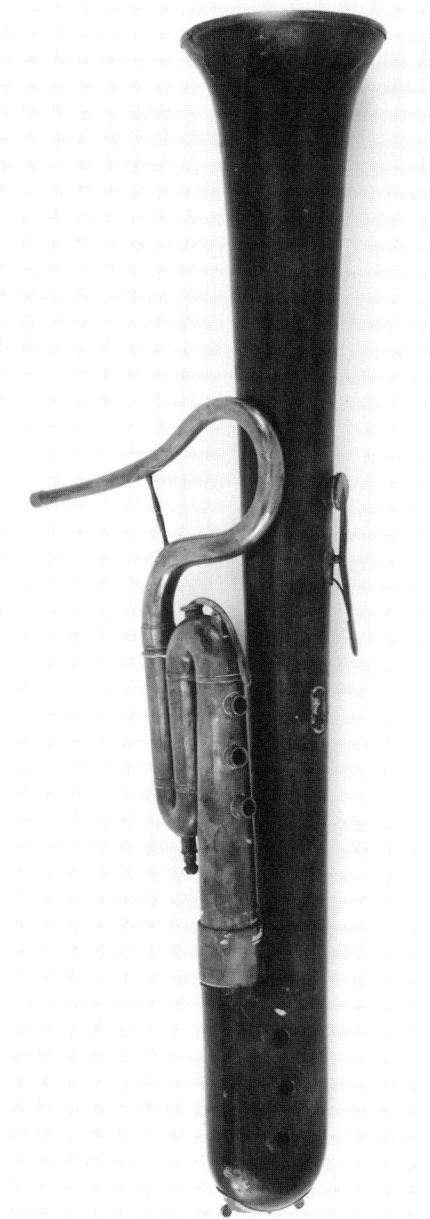

934

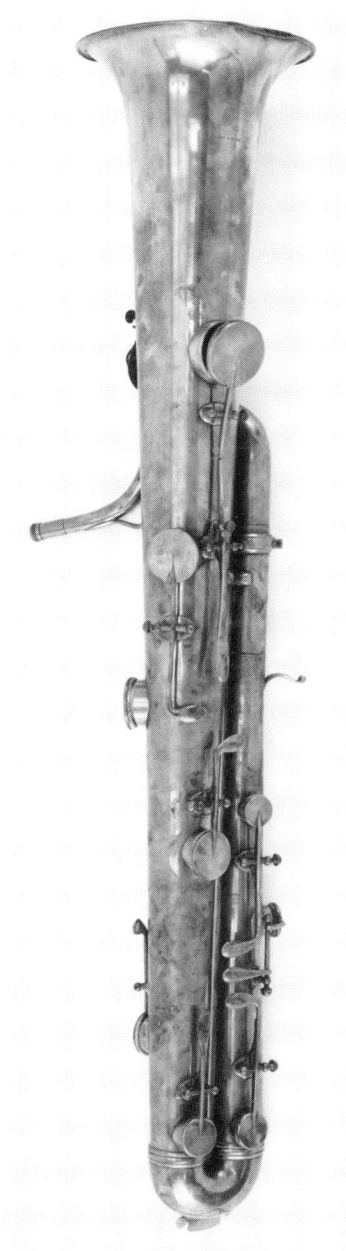

933

902
Russian bassoon
Lyon, ca. 1835
Dubois & Couturier (fl. 1835-1837)

Three dark stained maple body sections (one missing); brass crook, fittings, and painted dragon's head bell (missing). Three brass keys (extant sections with two), round flaps, one flat, one contoured to the body, mounted on pillars attached to plates. Crook with inner-outer U-slide.

1, 2: DUBOIS / & / COUTURIER / * à Lyon *

76 cm. (extant sections)
Receiver ⌀: 10.9 mm.

933
Alto Ophicleide (in E♭)
Paris, mid-19th century
Louis David (fl. 1827-1873)

Brass. Nine brass keys, modern cup type, mounted on pillars with adjusting screws, attached to plates, brass springs in slots on plates. Brass crook (clamp socket) with tuning U-slide.

DAVID A PARIS

91 cm.
Bell ⌀: 18.5 cm.
Receiver ⌀: 11.3 mm.

931
Bass Ophicleide (in B♭)
Barcelona, 19th century, third quarter
Bernareggi

Brass, painted (red, gold) dragon's head bell. Nine brass keys, modern cup type, mounted on pillars attached to elliptical plates, steel leaf springs on raised platforms. Circular coiled crook.

Bell ferrule: BERNAREGGI INSTRUMENTISTA DE [coat of arms] CAMARA DE S. M. A BARCELONA

121 cm.
Receiver ⌀: 12.5 mm.

Signal Horns

791
Alphorn
Switzerland, late 19th century
Maker unknown

Birch; wound with strips of bark. Hooked (upturned bell). Wooden mouthpiece.

148 cm.

792
Alphorn
Switzerland, late 19th century
Maker unknown

Birch; wound with strips of bark. Folded. Wooden mouthpiece.

104 cm.

1994
Winterhorn
Switzerland, modern
Maker unknown

Pine; bark stays. Curved; side-blown. Wooden mouthpiece, cut diagonally.

123 cm.

1373
Foghorn
Newfoundland, early 20th century
Maker unknown

Soldered sheet tin.

155 cm.

792

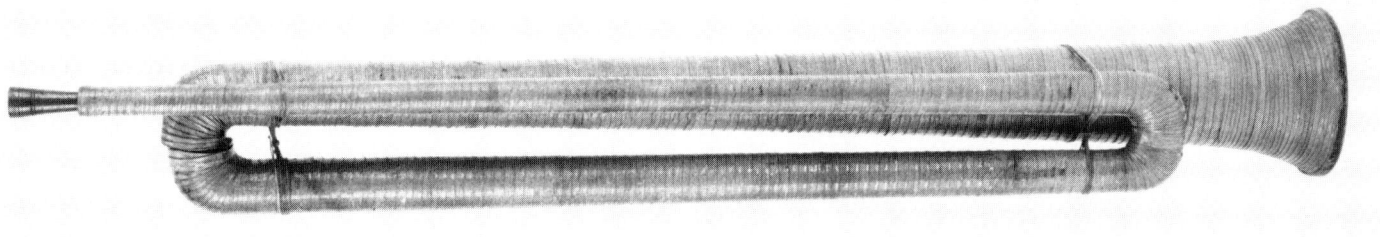

773

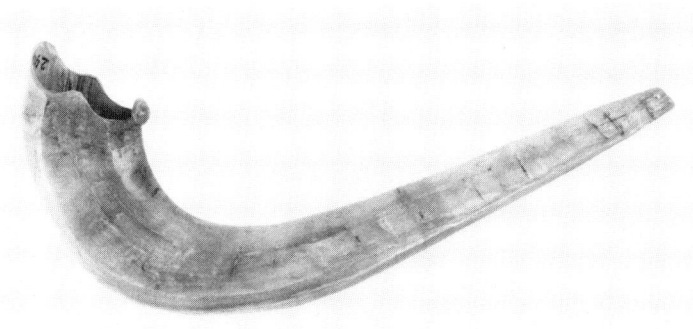

773
Shofar
Palestine

Ram's horn. No carvings or fittings.

30.8 cm.

768
Oliphant
France
Maker unknown

Ivory. Curved. Decoratively carved elephant tusk with hunting scenes, crown with coat of arms bearing three fleur-de-lys, three profiles within oval medallions inscribed: FRANCOIS. I, HENRI. II, FRANCOIS. II.

106 cm.
Mouthpiece O⌀: 26 mm.   I⌀: 21 mm.
    Depth: 7 mm.

777
Hunting Horn
Germany?

Cow's horn; decoratively carved ivory ferrule; decoration in sheet tin at finial; leather bell guard, receiver with leather bushing. End-blown.

38.5 cm.

779
Hunting Horn
Italy?

Cow's horn; iron rings for cord. Decoratively carved with hunting scene, coat of arms, various designs.

34 cm.

768 detail

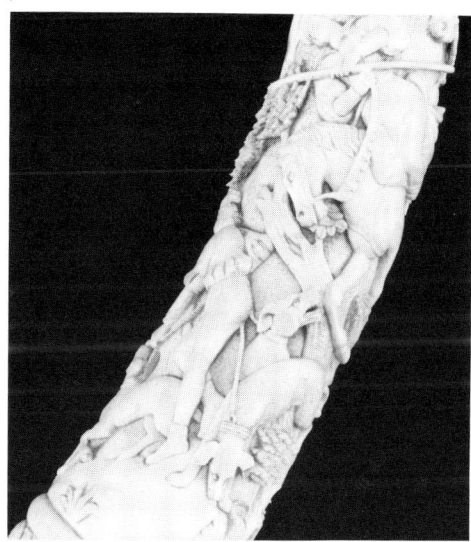

779

768

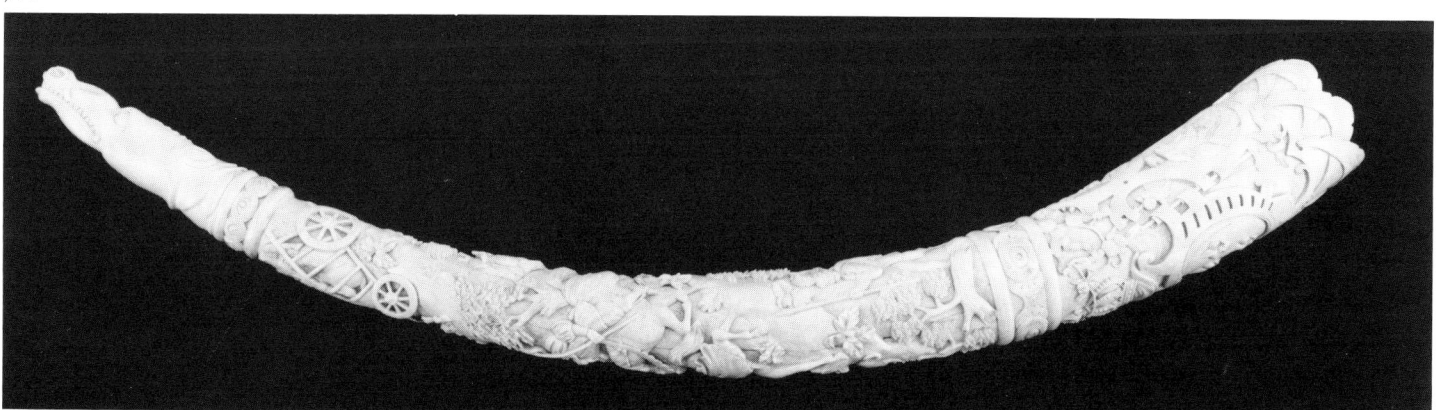

780
Hunting Horn
Argentina? 19th century

Ox horn; brass rings for cord; German silver bands, bell mount, decorative castings of hunting scene. Heart-shaped medallion in German silver (no inscription). Mouthpiece missing.

31.8 cm.

781
Hunting Horn
Germany? 19th century?

Cow's horn; leather finial, bell guard, two leather bands with German silver rings for braided cotton cord.

38.5 cm.

782
Hunting Horn
Milan, late 19th century
Giuseppe Pelitti (fl. ca. 1835-1893)

Cow's horn; German silver receiver (missing), mountings, rings for cord. German silver medallion (two lions; Milanese coat of arms) inscribed: PELITTI-MILANO.

50 cm.

807
Ruf-Horn
Germany? 19th century

Animal horn; two sections with threaded joint. Brass receiver and bell mount (missing).

31.8 cm.

808
Coach Horn (D), Straight
France? 19th century
No inscription

Brass. Two engraved ferrules.

99.7 cm.
Bell ⌀: 10.2 cm.
Receiver ⌀: 8.3 mm.

782

810
Coach Horn (F), Straight
Paris, mid-19th century
Etienne Francois Périnet (fl. 1829-1846)

Brass.

F. PERINET / 31 RUE COPERNIC / PARIS

130 cm.
Bell ⌀: 10 cm.
Receiver ⌀: 9 mm.

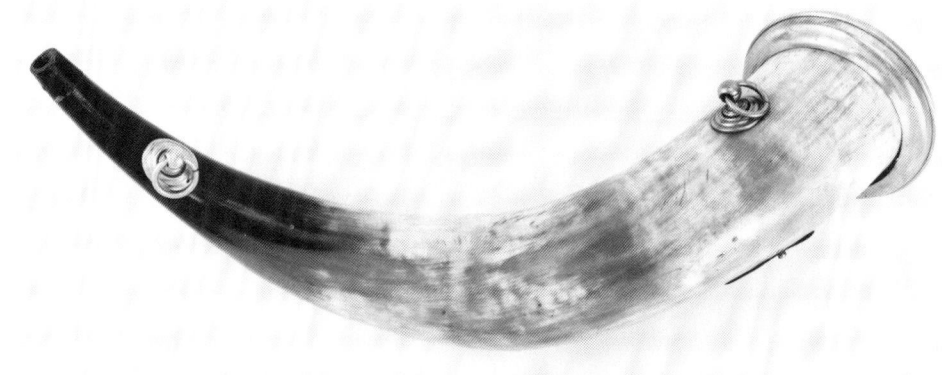

808

813
Coach Horn (G♭), Straight
England? 19th century
No inscription

German silver. Engraved ferrules.

65.8 cm.
Bell ⌀: 7.6 cm.
Receiver ⌀: 10 mm.

814
Coach Horn (B♭), Keyed, Straight
Italy? late 19th century
No inscription

Brass. Two brass keys, modern cup type, mounted in brass saddles, brass springs. Mouthpipe missing.

91 cm.
Bell ⌀: 9.8 cm.

816
Coach Horn (E♭), Keyed, Straight
Italy? late 19th century
No inscription

Brass. Two brass keys, modern cup type, mounted in brass saddles, brass springs. Similar to 814.

96 cm.
Bell ⌀: 8.7 cm.
Receiver ⌀: 11 mm.

818
Coach Horn (B♭), Keyed, Straight
Italy? late 19th century
No inscription

Brass. Two brass keys, modern cup type, mounted in brass saddles, brass springs. Similar to 814 and 816.

129 cm.
Bell ⌀: 10.5 cm.
Receiver ⌀: 11.7 mm.

851
Post Horn (G), Looped
England? 19th century
No inscription

Copper; brass mouthpiece. Bell section and mouthpiece soldered to body.

16.7 cm.
Bell ⌀: 7.5 cm.
Receiver ⌀: apprx. 8 mm.

851

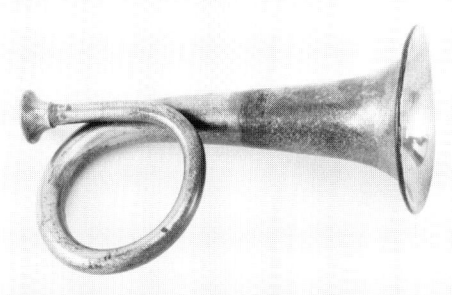

Horns

874
Waldhorn in D (Parforce-jagdhorn)
Dresden, 1775
Johann Gottfried Kersten (fl. 1775-1840)

Composite instrument (corpus not original). Brass. Two loops. Engraved bell garland (W: 3 cm.). Patched.

VERFERTIGT JOHANN GOTTFRIED KERSTEN / [coat of arms] / IN DRESDEN 1775

Corpus (oval): 53 x 48 cm.
Bell ⌀: 29 cm.
Receiver ⌀: 12 mm.

875
Cor de Chasse in D
Paris, ca. 1900
A. Leriche

Brass, interior of bell painted (black). Cylindrical tubes of graduated diameters with lapped joints.

A LERICHE / [crown mark] / PARIS

Corpus ⌀: 40 cm.
Bell ⌀: 26 cm.
Receiver ⌀: 7 mm.

878
Coiled Horn in D
France? late 19th century
No inscription

Brass. Mouthpipe bent toward the interior of single loop.

Corpus ⌀: 54 cm.
Bell ⌀: 30 cm.
Receiver ⌀: 10 mm.

874

874 detail

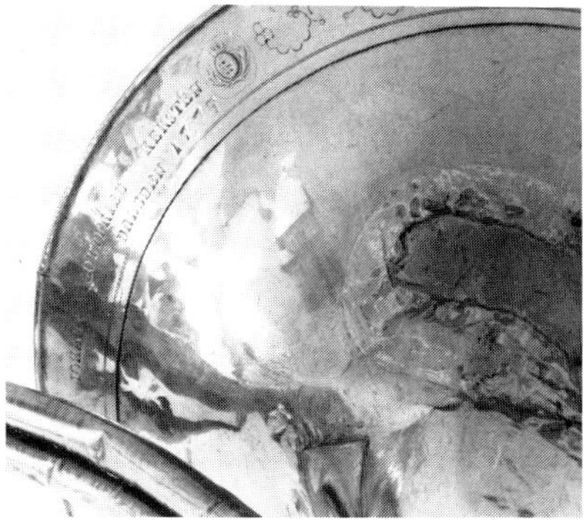

875 detail

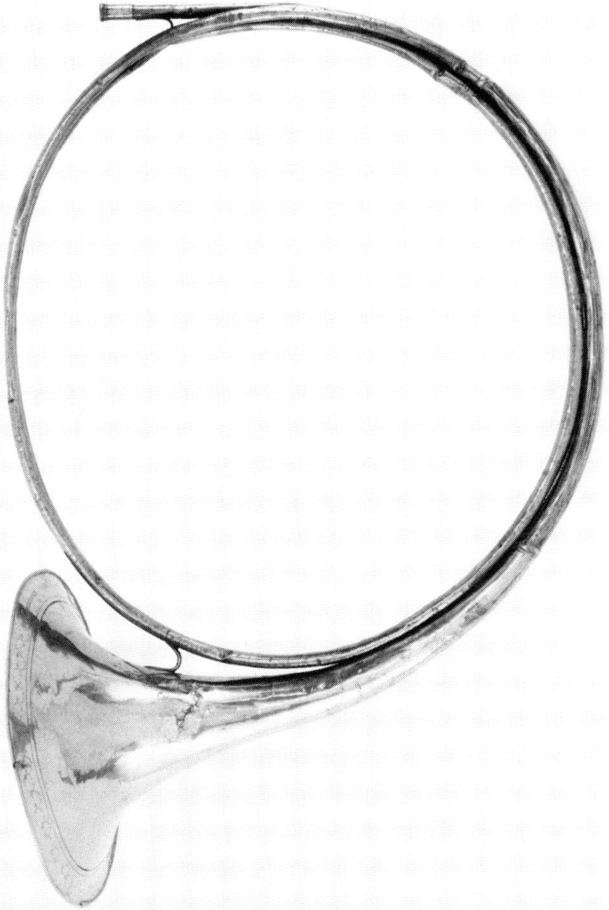

875

85

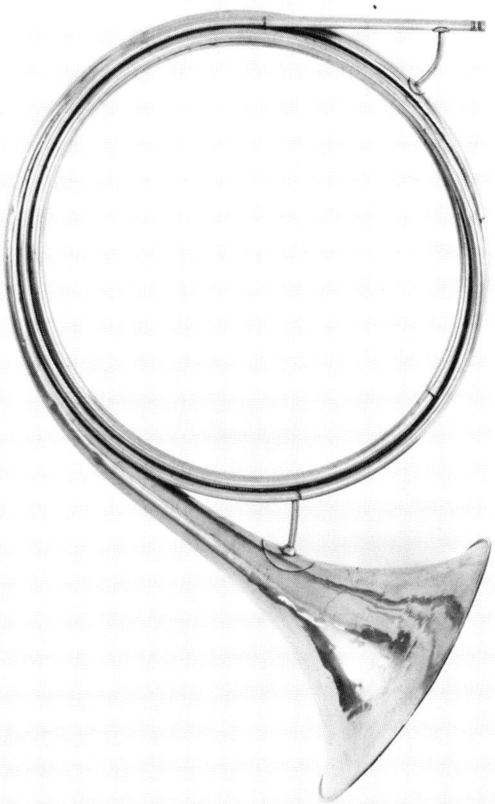

880 detail

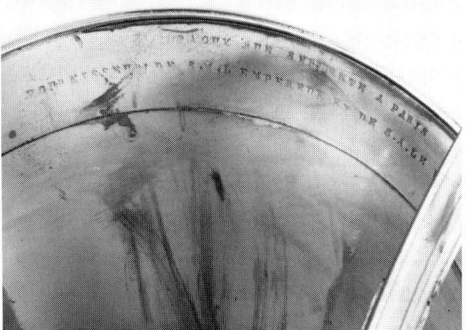

880

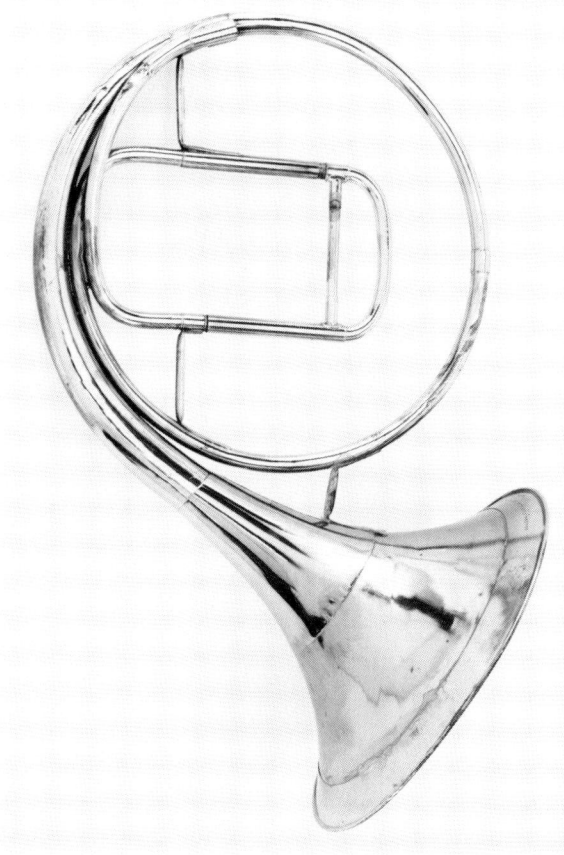

880
Orchestra Horn
Paris, 19th century, second quarter
Marcel-Auguste Raoux (1795-1871)

Brass. Eight terminal crooks (879 A-C, E, F, I-K) pitched (with duplications): E♭ (stamped: MB), E (Mi), G (Sol), A♭ (LaB), A (La).

RAOUX RUE SERPENT A PARIS / FOURNISSEUR DE S. A. L'EMPEROR ET DE J. J. LE VICE ROI D'EGYPT (within oval) T. O-C

Corpus ⌀: 34 cm.
Bell: 34 cm. (W, bell garland: 3 cm.)
Receiver ⌀: 8 mm.

879 D, H
Terminal crooks, B♭-alto

Brass. One loop; for 7 mm. receiver. Flat brass braces inscribed: A S.

O⌀: 11.5 cm.

879 G
Terminal crook, E♭

Brass. Two loops; for 8 mm. receiver. Brass plate (receiver) inscribed: MiB + 1.

O⌀: 27.9 cm.

881
Orchestra Horn
Vienna? early 19th century
No inscription

Brass, engraved ferrules; nickel-plated brace (later addition).

Corpus ⌀: 26.5 cm.
Bell: 28 cm.
Receiver ⌀: 11 mm.

882
Cor de Chasse in D (Helical Horn)
Paris, mid-19th century
Courtois Frère (fl. 1803-1844)

Brass, interior of bell painted (black). Nine loops in two layers. Cylindrical tubes of graduated diameters with lapped joints.

COURTOIS FRÈRE RUE DE CAIRE A PARIS

Corpus: O∅: 21 cm. I∅: 8.5 cm.
Bell ∅: 23.5 cm.
Receiver ∅: 8.5 mm.

883
Orchestra Horn (Inventionshorn)
Neukirchen, Saxony, early 19th century
C. W. Dürrschmidt

Brass. Interior inner/outer U-slide. Crooks and couplers missing.

C. W. Dürrschmidt Neukirchen in Sachsen

Corpus ∅: 28 cm.
Bell ∅: 27.5 cm. (W, bell garland: 2.4 cm.)
Receiver ∅: 11.5 mm.

883 detail

882

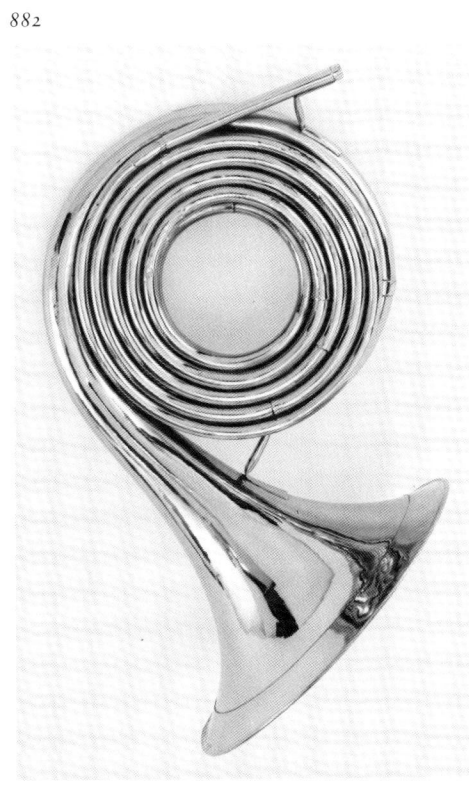

883

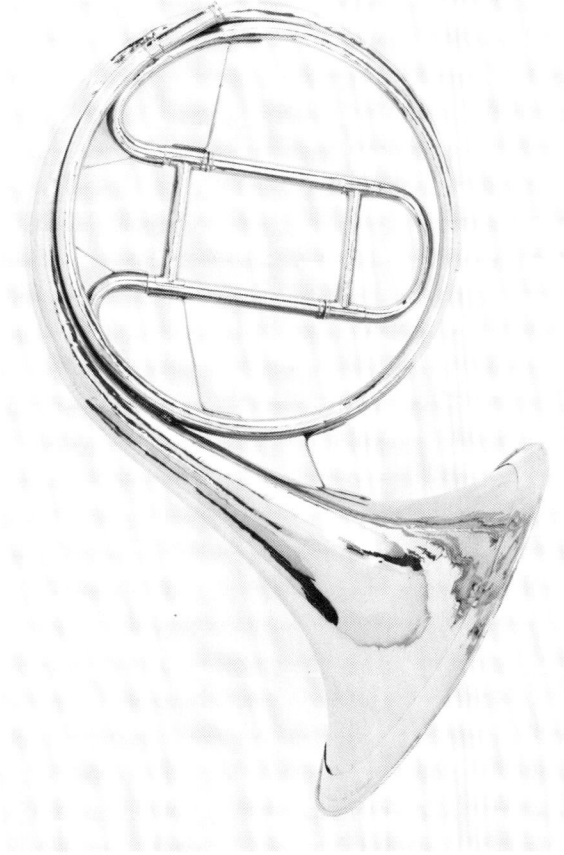

885

885
Orchestra Horn, Valved
Paris, late 19th century
Antoine Courtois-[Auguste] Mille
  (fl. 1880-1909)

Brass. Two detachable Périnet valves *(Sauterelle)*, top springs. U-slide (lacking) may be inserted in place of valve system. A-alto terminal crook extant.

ANTOINE COURTOIS & MILLE / MILLE SR / FACTEUR DU CONSERVATOIRE NATIONAL / 88 rue des Marais St. Martin / Paris

Corpus ⌀: 32.5 cm.
Bell ⌀: 28 cm.
Receiver ⌀: 7.5 mm.

886
Orchestra Horn, Valved
Austria? late 19th century
No inscription

Brass; German silver buttons, linkages, screws and caps. Three Vienna rotary valves, clock spring action.

Corpus ⌀: 33 cm.
Bell ⌀: 28.5 cm.
Receiver ⌀: 8 mm.

937
Alto-Tenor Saxtromba in E♭
Paris, mid-19th century
Adolphe (Antoine Joseph) Sax (1814-1894)

Brass. Three Périnet valves, bottom springs.
E♭ crook. U-slide.

No. 21130 / Adolphe Sax Breveté
 à Paris / F. teur de la M.son Mil.re de
 l'Empereur / [monogram:] A S (in cross
 stroke of letter S:) PARIS

73 cm.
Bell ⌀: 27.8 cm.
Receiver ⌀: 12.55 mm.

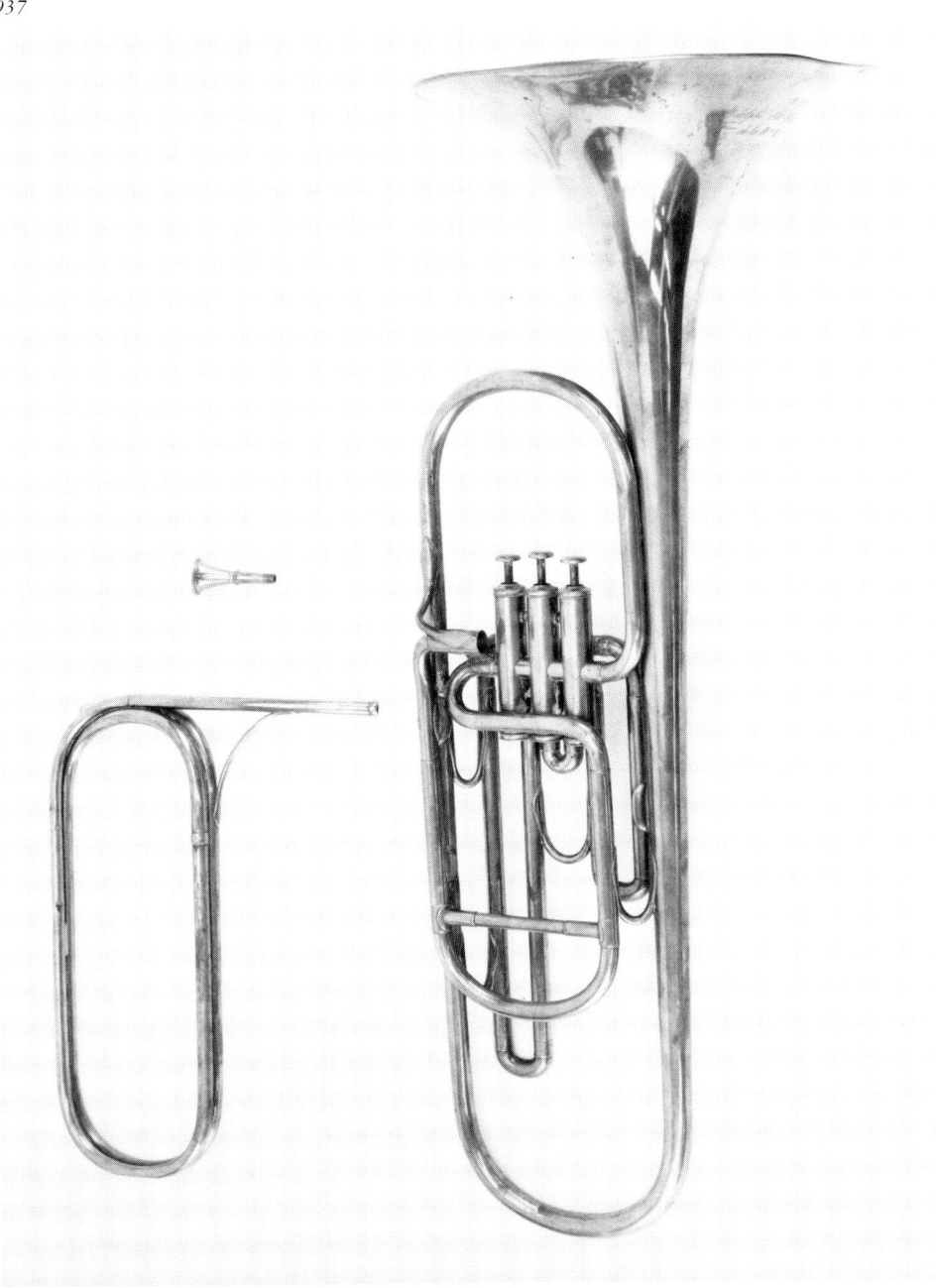

937

Bugles

822
Bugle in C
St. Petersburg, mid-19th century
Franz Eschenbach (1821-1898)

Brass. Single loop. Oval medallion with
Imperial Russian coat of arms on bell.

ESCHENBACH / S. PETERBURG (transliteration)

38.1 cm.
Bell ⌀: 8.2 cm.
Receiver ⌀: 11.5 mm.

822

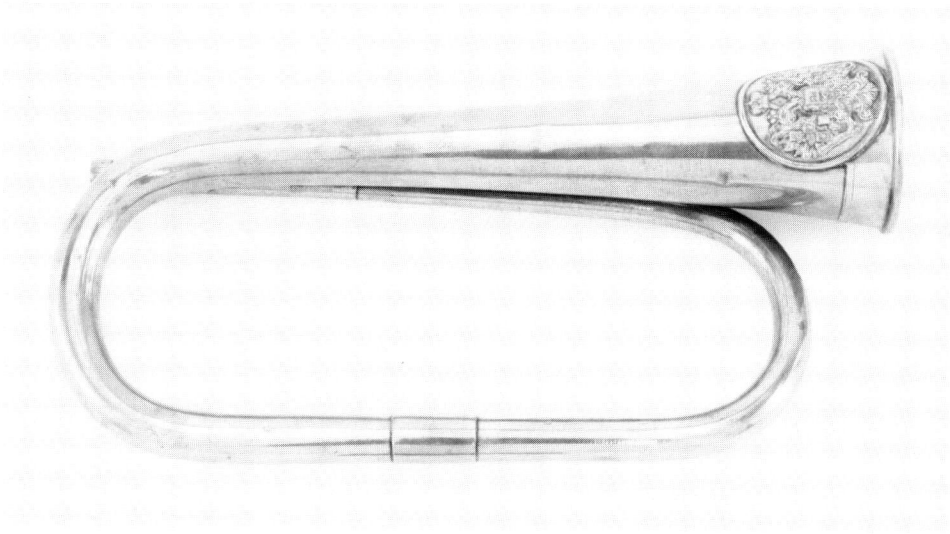

823
Bugle in D (D♭)
Berlin, mid-19th century
C. F. Lindenberg (fl. 1832-1847)

Brass; silver medallion without engraving; two brass rings for a blue silk cord with tassels. Single loop. Original mouthpiece.

.LINDENBERG. IN. BERLIN.

35.4 cm.
Bell ⌀: 10.3 cm.
Receiver ⌀: 11.6 mm.

852
Bugle in B♭ ("Buglet")
London, late 19th century
Henry Keat & Sons (fl. ca. 1845-1895)

Nickel-plated brass; nickel-plated clip and ring for a black cotton cord. Four loops. Original mouthpiece. Raised shield on bell, engraved: THORNTON / HEATH / B[ritish]. c[avalry].

THE / BUGLET / Prize Medal / 4 TURNS / BY APPOINTMENT TO THE WAR & INDIAN OFFICES / [seal of Great Britain] HY KEAT & SONS 105 / MATTHIAS RD / STOKE NEWINGTON G[REE]N N[ORTH] / London

16.5 cm.
Oval bell: 9 x 6.3 cm.
Receiver ⌀: 9.8 mm.

823

852
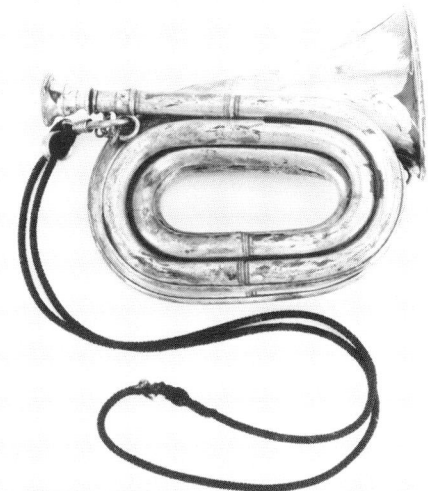

845

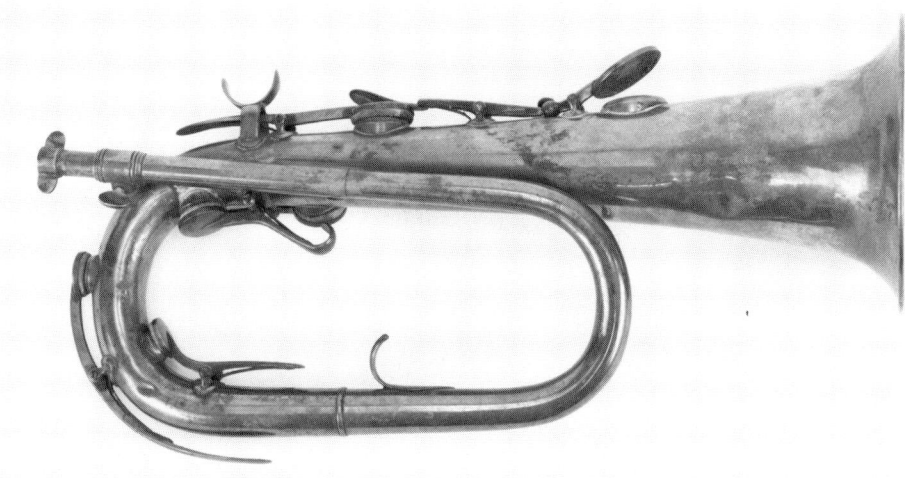

846

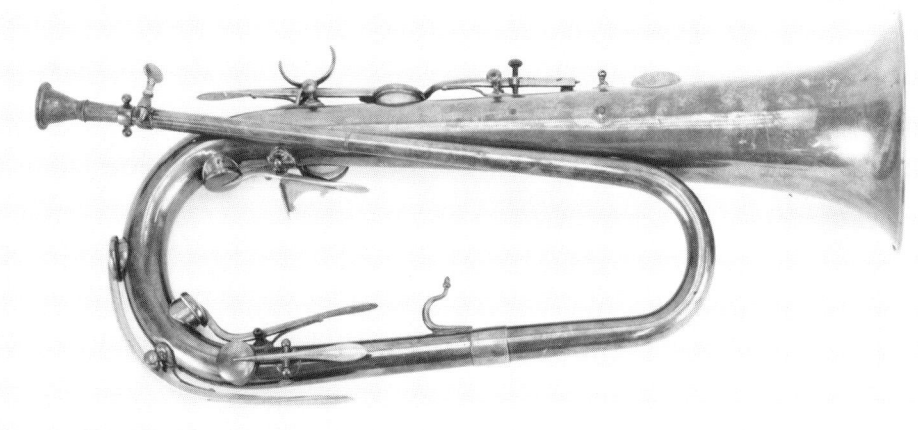

845
Keyed Bugle in E♭
Lyon, mid-19th century
Louis Müller (fl. ca. 1835-1867)

Brass. Seven brass keys (one open), modern cup type, mounted on pillars (Heyde 1982: 233, Design 22) attached to elliptical plates, steel leaf springs. Receiver I-slide with clamp. Open R4 key with ball and socket linkage.

[mark] / MÜLLER / BREVETE / A
 LYON / [mark]

38.3 cm.
Bell ⌀: 13.1 cm.
Receiver ⌀: 10.9 mm.

846
Keyed Bugle in B♭
France? mid-19th century
No inscription

Brass. Eight brass keys (one open), modern cup type, mounted on pillars with adjusting screws (Heyde 1982: 233, Design 25), seven attached to elliptical plates, one tear drop-shaped plate (see ibid., Design 27), brass leaf springs. Receiver I-slide with clamp. Open R4 key (missing) with screw device (closes the lowest tone hole); R th. key with alternate touch.

49.5 cm.
Bell ⌀: 14.5 cm.
Receiver ⌀: 10.6 mm.

847
Keyed Bugle in E♭
Brussels, 19th century, second quarter
B. Mahillon, jeune (fl. ca. 1835)

Brass. Six brass keys, modern cup type, mounted on pillars (Heyde 1982: 233, Design 22) attached to diamond-shaped plates, steel leaf springs. Receiver I-slide with clamp; funnel-shaped receiver. Open R4 key with ball and socket linkage.

Mahillon jeune / Bruxelles.

39.1 cm.
Bell ⌀: 14.5 cm.
Receiver ⌀: 9.3 mm.

848
Keyed Bugle in C
Mainz, mid-19th century
Klüh

Brass. Six brass keys (one open), flat, round flaps (Heyde 1982: 235, Design 3), mounted in saddles (see ibid., p. 233, Design 1), brass leaf springs. Receiver I-slide with clamp; funnel-shaped receiver. Open R4 key with screw device (closes the lowest tone hole).

On bell garland: Klüh Mainz

42.1 cm.
Bell ⌀: 16.3 cm.
Receiver ⌀: 11.4 mm.

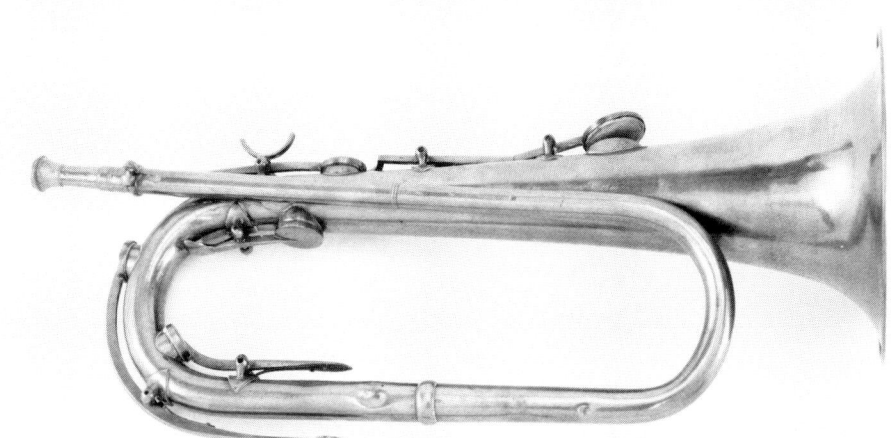

847

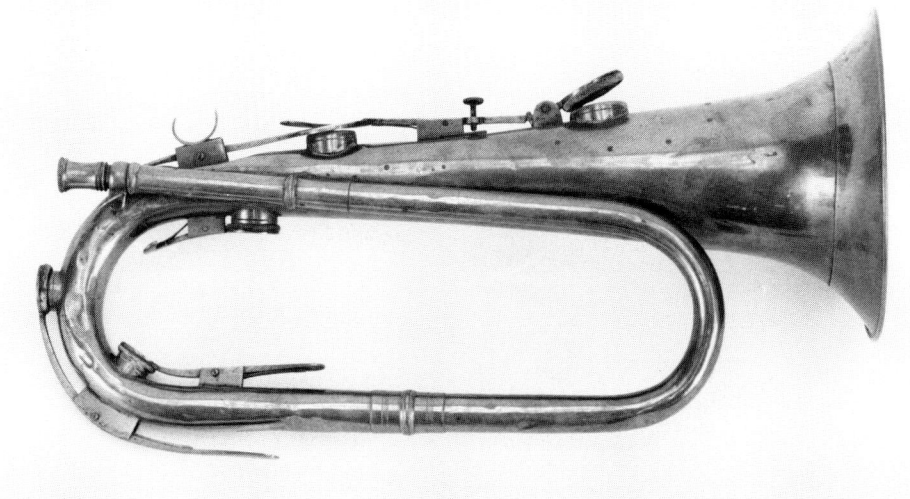

848

849
Keyed Bugle in C
England? mid-19th century
No inscription

Brass. Eight brass keys (one open), flat, round flaps (Heyde 1982: 235, Design 3), mounted in saddles (half recessed into key shanks), brass leaf springs. Receiver I-slide with clamp (screw missing). Open R4 key with screw device (screw missing). Rim of bell garland with decorative engraving (floral motif).

44.5 cm.
Bell ⌀: 18 cm.
Receiver ⌀: 12 mm.

844
Valved Bugle in B♭, Three Keys
Paris, mid-19th century
Adolphe (Antoine Joseph) Sax (1814-1894)

Brass. Long Berlin valves (L: 8 cm.), second valve with one horizontal and two parallel sloping passages; three brass keys, axle-mounted on pillars, touches adjacent to valves. Receiver I-slide (missing) with clamp. First button missing.

No. 24230 / Adolphe Sax Breveté à Paris / F.teur de la M.son Mil.re de l'Empereur

46.3 cm.
Bell ⌀: 14 cm.
Bore: 10 mm.

855
Valved Bugle in E♭
Boston, 19th century, third quarter
Graves & Co. (fl. 1849-1863)

German silver. String action rotary valves, top-mounted. Detachable lead pipe/valve section held in place by two screws on braces; third lever attached to strut soldered to cap of third valve.

Made by / GRAVES & CO. / Boston

32 cm.
Bell ⌀: 11.7 cm.
Bore: 10.8 mm.

844 detail

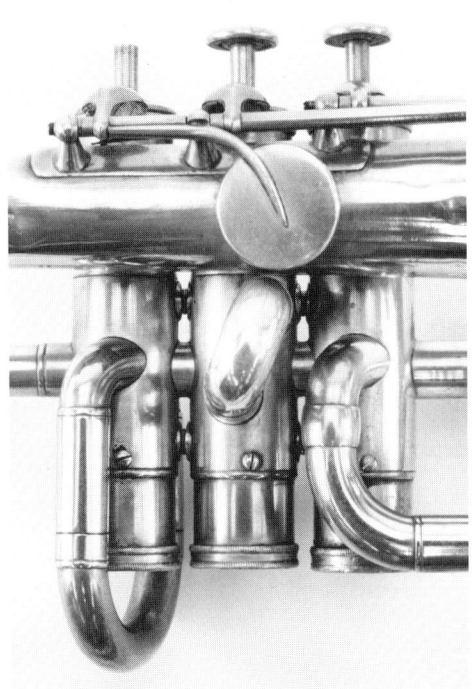

844

855

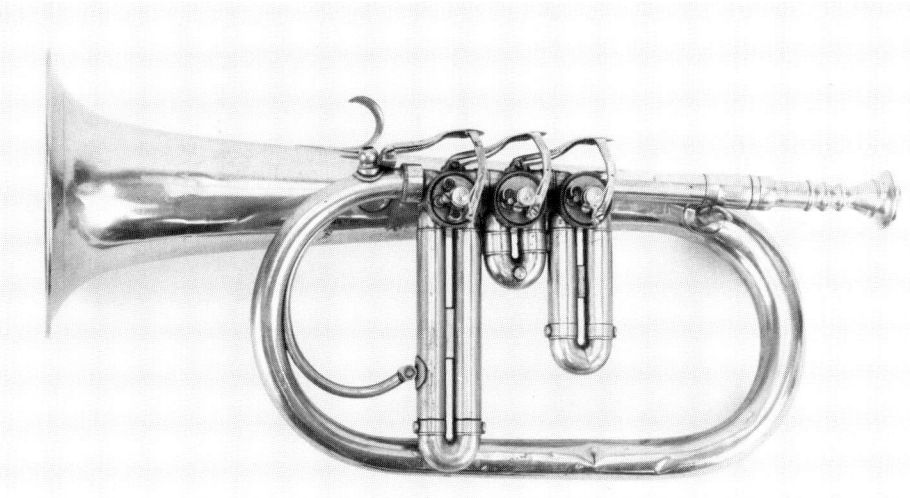

1785

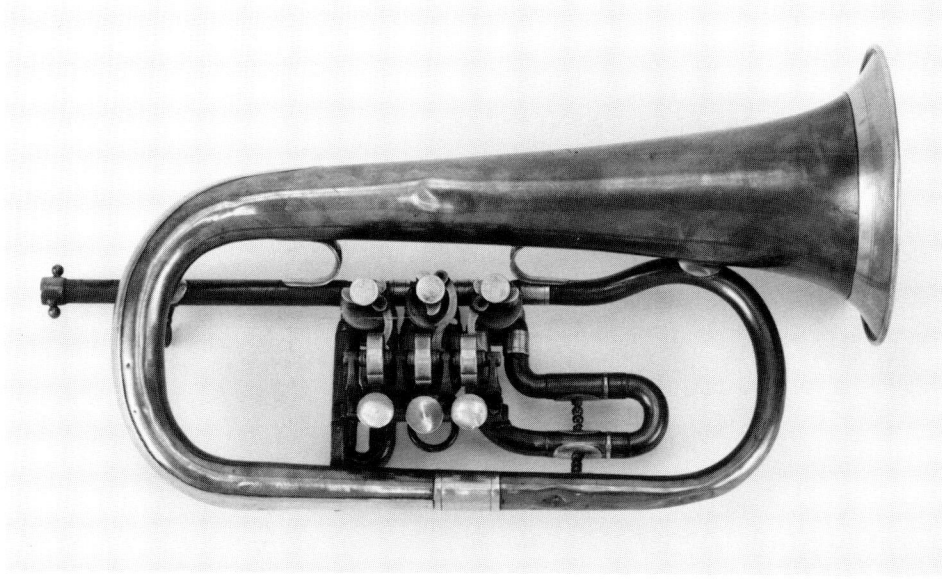

857
Valved Bugle (in B♭)
London, 19th century, third quarter
Fontaine Besson (fl. 1862-1873)

Brass. Périnet valves, bottom springs. Receiver I-slide (missing) with clamp; first valve missing. Second valve casing stamped: (within oval) BESSON / [five-pointed star] / BREVETE / (below oval) [serial number:] 28874; casings and stems stamped: 1, 2, 3.

(Within unfurled banner) 50 MEDALS OF HONOUR / [monogram:] F B / F. BESSON / BREVETÉ / 198 EUSTON ROAD / LONDON / [five-pointed star]

41.4 cm.
Bell ⌀: 14.4 cm.
Bore: 10.3 mm.

1785
Valved Bugle (in B♭) (Flügelhorn)
Austria? mid-19th century
No inscription

Brass; German silver fittings, linkages (Heyde 1982: 246, Design 7) and bell garland. Vienna rotary valves, clock spring action (Heyde, 1980: 229, Design 15; braces, see idid., p. 242, Design 26). Receiver I-slide with clamp. Original mouthpiece.

35.7 cm.
Bell ⌀: 13.8 cm.
Bore: 10.7 mm.

Reproductions of Roman Instruments

803
Cornu
Milan, 1883
Giuseppe Pelitti (fl. ca. 1835-1893)

Bronze corpus; wooden transverse brace. Poor state of preservation.

Corpus ∅: 128 cm.
Bell ∅: 14 cm.
Receiver ∅: 13 mm.

1364
Cornu
Milan, 1883
Giuseppe Pelitti (fl. ca. 1835-1893)

Painted brass, dragon's head bell. One small loop, circular corpus.

Corpus ∅: 78 cm.
Receiver ∅: 11.5 mm.

819
Cornu (E♭), Keyed
Milan, 1883
Giuseppe Pelitti (fl. ca. 1835-1893)

Brass; wooden transverse brace. Two brass keys, modern cup type, mounted in brass saddles, brass springs. Spear head decoration on brace.

Corpus ∅: 94 cm.
Bell ∅: 14.5 cm.
Receiver ∅: 12 mm.

820
Cornu (E♭), Keyed
Milan, 1883
Giuseppe Pelitti (fl. ca. 1835-1893)

Brass; wooden transverse brace. Two brass keys, modern cup type, mounted in brass saddles, brass springs. Spear head decoration on brace.

Corpus ∅: 77.5 cm.
Bell ∅: 14.5 cm.
Receiver ∅: 12.8 mm.

805
Lituus (E♭), Hooked
Milan, 1883
Giuseppe Pelitti (fl. ca. 1835-1893)

Painted brass (gold, red, black). Upturned bell. Two bulbous pommels. Mouthpiece soldered to corpus.

214 cm.
Bell ∅: 17 cm.

898
Tromba (B♭), Fanciful Shape
Milan, 1883
Giuseppe Pelitti (fl. ca. 1835-1893)

Brass. Three antique-style medallions on bell.

74 cm.
Bell ∅: 18 cm.
Receiver ∅: 13.9 mm.

1355
Double Horn (Tibia Impares)
Italy? late 19th century
No inscription

Brass. Two conical tubes, two bells, two receivers.

L: 65.8, 60.5 cm.
Bell ⌀: 12 cm.
Receiver ⌀: 10 mm.

1371
Tuba curva (C)
Italy? late 19th century
No inscription

Painted brass (black, gold). Narrow bore. Reinforcing tube. Mouthpiece soldered to corpus.

Corpus ⌀: 63 cm.
Bell ⌀: 12 mm.

898

1355

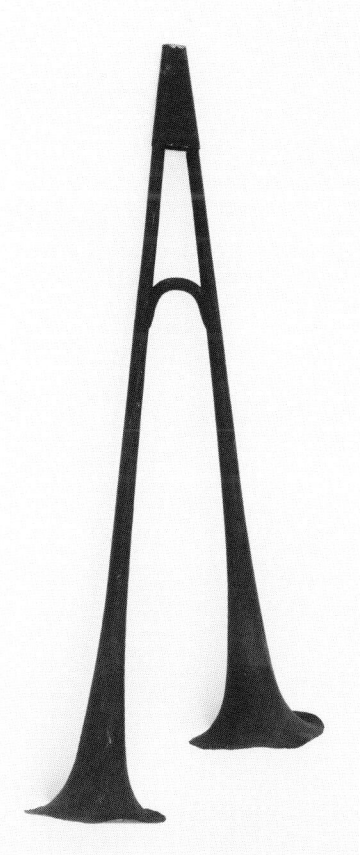

Trumpets

804
Buisine (C)
Italy, 1451
Petrus Asina Longa

Brass. Five brass ferrules, decorative pommel, and bell garland. Two leaf-shaped mounts for banner.

On bell garland: DI PETRUS ASINA LONGA
  MCDLI

124.2 cm.
Bell ⌀: 13.3 cm.
Receiver ⌀: 11.7 mm.

825
Natural Trumpet (D), Folded
Nürnberg, 1686
Johann Carl Kodisch (1654-1727)

Brass; red cord with tassel (replacement). Engraved brass ferrules, decorative pommel, and bell garland. Two leaf-shaped mounts with rings for cord. No crooks extant. Bell garland engraved with monogram: ICK.

On bell garland: MACHT. IOHAN / CARL.
  KODISCH / NURNBERG / 1686

69.9 cm.
Bell ⌀: 10.6 cm.
Receiver ⌀: 11.5 mm.

1759
Natural Trumpet (D) (Reproduction), Folded
Chicago, modern
Schilke Co.

Brass; red cord with tassel. Brass ferrules (engraved), decorative pommel. D crook.

65.1 cm.
Bell ⌀: 12.2 cm.
Receiver ⌀: 11.4 mm.

804

825 detail

825

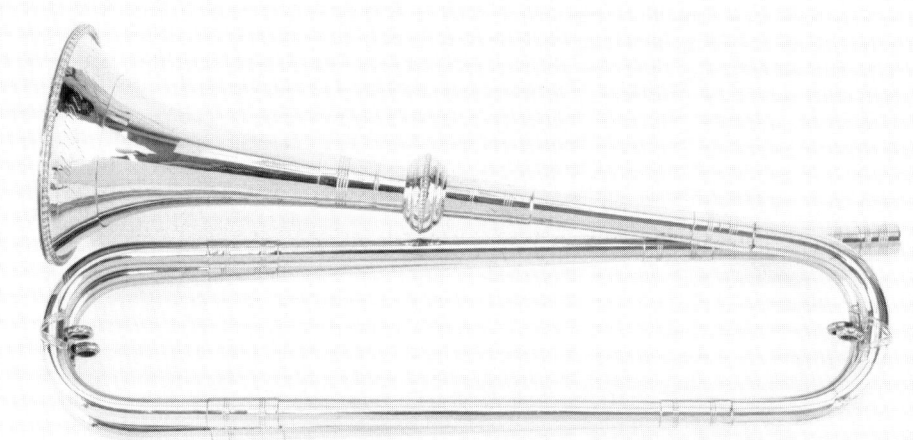

821

884

821
Cavalry Trumpet in E♭ (Kurztrompete)
Munich, mid-19th century
Michael Saurle (ca. 1790-ca. 1861)

Brass. Two loops. Single ornamental pommel; bell edge with beaded rope decoration; four rings for cord and tassels. Crooks or shanks missing.

On bell garland: MICHAEL SAURLE [flower mark] in München 1[---] (no date)

38 cm.
Bell ⌀: 10.6 cm.
Bore: 11.7 mm.

827
Cavalry Trumpet in E♭
France? late 19th century
No inscription

Brass. Two loops; U-slide (L: 7.8 cm.). Three rings for cord and tassels, one for chain attached to ring on mouthpiece.

44.3 cm.
Bell ⌀: 13 cm.
Bore: 11.3 mm.

884
Omnitonic Trumpet
Paris, mid-19th century
Jacques Christophe Labbaye, fils (fl. ca. 1834-1878)

Brass. Hoop-shaped; five separate receivers, stamped: MI FA, M[I]B, RE, S[I]B, UT; long inner/outer slide valve (handle stamped: FA / MI) connects one of five separate lengths of tubing (in sockets) to main tube. Inner/outer U-slide on main tube.

27.3 cm.
Bell ⌀: 12.3 cm.
Bore: 10.7 mm.

850
Keyed Trumpet in E♭
Lyon, 19th century, second quarter
Couturier, père (founded 1812)

Brass. Five brass keys, flat, round flaps (Heyde 1978: 148, Design 19), mounted on pillars with adjusting screws (Heyde 1982: 260, Design 16) attached to elliptical plates, steel leaf springs. Receiver I-slide with clamp.

[Maltese cross] / COUTURIER / à Lyon / [Maltese cross]

42.6 cm.
Bell ⌀: 12 cm.
Bore: 10.5 mm.

865
Trumpet in G, Valved
Austria? 19th century, second quarter
Anton Holly

Brass; nickel-plated fittings, buttons, guard, and bell garland. Vienna valves, clock spring action (Heyde 1982: 243, Design 2; linkages similar to Heyde 1980: 231, Design 5).

On bell garland: ANTON HOLLY [mark] PLZNI.

33.2 cm.
Bell ⌀: 12 cm.
Bore: 11.6 mm.

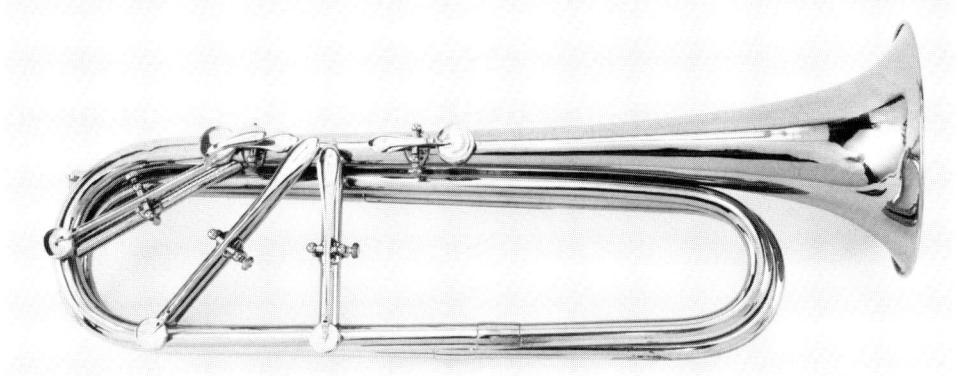

850

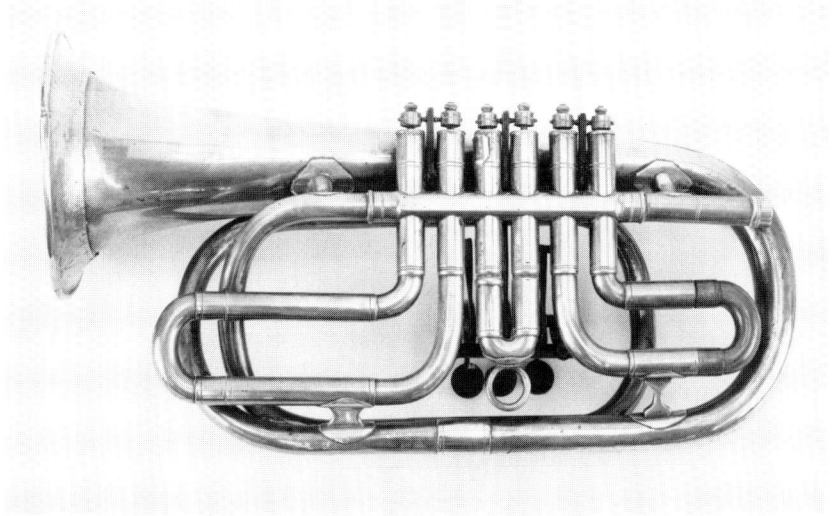

865

841
Bass Trumpet in D, Valved
Vienna, ca. 1850
Leopold Uhlmann (shop; fl. ca. 1834-1895)

Brass; German silver fittings, valve caps and screws (engraved, flower and stem), buttons, guard, and bell garland (vinestem engravings). Four Vienna rotary valves, clock spring action (Heyde 1980: 229, Design 15; linkages, see ibid., p. 232, Design 16). D crook with tuning bit. Two water keys.

Leopold Uhlmann / K: K: Hof / Instrumenten Fabrik in Wien

42 cm.
Bell ⌀: 15.4 cm.
Bore: 10.8 mm.

1741
Trumpet in B♭, Valved
Paris? 19th century, last quarter
Tourraine et Cie

Brass; mother-of-pearl button disks. Périnet valves, top springs. Extended U-slide with adjusting screw device on main tube. Valve casings stamped: 121, 122, 123.

(On cartouche) TOURRAINE / ET CIE

48 cm.
Bell ⌀: 11.6 cm.
Bore: 11.1 mm.

837
Straight Trumpet in B♭, Valved
France or Belgium, late 19th century
No inscription

Two brass sections; German silver mouthpipe, braces, fittings, and bell garland. Three Berlin valves; caps without perforation.

128 cm.
Bell ⌀: 12.8 cm.
Bore: 11.8 mm.

838
Straight Trumpet in F, Valved
France? late 19th century
No inscription

Two brass sections. Two Berlin valves. Receiver I-slide with clamp.

88.4 cm.
Bell ⌀: 13.5 cm.
Bore: 10.1 mm.

839
Straight Trumpet in F, Valved
France? late 19th century
No inscription

Two brass sections; German silver button. Single Berlin valve (min. 3rd). Shank (missing); two U-slides.

60.1 cm.
Bell ⌀: 11.3 cm.
Bore: 10 mm.

817
Fanfare Trumpet in A♭
Milan, late 19th century
Giuseppe Pelitti (fl. ca. 1835-1893)

Brass. Small portion of tube folded. Two decorative loops of tubing; pommel on bell section. Receiver I-slide with clamp.

* REGINA.DI.CIPRO. * / * / * G. PELITTI. MILANO. * / LA B.

128 cm.
Bell ⌀: 12.7 cm.
Receiver ⌀: 10.7 mm.

841
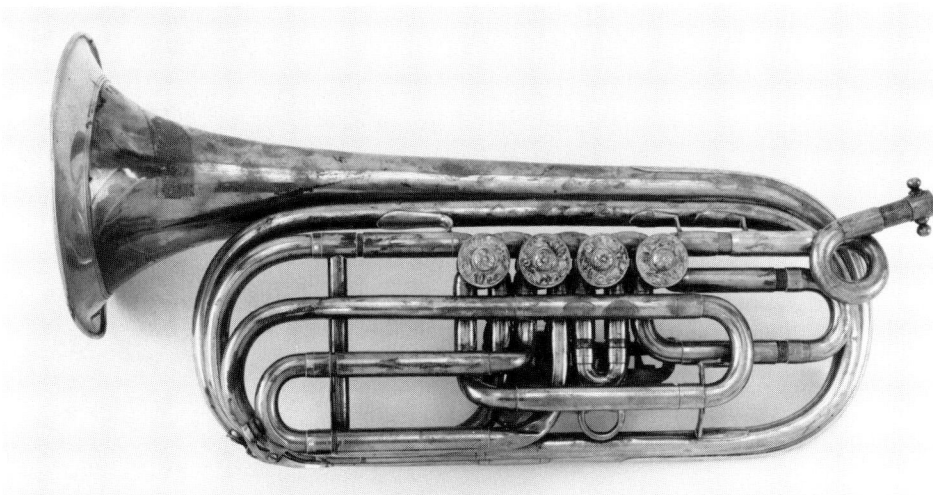

910
Fanfare Trumpet in A♭
Milan, late 19th century
Giuseppe Pelitti (fl. ca. 1835-1893)

Brass. Small folded portion; tube with two semicircular diversions. Two decorative loops of tubing; pommel on bell section. Receiver I-slide with clamp; single U-slide.

* REGINA.DI.CIPRO. * / * / * G. PELITTI. MILANO. * / LA B.

115 cm.
Bell ⌀: 13.4 cm.
Receiver ⌀: 10.5 mm.

828
Fanfare Trumpet in B♭ (B), Cruciform
Italy? late 19th century
No inscription

Brass. Single ring (missing) for chain attached to ring on mouthpiece.

88.6 x 43 cm.
Bell ⌀: 13.1 cm.
Receiver ⌀: 9.9 cm.

828

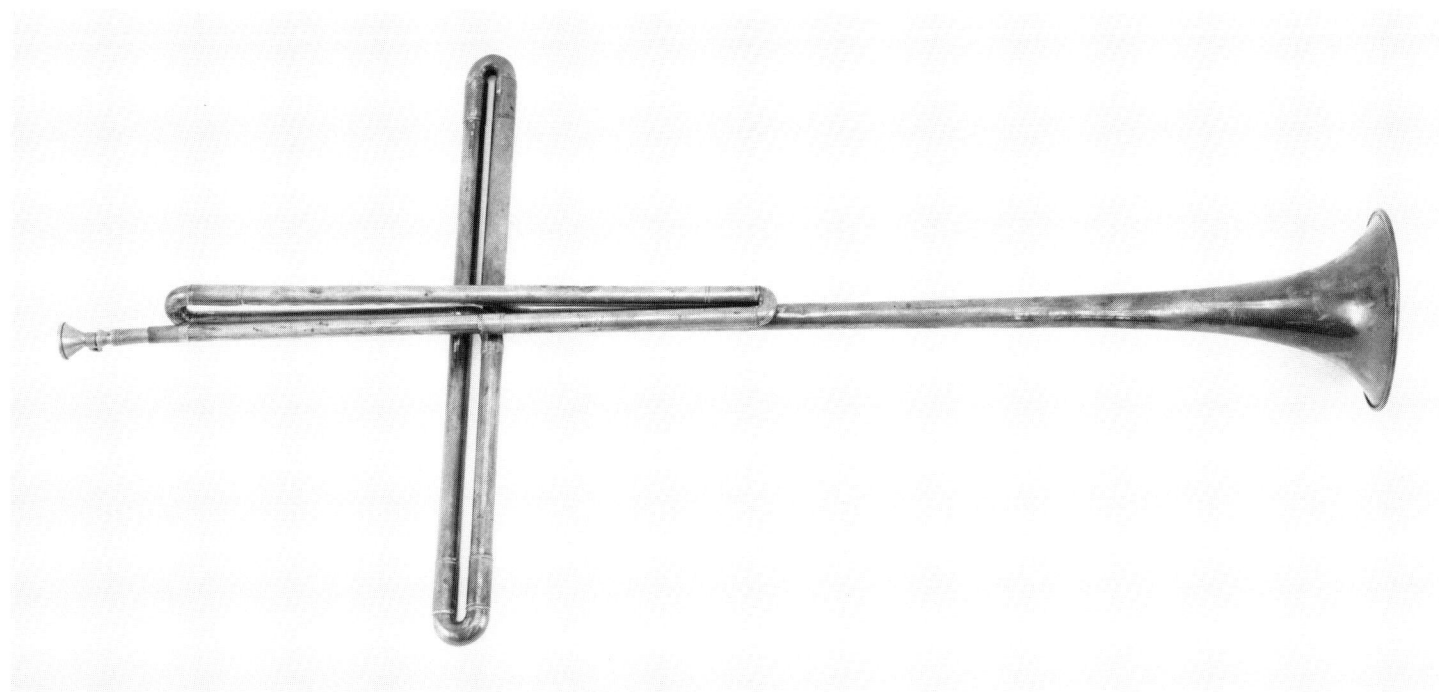

877

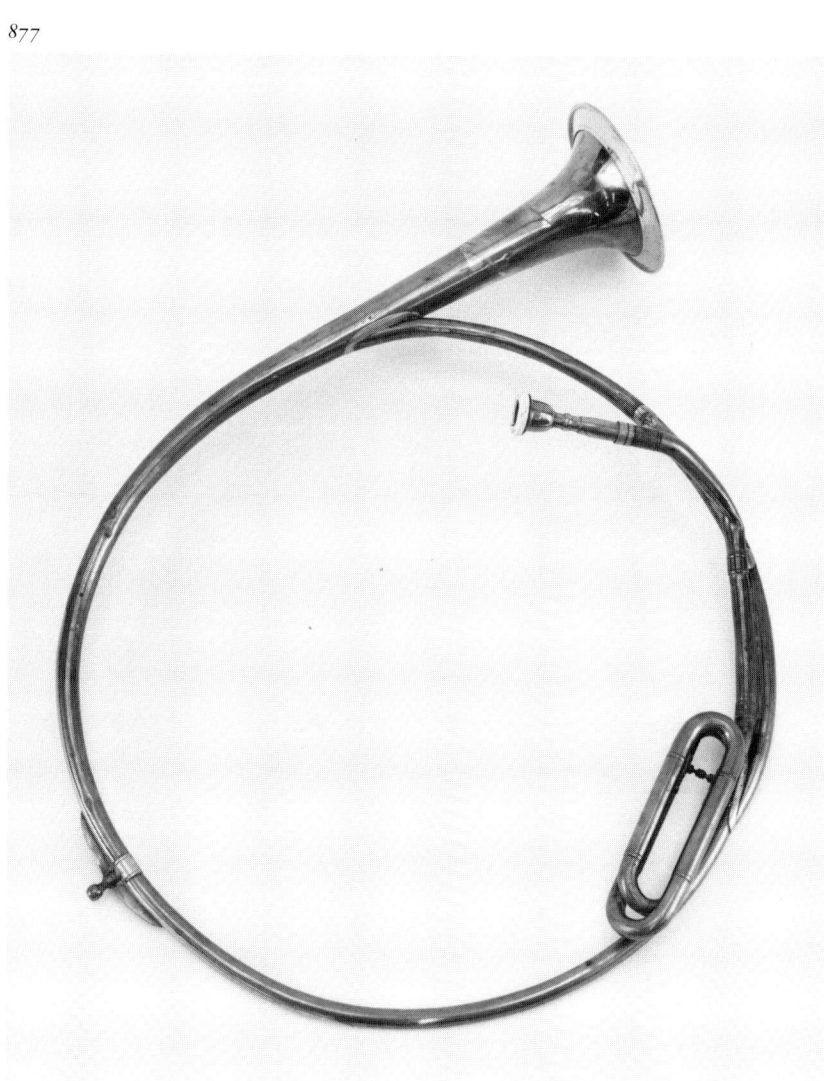

877
Fanfare Trumpet in E♭, Circular
Austria or Italy? late 19th century
No inscription

Brass; German silver fittings and bell garland; ivory lip on original mouthpiece. No tuning slide.

Corpus (oval): 42.9 cm.
Bell ⌀: 11.8 cm.
Receiver ⌀: 11 mm.

1359
Fanfare Trumpet (Tenor) in A
Bari, late 19th century
Fratelli Rossano (fl. ca. 1886)

Brass; German silver ferrules, fittings, guard, and bell garland. Folded (two loops); bulbous bell. Two brass rings for cord. Shank (missing).

Brevettata e Premiata Fabbrica / Fratelli
  Rossano Bari

87.7 cm.
Bell ⌀: 12.1 cm.
Receiver ⌀: 11.5 mm.

1971
Fanfare Trumpet in E♭
Italy? late 19th century
No inscription

Brass. Portion of tube folded. Single ferrule, pommel on bell section. U-slide.

114 cm.
Bell ⌀: 13.1 cm.
Receiver ⌀: 11 mm.

911
Fanfare Trumpet in E♭, Valved
Italy? late 19th century
No inscription

Brass; German silver fittings and button. One Périnet valve (perf. 4th), bottom spring. Shoulder mounted. U-slide; shank (missing).

119 cm.
Bell ⌀: 12.3 cm.
Receiver ⌀: 11 mm.

840
Fanfare Trumpet in A, Valved
Milan, late 19th century
Camillo Sambruna (fl. ca. 1886-1906)

Brass; German silver buttons. Serpentine bell section. Périnet valves, bottom springs. Receiver I-slide with clamp. Second valve casing stamped: 258; receiver stamped: 103.

[coat of arms] / C. SAMBRUNA / MILANO / 12

86 cm.
Bell ⌀: 9.9 cm.
Bore: 11.55 mm.

1971

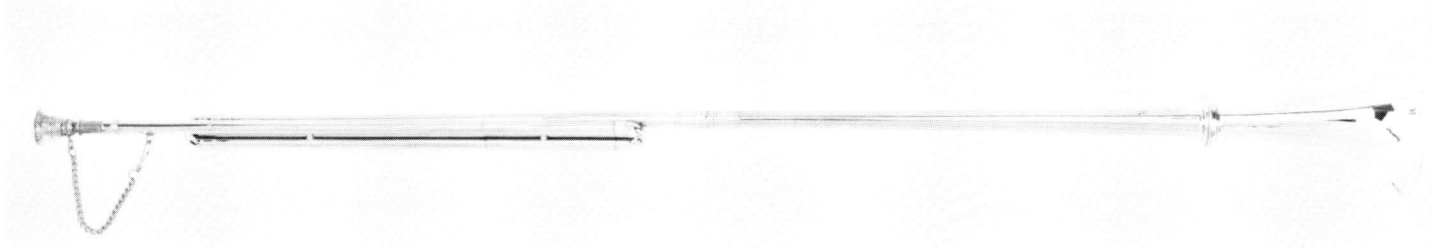

840

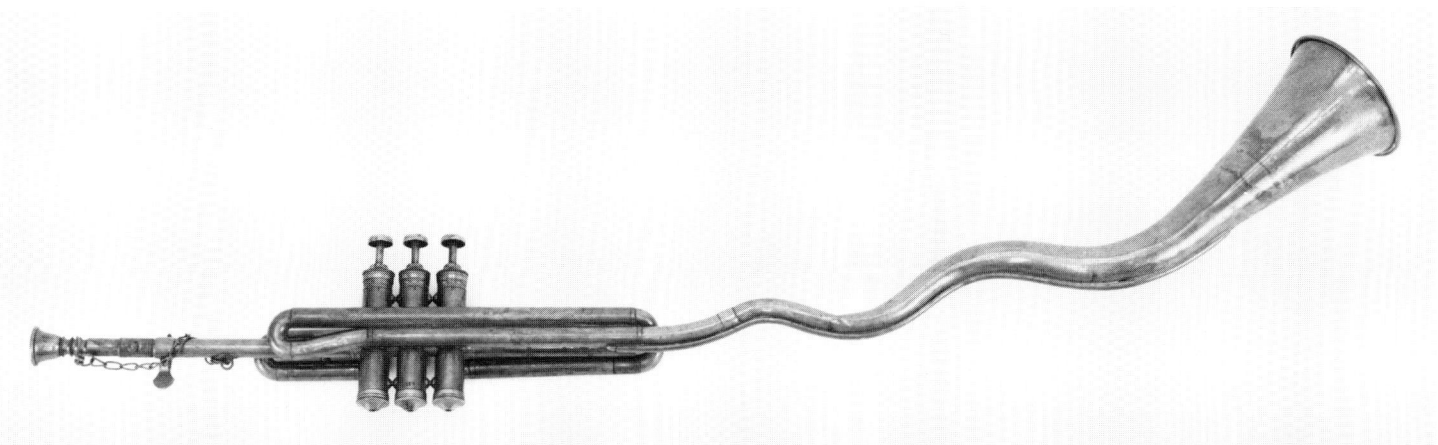

842
Fanfare Trumpet in B♭, Valved
Naples, late 19th century
A. Abbate & Figlio (fl. ca. 1890-1899)

Brass; German silver buttons and fittings.
Hooked (upturned bell). Périnet valves,
bottom springs. Receiver I-slide with clamp.

Ballo Rodope / A. Abbate & figlio Napoli

84 cm.
Bell ⌀: 11.8 cm.
Bore: 11.7 mm.

842

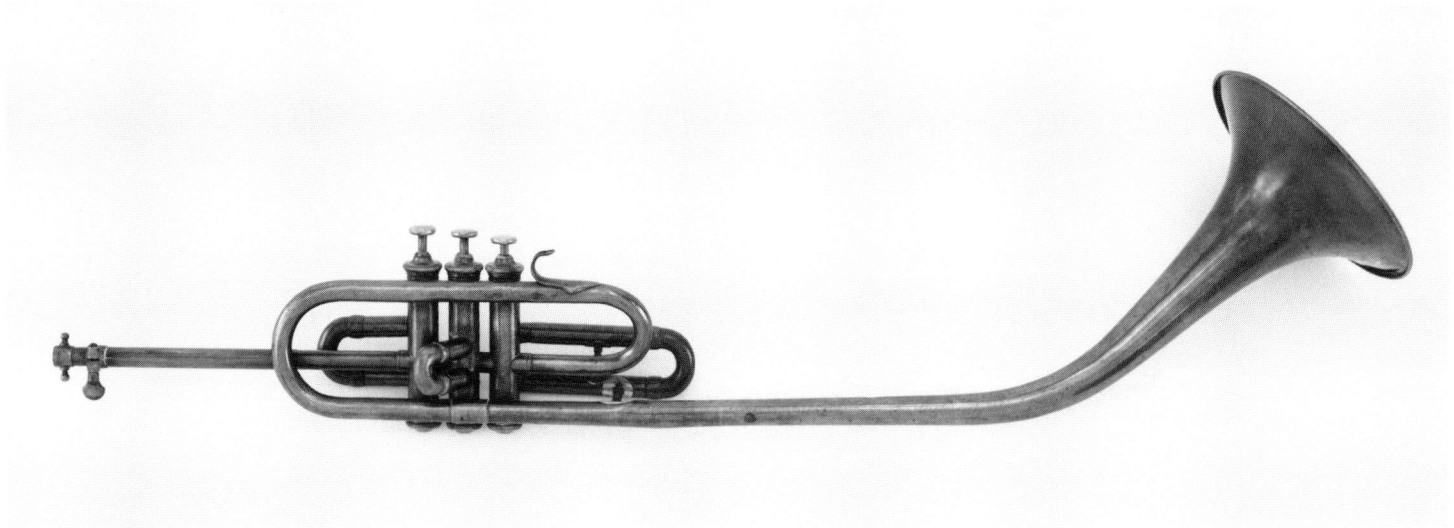

921
Fanfare Trumpet (Tenor) in B♭, Valved
Naples, late 19th century
A. Abbate & Figlio (fl. ca. 1890-1899)

Brass; German silver buttons and fittings.
Hooked (upturned bell). Périnet valves,
bottom springs. Receiver I-slide with clamp.

Ballo Rodope / A. Abbate & figlio Napoli

86.8 cm.
Bell ⌀: 22.2 cm.
Bore: 12.5 mm.

921

925

924
Fanfare Trumpet in B♭, Valved
Milan, late 19th century
Giuseppe Pelitti (fl. ca. 1835-1893)

Brass; painted dragon's head bell. Périnet valves, bottom springs. Receiver I-slide with clamp.

85.7 cm.
Bore: 10.8 mm.

925
Fanfare Trumpet in B♭, Valved
Milan, late 19th century
Giuseppe Pelitti (fl. ca. 1835-1893)

Brass; painted dragon's head bell. Périnet valves, bottom springs. Receiver I-slide with clamp. Restored. Very similar to 924.

85.1 cm.
Bore: 10.9 mm.

1354
Fanfare Trumpet in D, Valved
Milan, late 19th century
Giuseppe Pelitti (fl. ca. 1835-1893)

Painted brass. Serpentine corpus. Périnet valves, bottom springs. Receiver I-slide with clamp.

[coat of arms] / G. PELITTI. MILANO / * /
   BALLO TEODORA

71.1 cm.
Bell ⌀: 15.3 cm.
Receiver ⌀: 10.7 mm.

1357
Fanfare Trumpet in D, Valved
Milan, late 19th century
Giuseppe Pelitti (fl. ca. 1835-1893)

Painted brass. Périnet valves, bottom springs. Receiver I-slide with clamp.

[coat of arms] / G. PELITTI. MILANO / * /
   BALLO TEODORA

155 cm.
Bell ⌀: 12 cm.
Receiver ⌀: 12 mm.

Trombones

887
Treble Slide Trombone in B♭
London, 19th century, last decade
Besson & Co. Ltd. (founded ca. 1851)

Brass; inner slide extensions in German silver. No water key. Serial number: 7547; receiver stamped: BESSON & CO / BREVETES.

CHICAGO / BORE / (within unfurled banner) 50 MEDALS OF HONOUR / (below banner) [monogram:] F B / BESSON & CO / "Prototype" / 198 EUSTON ROAD / LONDON / [five-pointed star] / ENGLAND / C. FISCHER / 6. 4TH AV. N.Y. / SOLE AGENT U. STATES

52.8 cm.
Bell ⌀: 11.8 cm.
Bore: 11.65 mm.

887

888
Alto Slide Trombone in E♭
Leipzig, 19th century, second quarter
Johann Gottlob Schmidt (1777-1849)

Brass. No water key; holder for lyre (later addition). Ferrules decoratively cast; engraved bell garland (oak leaf and acorn motif).

J. G. SCHMIDT / IN LEIPZIG

85 cm.
Bell ⌀: 15.7 cm.
Bore: 10.05 mm.

1478 (formerly 887 A)
Alto Trombone in F
France? late 19th century
No inscription

Brass. No water key. U-bends with decoratively engraved guards (brass).

72 cm.
Bell ⌀: 12.5 cm.
Bore: 11.3 mm.

889
Tenor Slide Trombone in B♭
France? 19th century, third quarter
Inscription obliterated

Brass. No water key; both branches of inner slide shortened; bell removed, replaced with brass ring (ring and bell flare painted black). Raised silver label on terminal ring stamped: TREPAT EN BARCELONA (Leopoldo Franciolini, dealer?)

100.5 cm.
Bell ⌀: 11.3 cm.
Bore: 10 mm.

888

890
Tenor Slide Trombone in B♭
Germany? late 17th / early 18th century
No inscription

Brass. No water key; outer slide U-bend with ring for ornamental cord. Braces decoratively cast and engraved; engraved bell garland. Inner slide extended (brass); screw clamp on bell section (added at restoration).
Mouthpiece (modern replacement).

109 cm.
Bell ⌀: 11.35 cm.
Bore: 9.55 mm.

890 detail

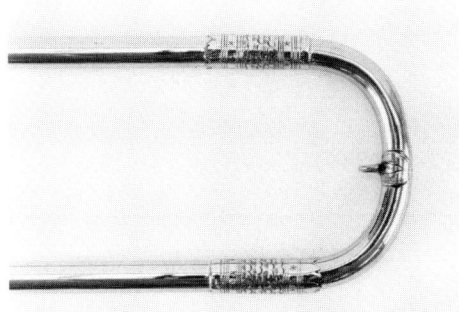

890

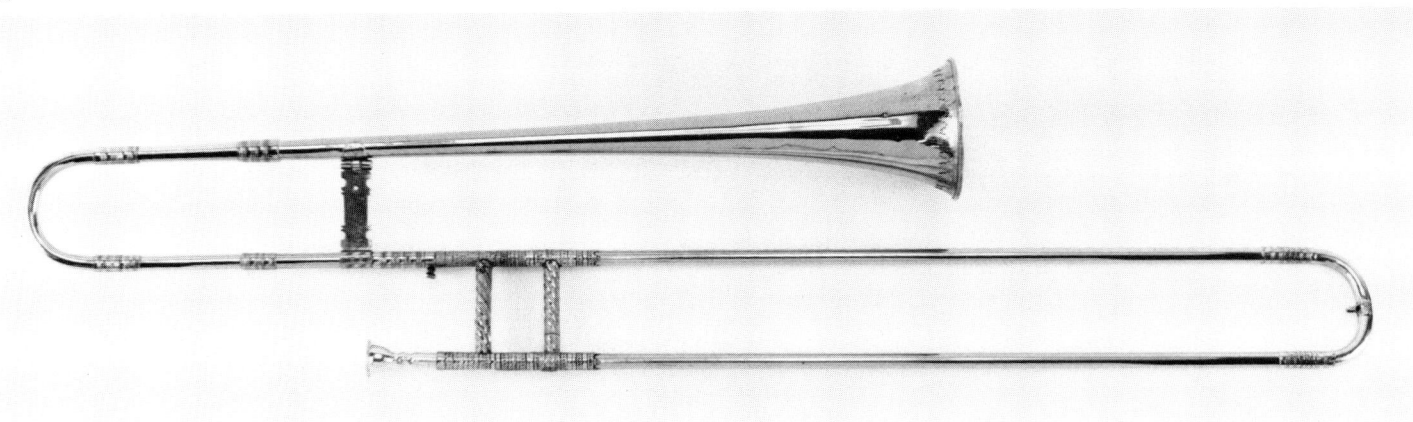

891
Tenor Slide Trombone in B♭
Paris, ca. 1905
Fontaine Besson (founded ca. 1882)

Brass; inner slide extensions in German silver. No water key. Stamped: (within oval) F. BESSON / [five-pointed star] / BREVETÉ. Serial number: 436. Ferrules decoratively cast (vinestem motif).

(Within unfurled banner) SYSTEME PROTOTYPE / (below banner) [monogram:] F B / F. BESSON / BREVETÉ / S.G.D.G. / 96 RUE D'ANGOULÊME / PARIS. / [five-pointed star] / GRAND PRIX / PARIS 1900 / ST LOUIS 1904 / LIÈGE 1905

118 cm.
Bell ⌀: 14.8 cm.
Bore: 11.7 mm.

1968
Tenor Slide Trombone in B♭
Grand Rapids, Mich., early 20th century
J. W. York and Sons (fl. ca. 1918)

Nickel-plated brass (brushed); inner slide extensions in German silver. Alternate bell section U-slides for high and low pitch. Original mouthpiece. Outer slide and mouthpiece stamped: YORK & SONS (mouthpiece: / 13); inner, outer slides with serial number: 23374; bell section and both slides with serial number: 736.

(On cartouche) PROFESSIONAL / Made by / J. W. YORK / AND SONS / Grand Rapids / Mich.

112 cm.
Bell ⌀: 18.1 cm.
Bore: 11.95 mm.

891

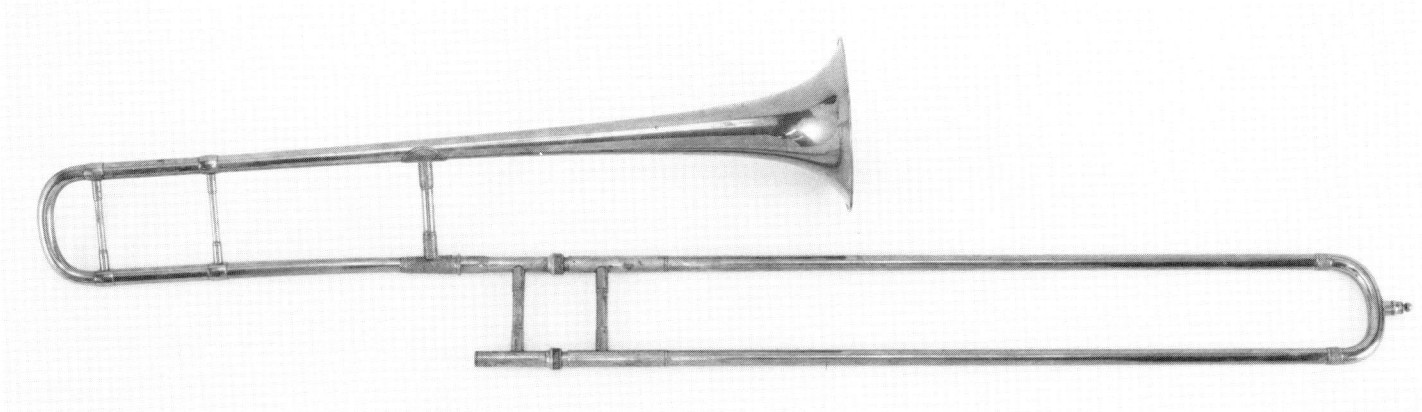

893
Bass Slide Trombone in F
Erfurt, late 19th century
Johann Eduard Kruspe (1831-1919)

Brass; nickel-plated fittings and bell rim. Jointed brass handle with wooden knob (controls slide in lowest position); inner slide extensions in German silver. Ferrules decoratively cast; small, raised shells along edge of engraved bell garland (oak leaf and acorn motif).

Ed. Kruspe / Herzgl. L. M. Hoflieferant / Erfurt / Filiale C. Kruspe. Leipzig

141 cm.
Bell ⌀: 25.5 cm.
Bore: 14.35 mm.

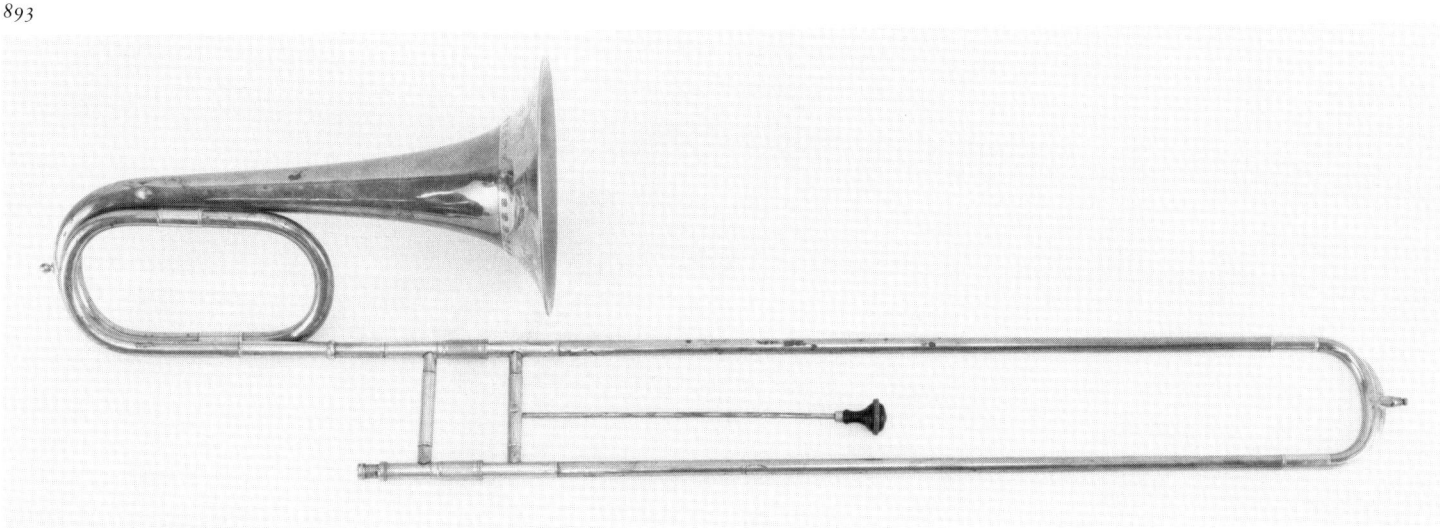
893

897
Double Slide Bass Trombone in G
Paris, ca. 1823
André Antony Schmittschneider
 (fl. ca. 1820-1831)

Copper. Upturned bell; no water key. Slide incorporates four telescopes.

Schmittschneider Inventor. Breveté du Roi
 Médaille d'Argent 1823 Paris

71 cm.
Bell ⌀: 17.8 cm.
Bore: 11.35 mm.

1962
Alto Valved Trombone in E♭
France? 19th century, last quarter
Maker unknown (Charles H. Parsons & Co.,
 dealer)

Brass. Périnet valves, bottom springs. Short model. Shield on bell, engraved: CHAS. H. / PARSONS / & CO. / NEW-YORK.

61 cm.
Bell ⌀: 15.3 cm.
Bore: 12.3 mm.

897

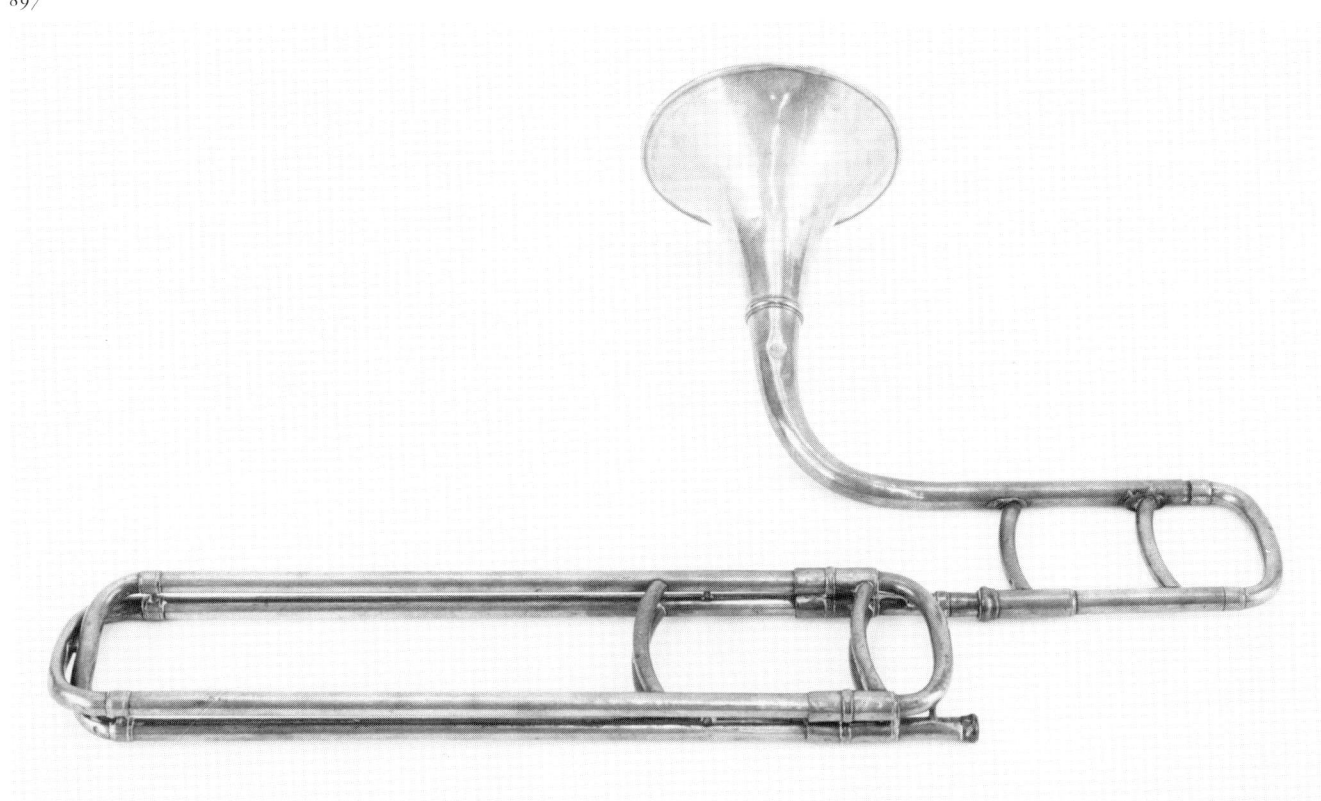

892
Tenor Valved Trombone in B♭
London, mid-19th century (after 1866)
Henry Keat and Sons (fl. ca. 1845-1895)

Brass. Périnet valves, bottom springs. Short model.

HENRY KEAT & SONS / 105 / MATTHIAS RD / STOKE NEWINGTON G[REE]N N[ORTH] / LONDON / N

74 cm.
Bell ⌀: 17.7 cm.
Bore: 11.8 mm.

896
Tenor Valved Trombone in B♭,
  Independent pistons and tubes
Paris, ca. 1870
Adolphe (Antoine Joseph) Sax (1814-1894)

Brass. Six Périnet valves, bottom springs. Three valves for each hand, placed at right angle, corresponding to positions 1 to 6 on a slide. U-slide on main tube. Caps with three perforations in triangular configuration.

SEUL / GRAND PRIX / 1867 / [monogram:] A S (in cross stroke of letter S:) PARIS / No. 30179 / Nouveau Trombone Sax / Adolphe Sax F.teur Breveté / de la M.son Mil.re de l'Empereur / 50 rue St. Georges à Paris

65.8 (bell axis) x 62.53 cm.
Bell ⌀: 15.1 cm.
Bore: apprx. 11.8 mm.

1363
Tenor Valved Trombone in B♭,
  Independent pistons and tubes
Brussels? 19th century, last quarter
Mahillon shop?

Brass. Six Périnet valves, bottom springs. Valves configured like 869. U-slide on main tube. Caps without perforations. Bell section missing.

66.5 cm.
Bore: 12.05 mm.

892

896

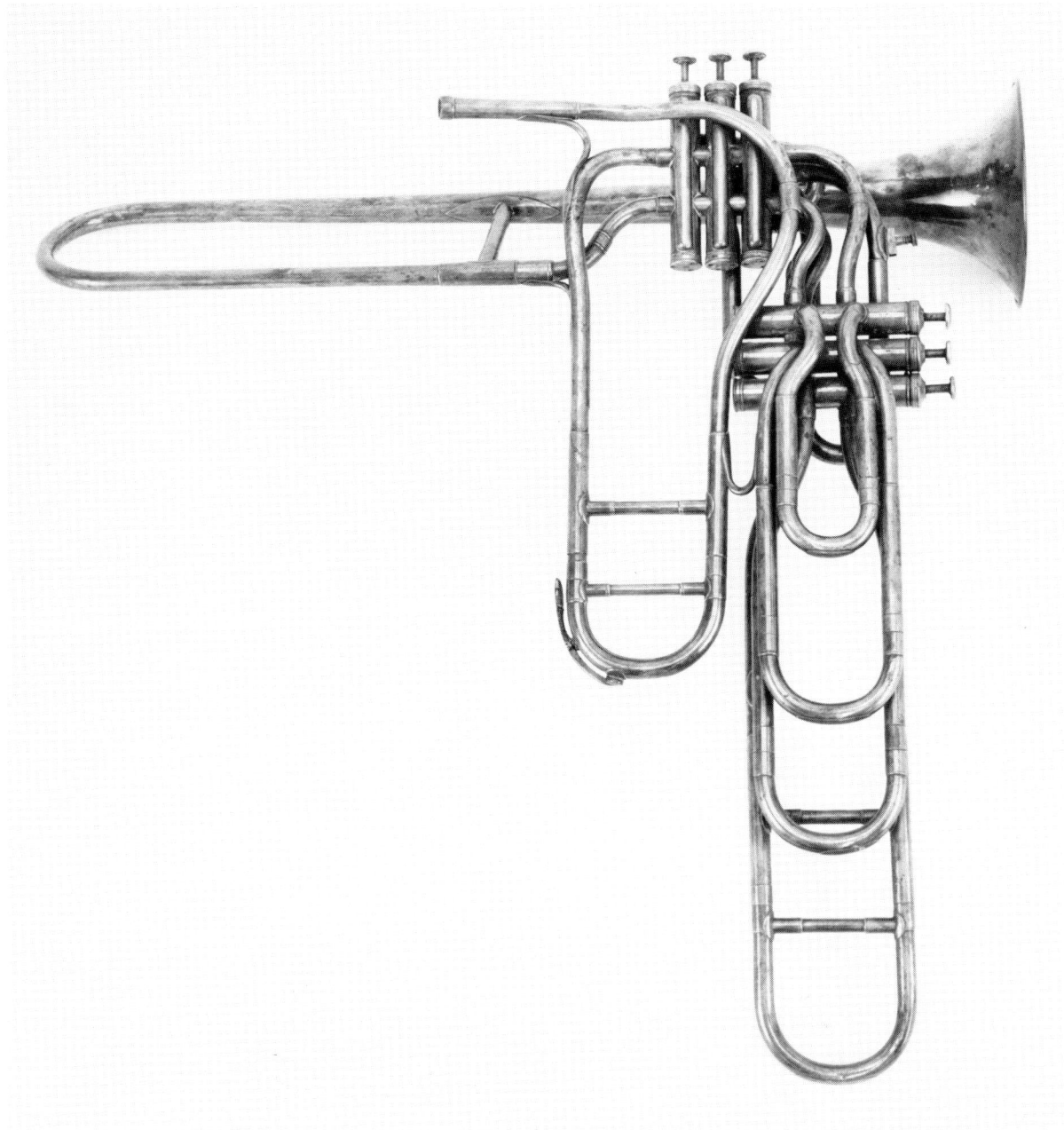

894

895

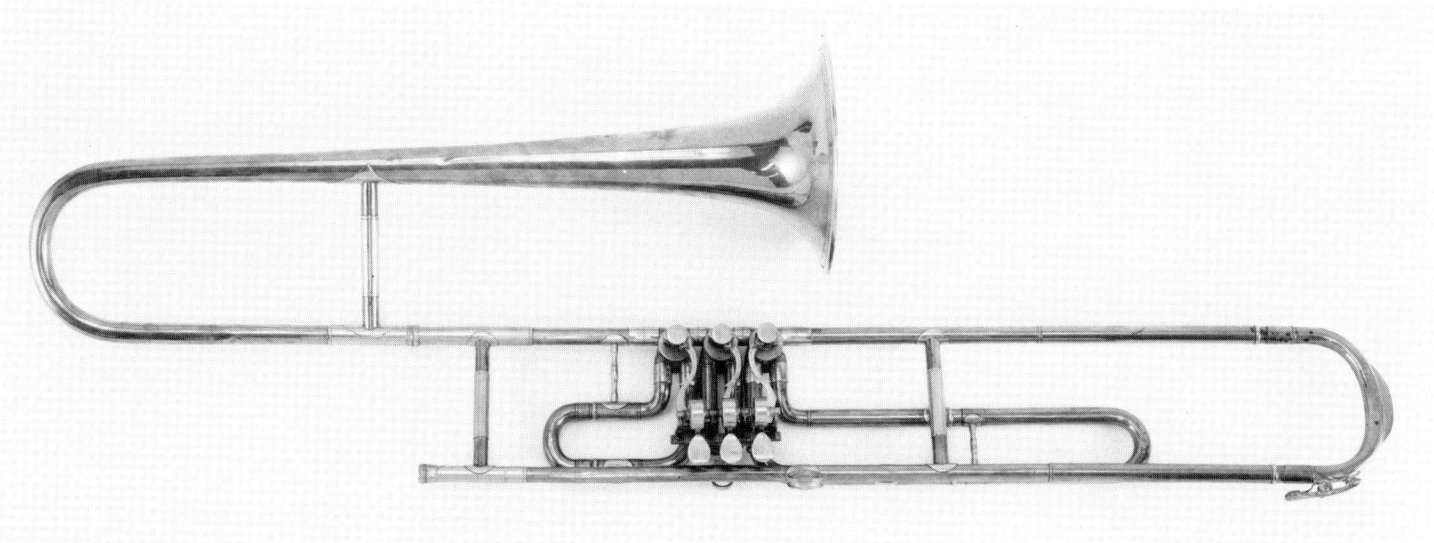

894
Bass Valved Trombone in F
Paris, 19th century, after 1878
Antoine Courtois-[Auguste] Mille (fl. 1880-1909)

Brass; silver-plated rim on original mouthpiece (inscribed: ANTOINE COURTOIS / Breveté / 88 rue des Marais St. Martin / Paris); nickel-plated buttons. Périnet valves, bottom springs. Short model. U-slide on main tube. Engraved braces and ferrules on bell section (floral motif). Bell stamped: 6 / 62ND BAND. Mouthpiece engraved by former owner: Bs. Trom. / 2607.

(Within oval) MÉDAILLE / DE / IRE CLASSE / EXPOSITION / UNIVERSELLE / 1856 / (below oval) Médaille / LONDRES 1862 / Exposition Universelle / PARIS 1867 / Médaille d'Honneur / EN ARGENT / ANTOINE COURTOIS & MILLE / Breveté / FACTEUR DU CONSERVATOIRE NATIONAL / 88 rue des Marais St. Martin / Paris / IER PRIX / GRANDE MÉDAILLE D'OR / EXPOSITION DE MOSCOU 1872 / & MÉDAILLE D'OR PARIS 1878 / S. ARTHUR CHAPPELL / Sole Agent / 52 New Bond Street / London

108 cm.
Bell ⌀: 19.6 cm.
Bore: 12.3 mm.

895
Bass Valved Trombone in F
Erfurt, late 19th century
Johann Eduard Kruspe (1831-1919)

Brass; German silver fittings, braces, buttons, valve caps and screws, and bell rim. Long model. Three Vienna rotary valves, clock spring action (similar to Heyde 1980: 228, Design 12; linkages, see ibid., p. 232, Design 15). U-slide on main tube.

E. KRUSPE / IN / ERFURT

113 cm.
Bell ⌀: 19 cm.
Bore: 11.9 mm.

1356
Bass Trombone in F, Valved
Milan, late 19th century
Giuseppe Pelitti (fl. ca. 1835-1893)

Painted brass. Périnet valves, bottom springs. Serpentine.

110 cm.
Bell ⌀: 17.8 cm.
Receiver ⌀: 12 mm.

Cornets

853
Cornet in E♭
Paris, 19th century, third quarter
Henry Gunckel

Brass. Périnet valves, top springs. Receiver I-slide (missing) with clamp; no tuning slide on main tube. Second button missing.

[Two-masted ship, bow inscribed:] PARIS / Henry Gunckel / PARIS / Lyon & Healy / CHICAGO / SOLE AGENTS

30 cm.
Bell ⌀: 12 cm.
Bore: 11.05 mm.

854
Pocket Cornet in B♭
England? late 19th century
No inscription

Brass. Périnet valves, bottom springs. Shanks missing. Knobbed caps. Inscription on bell obliterated; second valve casing stamped: s.

23 cm.
Bell ⌀: 9.6 cm.
Bore: 11.1 mm.

854

856
Cornet in B♭
Boston, 19th century, third quarter
Hall and Quinby (fl. 1866-1869; 1872-1875)

German silver. String action rotary valves, side-mounted. Shanks missing.

(On cartouche) Made by / Hall & Quinby / Boston

33.1 cm.
Bell ⌀: 12.1 cm.
Bore: 10.9 mm.

858
Cornet in E♭
Cincinnati, Ohio, late 19th century
Rudolph Wurlitzer and Bro. (fl. ca. 1887)

Brass. Périnet valves, top springs. Receiver I-slide with clamp; second valve U-slide missing. Buttons, third valve stem missing. Second valve casing stamped: Q.

R. Wurlitzer & Bro. / Manuf. / Cincinnati O.

30.2 cm.
Bell ⌀: 11.9 cm.
Bore: 11.7 mm.

859
Cornet in E♭
Austria or Germany? late 19th century
No inscription

Brass; German silver fittings. Berlin valves. Receiver I-slide (missing) with clamp. Second button missing.

29.9 cm.
Bell ⌀: 12.4 cm.
Bore: 11 mm.

856

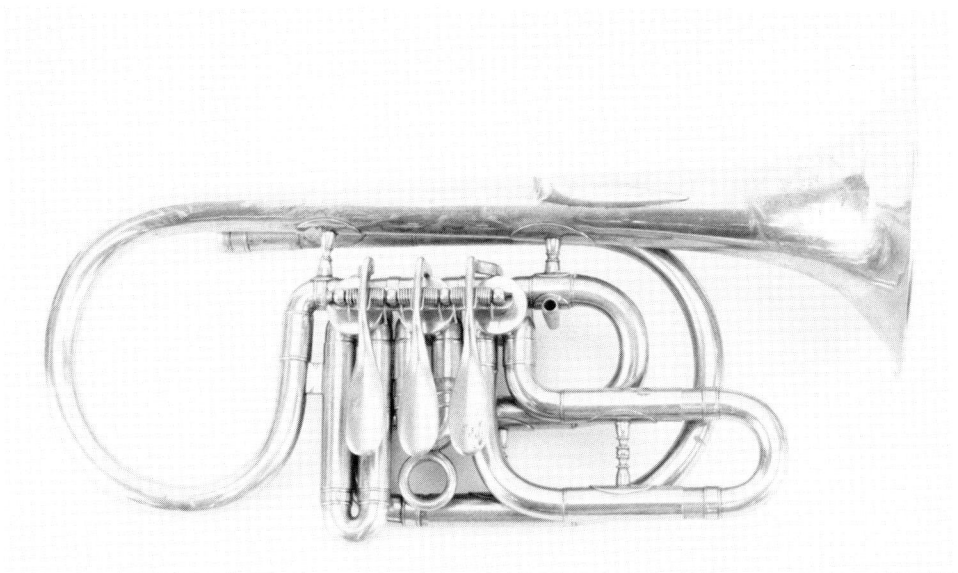

860
Cornet in E♭
Elkhart, Ind., 1876
Conn and Dupont (fl. 1875-1887)

Silver-plated brass. Périnet valves, top springs. Receiver I-slide with clamp; no tuning slide on main tube. Knobbed caps (second replaced). Serial number: 471.

(On cartouche) Superior Class / MADE BY / CONN & DUPONT / ELKHART, IND.

32 cm.
Bell ⌀: 12.2 cm.
Bore: 11.6 mm.

861
Cornet in B♭
Austria or Germany? late 19th century
No inscription

Brass; German silver fittings. Berlin valves. Very similar to 859.

31.5 cm.
Bell ⌀: 12.6 cm.
Bore: 11.1 mm.

862
Cornet in E♭, Bell Over-the-Shoulder
U.S.A., 19th century, third quarter
No inscription

German silver. String action rotary valves, top-mounted. Receiver I-slide with screw adjustment mechanism; no tuning slide on main tube. Three keys, second valve U-slide missing. Poor state of preservation.

61 cm.
Bell ⌀: 12.1 cm.
Bore: 11.45 mm.

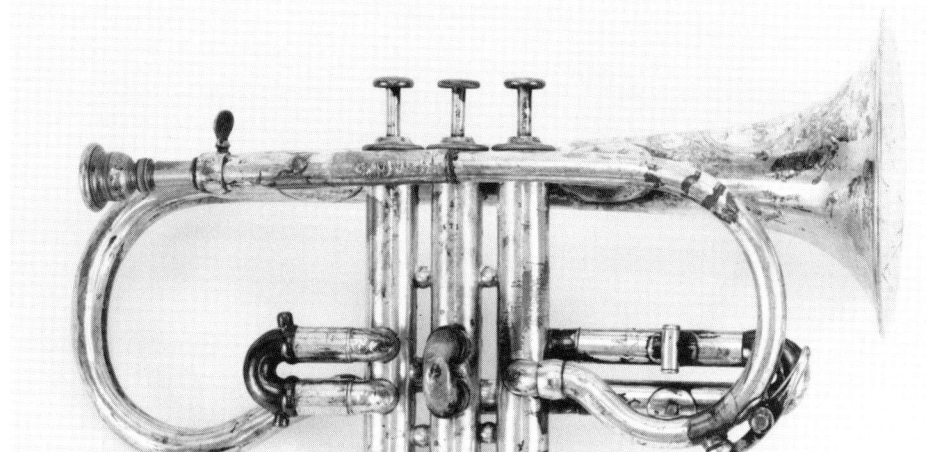
860

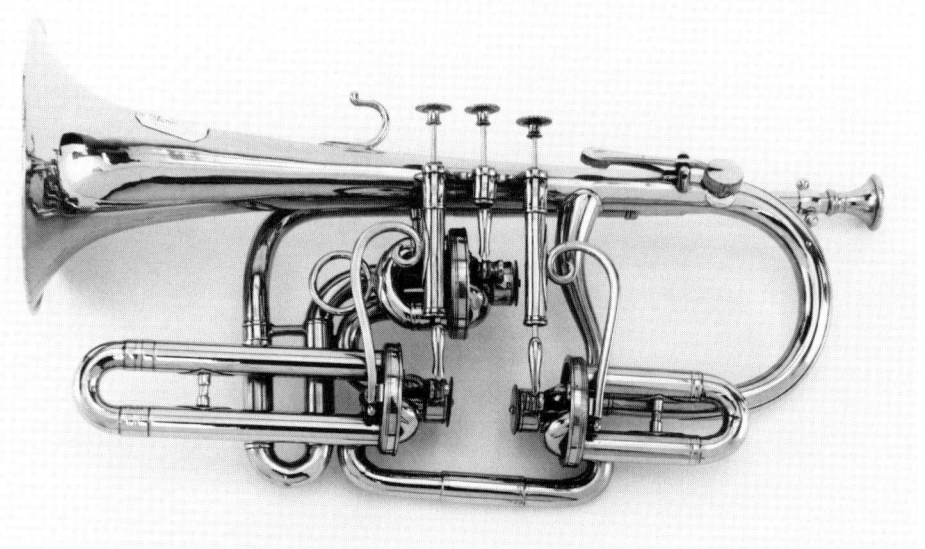
863

863
Cornet in B♭ (Patent Lever Cornopean)
London, mid-19th century
John Augustus Köhler (Kohler)
  (fl. 1834-1863)

Brass, silver-plated buttons and valve stems. Shaw disc valves, Macfarlane's clapper key (for whole tone trill); tone hole with silver patch. Original B♭ shank, mouthpiece. Serial number: 108.

On silver medallion: BY HER MAJESTY / ROYAL LETTERS PATENT / J. SHAW INVENTOR / [British coat of arms] / KOHLER.SOLE.MAKER / 35 HENRIETTA ST.T / COVENT GARDEN   LONDON

37.5 cm.
Bell ⌀: 12.4 cm.
Bore: 11.2 mm.

864
Cornet in B♭
France? ca. 1870
Maker unknown (C. J. Whitney & Co., dealer [fl. 1866-1874])

Brass. Pérenet valves, top springs. Shanks, first and second buttons missing.

EX CELSIOR / C. J. WHITNEY & CO. / DETROIT / MICH.

31.7 cm.
Bell ⌀: 12.4 cm.
Bore: 11.55 mm.

866
Cornet in B♭
Vienna, late 19th century
Ignaz Stowasser (fl. 1838-1914)

Brass; German silver fittings, linkages (Heyde 1980: 232, Design 14), buttons, and bell garland. Vienna rotary valves with clock spring actions. Engraved screw caps (floral motif).

On bell garland: *Ignaz Stowasser k.k. auschl. Prix* [Austro-Hungarian Imperial coat of arms] *Musik Instrum. Fabrick. in Wien*

32 cm.
Bell ⌀: 12.1 cm.
Bore: 10.95 mm.

866 detail

866

1494 (formerly 856 A)
Cornet in E♭, Teardrop
New York, ca. 1870
Schreiber Cornet Mfg. Co. (founded 1867)

Nickel-plated brass. String action rotary valves, top-mounted. Receiver I-slide with clamp (screw missing). Key lever rod mechanism attached to valve casings with unusual wishbone-shaped mounts.

On raised shield: SCHREIBER CORNET MFG. CO. / (portrait, inventor?) PATENTED BY L. SCHREIBER SEP.12 1865 / N Y / U S

63.2 cm.
Bell ⌀: 12.4 cm.
Bore: n.a.

1494

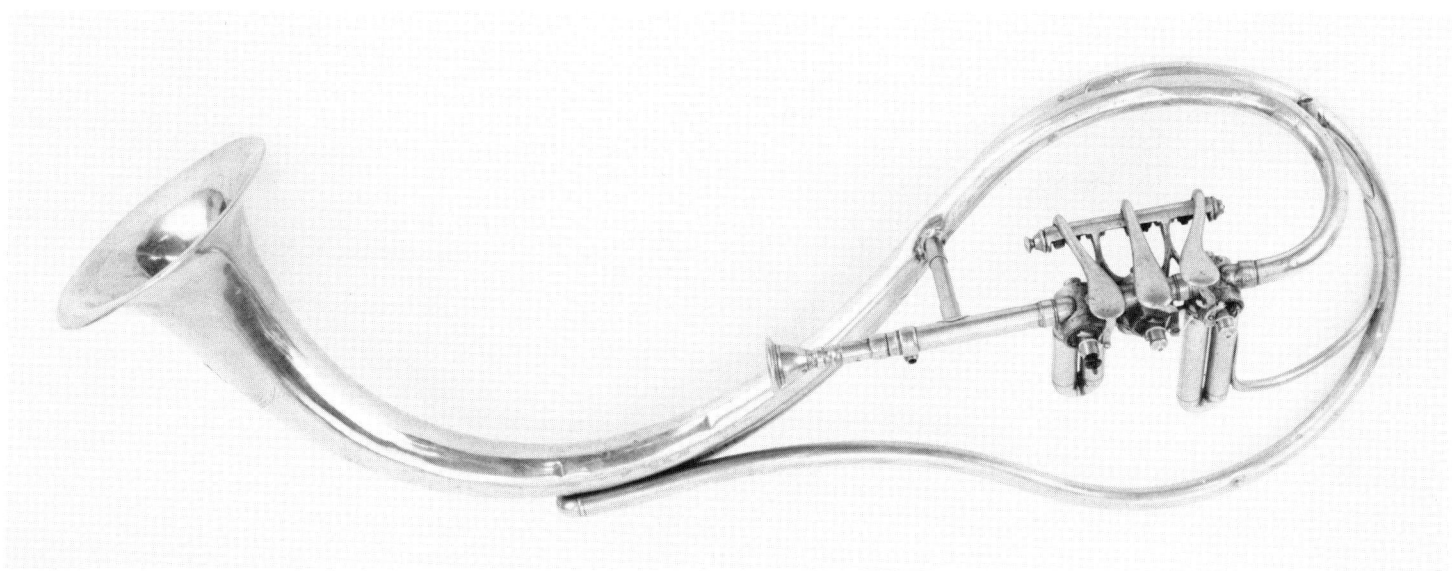

1559 (formerly 863 A)
Cornet in B♭
France? ca. 1850
No inscription

Brass; German silver fittings; Stoelzel piston valves. F, G, and A♭ crooks; B♭, A shanks, second and third buttons missing. Four mouthpieces. Wooden case (1559 A).

26.8 cm.
Bell ⌀: 13.5 cm.
Bore: 11.3 mm.

1559

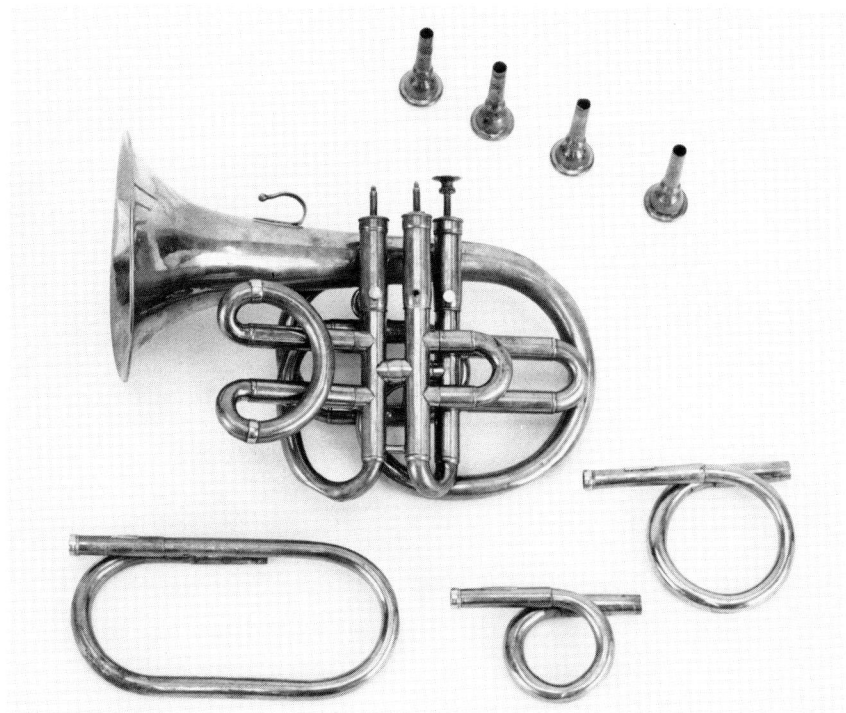

1560 (formerly 864 A)
Cornet in B♭
London, 19th century, last decade
Besson and Co. Ltd. (founded ca. 1851)

Silver-plated brass; mother-of-pearl buttons. Périnet valves, top springs (casings stamped: 16, 17, 18). Extensive engravings (floral motif; cupid playing transverse flute on bell). Outfit includes C crook (floral engravings) with receiver I-slide and clamp, B♭, A shanks (floral engravings), alternate main tube U-slide for high and low pitch (engraved fittings). Second valve casing stamped: (within oval) BESSON & CO / [five-pointed star] / BREVETE / (below oval) [serial number:] 74975; B♭ and A shanks stamped with number: 975. Bell with owner's monogram: FCOP. Mouthpiece stamped: 18 / BESSON & CO / Prototype. Velvet-lined leather case (1560 A).

CHICAGO BORE / (within unfurled banner) 50 MEDALS OF HONOR / [monogram:] F B / BESSON & CO / "Prototype" / 198 EUSTON ROAD / LONDON / [five-pointed star] / ENGLAND / C. FISCHER / 6 4TH AV. N.Y. / SOLE AGENTS U. STATES

33 cm.
Bell ⌀: 11.8 cm.
Bore: 11.45 mm.

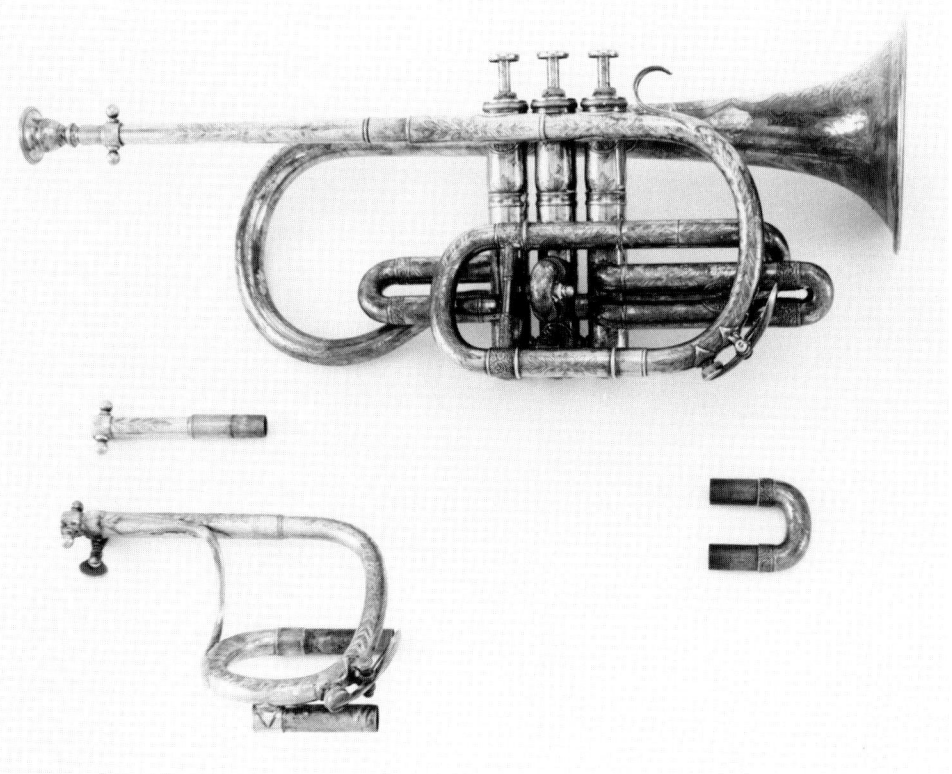

1560

1561
Cornet in B♭
London, 19th century, last decade
Besson and Co. Ltd. (founded ca. 1851)

Silver-plated brass. Périnet valves, top springs (casings stamped: 34, 35, 36). B♭ (missing), A shanks. Second valve casing stamped: (within oval) BESSON & CO / [five-pointed star] / BREVETE / (below oval) [serial number:] 64953; shanks stamped with number: 953. Mouthpiece stamped: BESSON & CO / Prototype. No decorative engravings. (a' 440)

CHICAGO BORE / (within unfurled banner) 50 MEDALS OF HONOR / [monogram:] F B / BESSON & CO / "Prototype" / 198 EUSTON ROAD / LONDON / [five-pointed star]

32.7 cm.
Bell ⌀: 11.8 cm.
Bore: 11.6 mm.

1740
Cornet in B♭
England? late 19th century
No inscription

Silver-plated brass. Périnet valves, top springs. Engraved mounts (vinestems, floral motif); intricate decorative knurling on caps. B♭ and A shanks. Wishbone (double) water key.

31.4 cm.
Bell ⌀: 12.5 cm.
Bore: 11.55 mm.

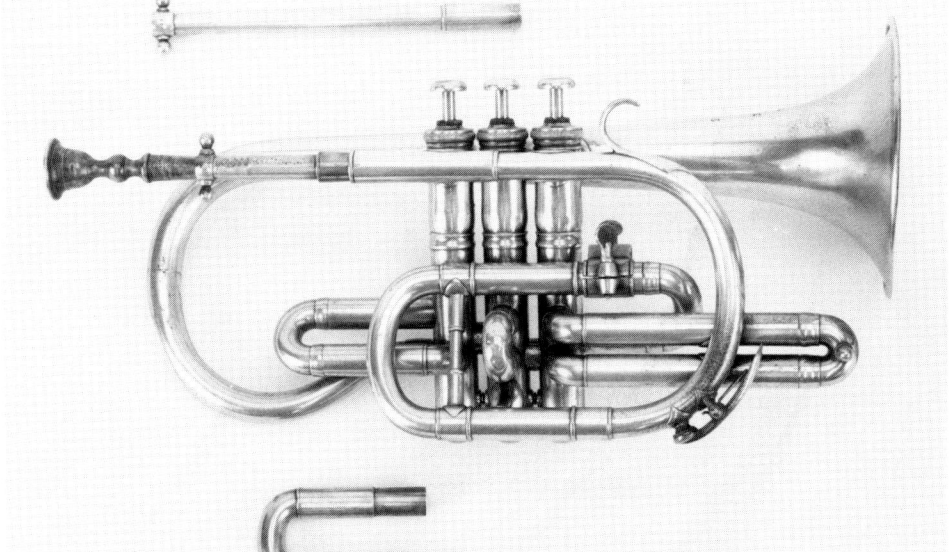

1561

1904
Cornet in B♭
Manchester, mid-19th century
Joseph Higham (1818-1883)

Brass; German silver buttons. Périnet valves, top springs. B♭, A shanks; alternate main tube U-slide (inner/outer) for high and low pitch. Split wishbone (double) water key. Serial number (second valve casing): 49576. Original mouthpiece, stamped: J.HIGHAM / MAKER. Wooden case (1904 A).

LYON & HEALY / SOLE AGENTS / CHICAGO / PATENT / CLEAR BORE / [seal of Great Britian] / EXHIBITION / PRIZE MEDALS / AWARDED / TO / J. HIGHAM / MAKER / 127 / STRANGEWAYS / MANCHESTER / ENGLAND / [embossed British seal]

31.9 cm.
Bell ⌀: 12.3 cm.
Bore: 11.5 mm.

1904

Alto Horns

867
Alto Horn in E♭
London, late 19th century
Henry Distin & Co. (fl. ca. 1862-1885)

Brass. Périnet valves, bottom springs. E♭ crook.

HENRY DISTIN & CO / MAKERS / 9 & 10 GT NEWPORT ST / LEICESTER SQUARE / LONDON

53.4 cm.
Bell ⌀: 15.6 cm.
Bore: 11.6 mm.

867

868
Alto Horn in E♭
London, 19th century, last quarter
Rivière & Hawkes (fl. 1875-1889)

Brass. Périnet valves, bottom springs. Extended U-slide on main tube.

RIVIÈRE & HAWKES / 28 / Leicester Square / London

48.9 cm.
Bell ⌀: 16.3 cm.
Bore: 12 mm.

868

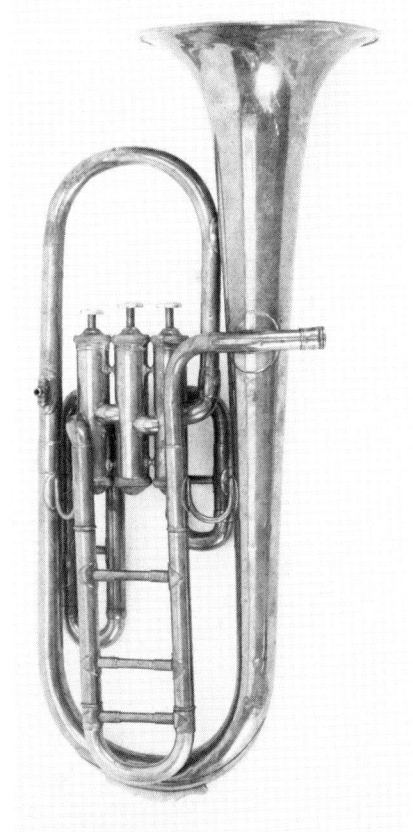

869

Alto Horn in F
Paris, ca. 1875
Antoine Courtois (fl. 1840-1880)

Brass. Périnet valves, bottom springs. F crook. Engraved with intials X / R H.

5 (upside-down) / (within oval) MÉDAILLE 1ER CLASSE / EXPOSITION / UNIVERSELLE / 1855 / (below oval) Médaille / LONDRES 1862 / Exposition Universelle / PARIS 1867 / Médaille d'Honneur / EN ARGENT / ANTOINE COURTOIS / Breveté / FACTEUR DU CONSERVATOIRE NATIONAL / 88 rue des Marais St. Martin / Paris / 1ER PRIX / GRANDE MÉDAILLE D'OR / EXPOSITION DE MOSCOU / 1872 & Paris 1873 / S. ARTHUR CHAPPELL / Sole Agent / 52 New Bond Street / London / ALTO / FA & MI♭

48.2 cm.
Bell ⌀: 18.2 cm.
Bore: 11.3 mm.

869

870

Alto Horn in E♭
Paris? late 19th century
Maker unknown (Harry Wilson, dealer)

Brass. Périnet valves, bottom springs. Stamped, receiver: A J; second valve casing: (within starburst design) C; second valve stem: U. High pitch.

"HARMONIOUS" / HARRY WILSON / Covered Market / LEEDS / MADE IN FRANCE

52.7 cm.
Bell ⌀: 18.2 cm.
Bore: 11.6 mm.

871
Alto Horn in E♭, Circular
Paris, 19th century, third quarter
Nic.-Firmin Michaud (ca. 1837-1872)

Brass. Périnet valves, bottom springs. E♭ crook.

(Upside-down) MICHAUD / BREVETÉ / (within circle) [monogram:] N F M / (below circle) 10 ET 12 / RUE DE SARTINE / PARIS

36 cm.
Bell ⌀: 17.8 cm.
Bore: 11.7 mm.

872
Alto Horn in E♭, Circular
France? 19th century, third quarter
No inscription

Brass. Périnet valves, bottom springs.

47.6 cm.
Bell ⌀: 18.2 cm.
Bore: 11.2 mm.

873
Alto Horn in F, Upturned Bell
France? mid-19th century
No inscription

Brass. Stoelzel piston valves with restraining screws. Articulated bell section, threaded joint (stamped: E 3267). U-slides marked with lines. E crook extant; F crook missing. Restored.

36 x 42.4 cm.
Bell ⌀: 18.8 cm.
Bore: 11.7 cm.

871

873

Baritones

900
Baritone in E♭ (Tenor Saxhorn)
Paris, 19th century, fourth quarter
Adolphe (Antoine Joseph) Sax (1814-1894)

Silver-plated brass. Three Périnet valves, bottom springs (top mounted), two Berlin valves (side mounted). Water key on first U-slide. Crook marked with lines.

No 40649 / Ad. Sax & Cie F.teur Breveté / 26 rue de Rocroy et 39 r[ue]. du Dunkerque / à Paris / SEUL / GRAND PRIX / 1867 / [monogram:] A S (within cross stoke of s:) PARIS

64 cm.
Bell ⌀: 17.2 cm.
Bore: 11.7 mm.

901
Baritone in B♭/C
France? late 19th century
No inscription

Brass. Périnet valves, bottom springs. Extended U-slide on main tube.

65 cm.
Bell ⌀: 20.3 cm.
Bore: 12 mm.

932
Baritone in B♭
U.S.A., late 19th century
No inscription

Brass; German silver fittings and levers; steel coiled springs. String action rotary valves, side-mounted. High pitch.

80 cm.
Bell ⌀: 19.4 cm.
Bore: 13 mm.

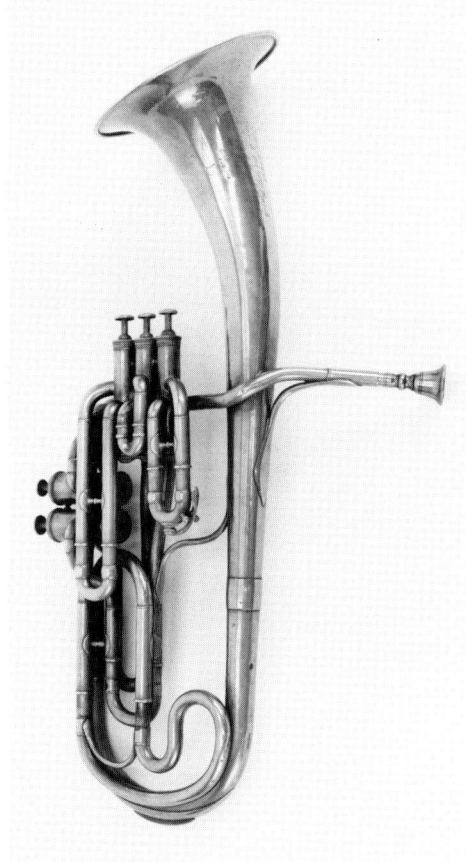

900

939
Baritone in B♭
London, late 19th century
Henry Potter & Co. (fl. 1858-1904)

Brass; German silver buttons. Périnet valves, bottom springs. High pitch.

HENRY POTTER & CO / MAKERS / 30 Charing Cross. / London

64 cm.
Bell ⌀: 23.2 cm.
Bore: 12.1 mm.

939

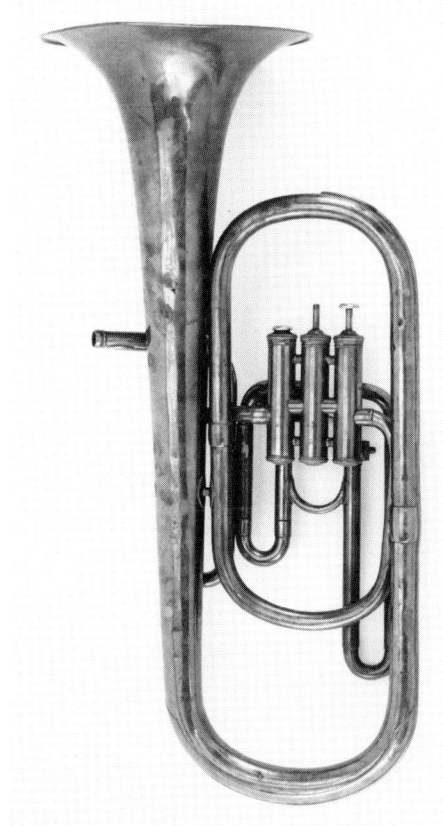

942

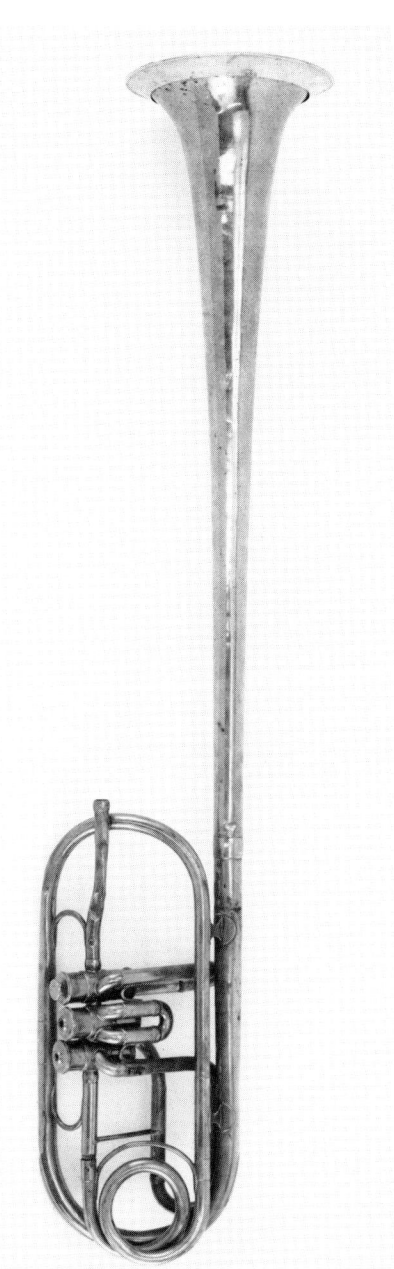

942
Baritone in B♭, Bell Over-the-Shoulder
France? 19th century, third quarter
No inscription

Brass; German silver bell garland. Berlin valves. Circular coiled crook on main tube.

102.5 cm.
Bell ⌀: 18.8 cm.
Bore: 12 mm.

944
Baritone in B♭/C
Paris, mid-19th century
Pierre Louis Gautrot (fl. 1845-1884)

Brass; German silver buttons, linkages, caps, screws, guard, and bell garland (engraved). Five rotary valves, four with clock spring action, one without mechanical linkage (wing nut attached directly to valve; cap stamped: F[irmé] O[uvert], indicating closed and open position).

Gautrot Breveté / à Paris / [monogram:] P L G / CANONGIA & CA / Rua nova do Almada No 66 & 67 / à LISBO[N]A

102 cm.
Bell ⌀: 21.4 cm.
Bore: 12.45mm.

944

Euphoniums

936
Euphonium in B♭, Oval
Frankfurt, 19th century, last quarter
(Ferdinand) Julius (Hermann) Altrichter
   (1842-1915)

Brass; German silver fittings, buttons, valve linkages, caps, braces, and bell garland. Vienna rotary valves, clock spring action. Shortened U-slide on main tube.

On German silver shield: [seal] / J. Altrichter / Frankfurt a / O. / Hof-Instrumenten-Fabrik / Sr. Königl. Hoheit / d. Prinzen Friedr. Carl v. Preussen

73.4 cm.
Bell ⌀: 22.3 cm.
Bore: 12.9 mm.

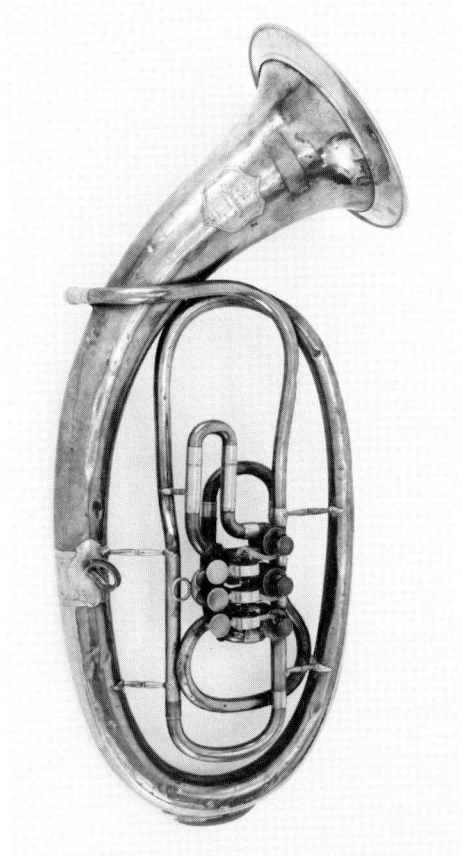

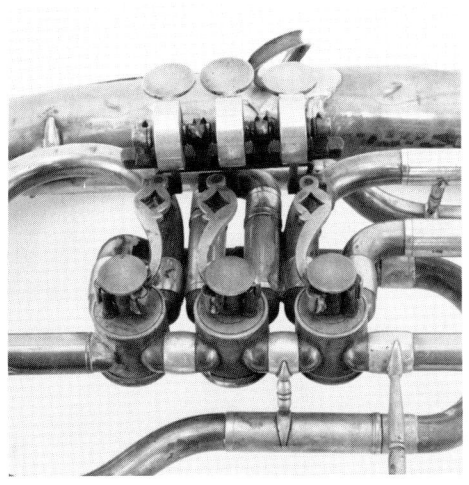

936 detail

940
Euphonium in B♭
London, 19th century, third quarter
F. Besson (fl. 1862-1873)

Brass. Four Périnet valves, bottom springs (three top-, one side-mounted). Serial number (second valve casing): 27386. Second and fourth (side) valve casings stamped: (within oval) F. BESSON / [five-pointed star] / BREVETÉE.

1/83 / (within unfurled banner) 50 MEDALS OF HONOUR / (below banner) [monogram:] F B / F. BESSON / BREVETÉ / 198 EUSTON RD / LONDON / [five-pointed star]

68.5 cm.
Bell ⌀: 24.7 cm.
Bore: 14.3 mm.

940

941
Euphonium in B♭, Bell Over-the-Shoulder
U.S.A., 19th century, third quarter
No inscription

Brass; nickel-plated bell garland; nickel-plated brass levers (one missing). Adams twin-vane valves, string action with adjusting screws, top-mounted. Bell section with threaded joint (stamped: 2).

105 cm.
Bell ⌀: 24 cm.
Bore: 13.15 mm.

943
Euphonium in B♭, Bell Over-the-Shoulder
U.S.A., late 19th century
No inscription

Brass. String action rotary valves, top-mounted.

104 cm.
Bell ⌀: 24 cm.
Bore: 13.7 mm.

947
Euphonium in B♭
Vienna, late 19th century
Leopold Uhlmann & Sohn (fl. 1834-1895)

Brass; nickel-plated fittings, guard, and bell garland; German silver buttons (vinestem engravings), caps, and screws (two missing; engraved, floral motif). Vienna rotary valves (Heyde 1980: 229, Design 15). Engraved brass linkages (vinestem).

Nickel-plated shield: (cartouche bearing coat of arms) K: K: Hof / Instrumenten Fabrik / Leopold Uhlmann & Sohn / IN WIEN

75 cm.
Bell ⌀: 22 cm.
Bore, U-slide, O⌀: 14.8 mm.

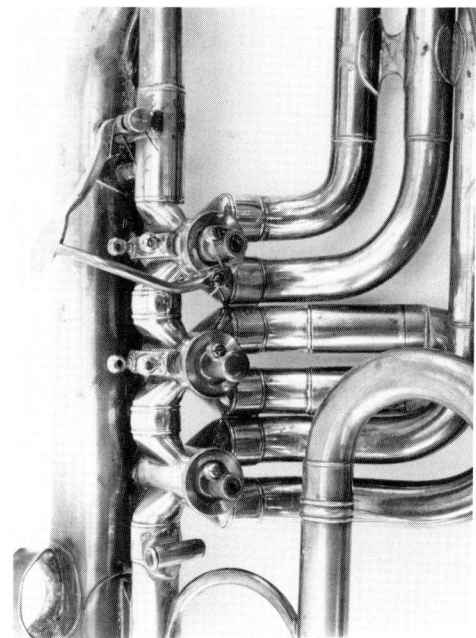

941 detail

941 943 947

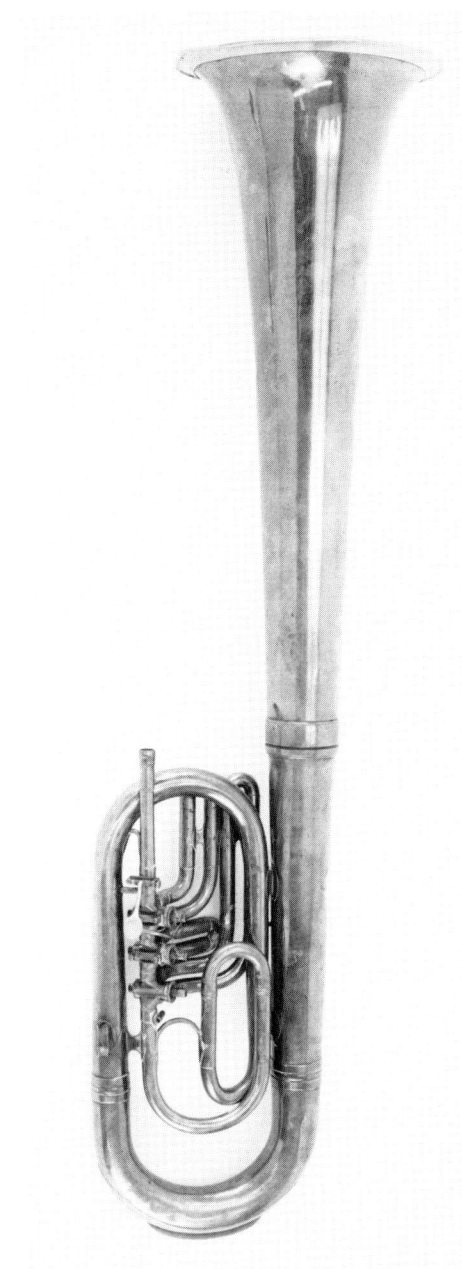
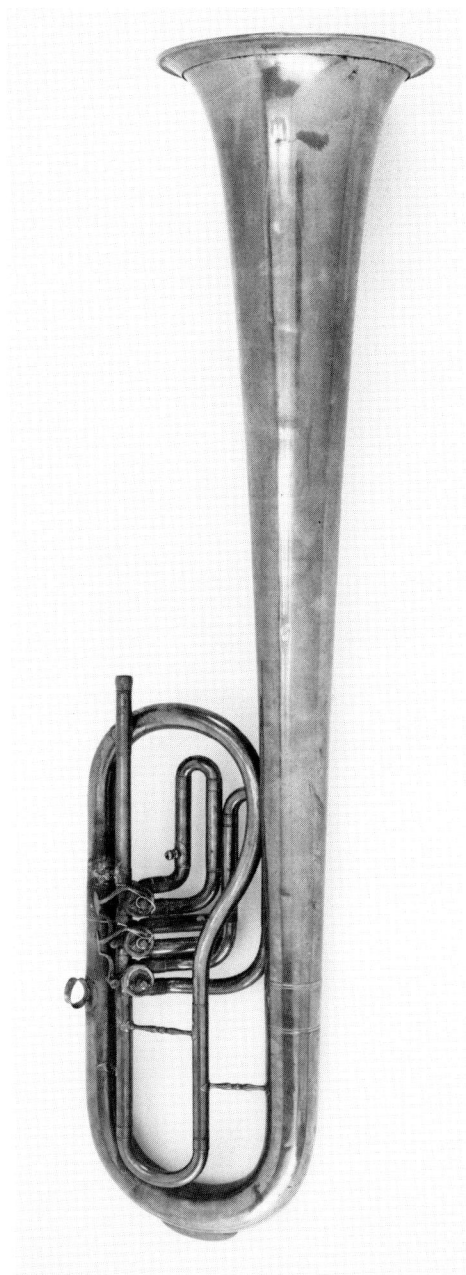
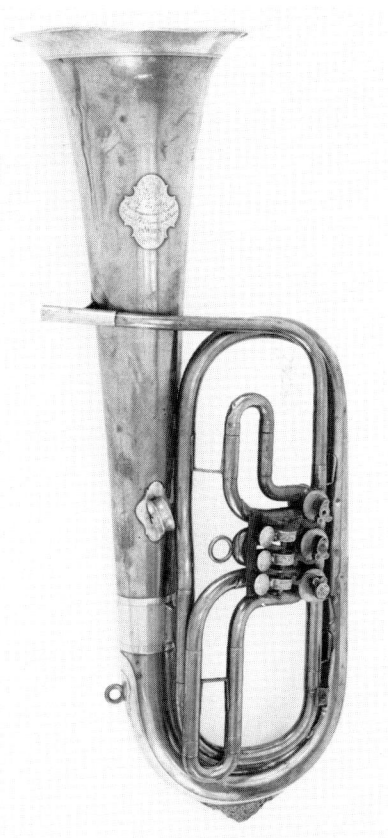

Tubas

945
Tuba in F
Bremen, mid-19th century
C. Anton Langhamer (fl. ca. 1875-1910)

Brass; nickel-plated fittings, buttons, guard, and bell garland (engraved, floral motif). Berlin valves, early type. No U-slide on second valve tube; no water key.

Nickel-plated shield: (cartouche) A. Langhamer / Instr: in / Bremen

85 cm.
Bell ⌀: 20.7 cm.
Bore (O⌀): 16.3 mm.

946
Tuba in E♭
Paris? late 19th century
Joseph Wallis & Sons Ltd. (fl. 1887-1928)

Brass. Périnet valves, bottom springs. Second valve casing stamped: (within starburst design) C.

J. Wallis & Sons Ltd / Paris / and / London , No. W

72 cm.
Bell ⌀: 29.5 cm.
Bore: 14.5 mm.

1370
Tuba in E♭, Bell Over-the-Shoulder
Austria or Germany? late 19th century
No inscription

Brass. Four Berlin valves (three top-, one side-mounted). U-slides marked with lines; inlet altered. D♭ crook extant. No water key.

146 cm.
Bell ⌀: 26.5 cm.
Bore: 15.15 mm.

1784
Tuba in E♭, Bell Over-the-Shoulder
Boston, 19th century, third quarter
Elbridge G. Wright (fl. 1841-1871)

German silver. Four string action rotary valves placed at a right angle (three top-, one side-mounted). No water key.

Made by / E. G. WRIGHT / BOSTON

145 cm.
Bell ⌀: 28 cm.
Bore, U-slide, O⌀: 17.6 mm.

945

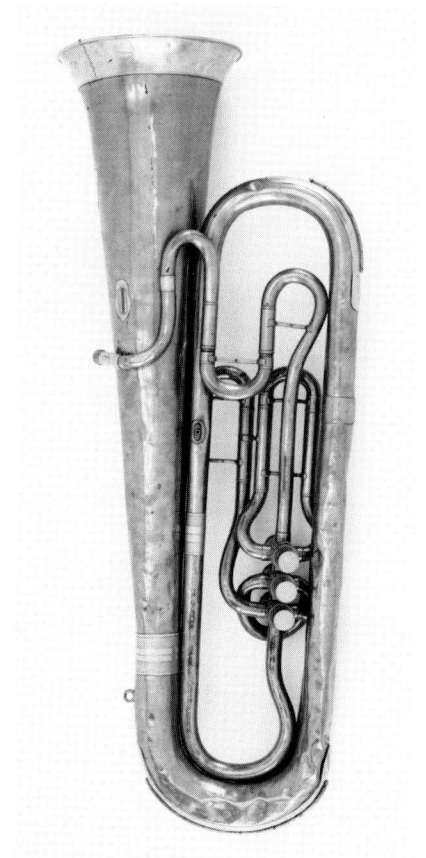

1784

1934
Tuba in B♭
Cleveland, Ohio, 20th century
H. N. White & Co.

Nickel-plated brass (brushed); mother-of-pearl button disks. Périnet valves, bottom springs. Alternate U-slide (with water key) for high pitch. Serial number: 23622.

(On cartouche) KING / MADE BY / N. H. WHITE / CLEVELAND / OHIO

67.5 cm.
Bell ⌀: 27.8 cm.
Bore: 14.2 mm.

948

948
Helicon in E♭
Chicago, late 19th century
J. Bader & Co.

Brass; German silver fittings, key levers, and caps. String action rotary valves, side-mounted. Receiver with clamp.

J. BADER & CO. CHICAGO

97 cm.
Bell ⌀: 30 cm.
Bore: 15.15 mm.

949
Helicon in B♭
London, late 19th century
S. Arthur Chappell (fl. 1863-1906)

Brass. Périnet valves, bottom springs. Felt-wrapped leather shoulder rest. Patched.

S. ARTHUR CHAPPELL / 52 NEW BOND ST / LONDON N. W.

101 cm.
Bell ⌀: 39 cm.
Bore: 16.85 mm.

913
Pelittone Fagattone (Contrabass) (BB♭)
Milan, late 19th century
Giuseppe Pelitti (fl. ca. 1835-1893)

Painted (gold) brass. No valves. Sinuous shape with upright bell; two transverse braces. Mouthpiece soldered to corpus.

Within painted oval: Contrabasso / Pelittone / Fagattone

319 cm.
Bell ⌀: 46 cm.

949

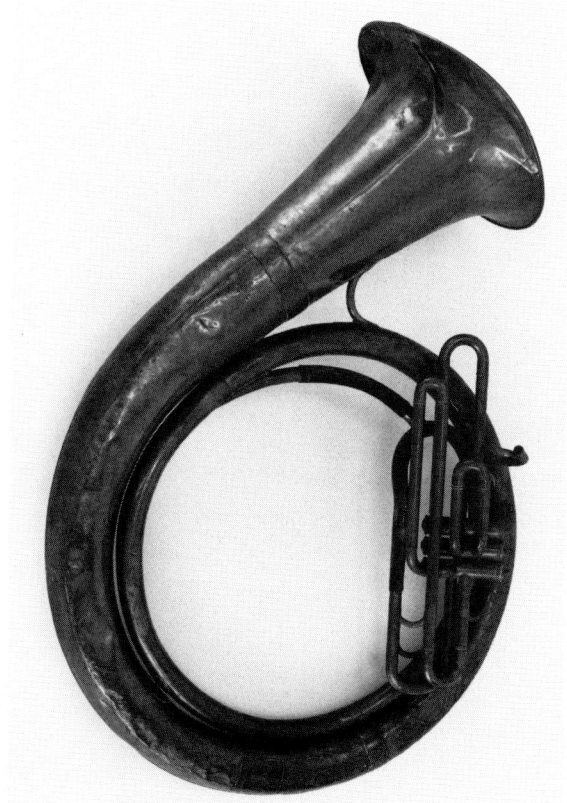

Trombe

930
Tromba (G♭)
Italy? late 19th century
No inscription

Painted (black) brass corpus; patinated brass mouthpipe, U-bend, and bell; German silver receiver. Elongated U-shape; hooked bell section. Two rings for cord.

70.5 cm.
Bell ⌀: 24 cm.
Receiver ⌀: 12.5 mm.

1358
Tromba (B♭)
Milan, late 19th century
Giuseppe Pelitti (fl. ca. 1835-1893)

Painted (gold) brass. Small portion of tube folded. Two ornamental bosses.

CORNET IN SI B / EXCELSIOR / G. PELITTI. MILANO.

93.3 cm.
Bell ⌀: 12.6 cm.
Receiver ⌀: 9.6 mm.

1360
Tromba (D)
Milan, 1884
Giuseppe Pelitti (fl. ca. 1835-1893)

Painted (silver, gold) brass. Portion of tube folded; two semicircular diversions. Ring on mouthpipe; bulbous ferrule; bulbous boss on bell section.

[coat of arms] / * * / G. PELITTI. MILANO. / 1884 / BALLO METEMESICOSIS / * / RE

124.5 cm.
Bell ⌀: 15.3 cm.
Receiver ⌀: 10.4 mm.

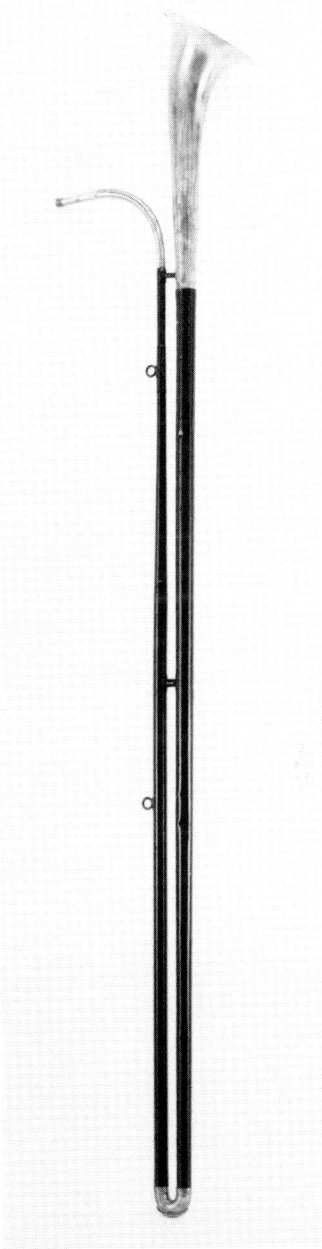

930

908
Tromba (E♭), Valved
Italy? late 19th century
No inscription

Brass; German silver fittings. Tube with semicircular diversion, symmetrical brace. One Périnet valve (P4), bottom spring. Receiver I-slide with clamp. Large pommel on bell flare.

134 cm.
Bell ⌀: 15 cm.
Receiver ⌀: 10.4 mm.

1367
Tromba (E♭)
Italy? late 19th century
No inscription

Painted brass (black corpus, gold bell section). Curved tube with symmetrical brace, two transverse struts. Bulbous boss on bell section.

201 cm.
Bell ⌀: 16.2 cm.
Receiver ⌀: 11.7 mm.

809
Tromba (B♭), Folded
Milan, late 19th century
Giuseppe Pelitti (fl. ca. 1835-1893)

Painted (gold) brass. Two bends. U-slide. Ring on mouthpipe; bulbous boss on bell section.

SI B / * / TROMBA BASSA DI CANIO / EXCELSIOR. / G. PELITTI. MILANO / *

122 cm.
Bell ⌀: 15.4 cm.
Receiver ⌀: 11 mm.

912
Tromba (B), Folded
Italy? late 19th century
No inscription

Two brass sections. Four bends (trombone shape). Mouthpiece soldered to body.

191 cm.
Bell ⌀: 15 cm.

916
Tromba (F), Folded
Milan, late 19th century
Giuseppe Pelitti (fl. ca. 1835-1893)

Brass. Six bends. U-slide. Ring on mouthpipe; two rings for cord.

On brass medallion: PELITTI / [coat of arms with central crescent] / MILANO / (below medallion) FA. BASSO.

70.1 cm.
Bell ⌀: 11.4 cm.
Receiver ⌀: 11.5 mm.

1366
Tromba (E♭), Folded
Italy? late 19th century
No inscription

Brass. Two bends.

100 cm.
Bell ⌀: 25.2 cm.
Receiver ⌀: 9 mm.

1368
Tromba (E♭), Folded
Milan, late 19th century
Giuseppe Pelitti (fl. ca. 1835-1893)

Painted (grey, gold, red) brass. Three bends, single coil in bell flare. U-slide with ring.

[coat of arms with seal of commune of Milan] / * * / G. PELITTI. MILANO / 52743

81 cm.
Bell ⌀: 15.7 cm.
Receiver ⌀: 10 mm.

917
Tromba (D), Serpentine
Italy, late 19th century
Maker unknown

Brass. Corpus with six bends.

CAMPIONE. / TROMBA. / N.4

90 cm.
Bell ⌀: 12.2 cm.
Receiver ⌀: 10 mm.

811
Tromba (B♭), Looped
Milan, late 19th century
Camillo Sambruna (fl. 1886-1906)

Brass. Two loops. Receiver I-slide with clamp. Engraved ferrules; ring on mouthpipe.

[coat of arms with seal of commune of Milan] / C. SAMBRUNA / MILANO / 5

104 cm.
Bell ⌀: 17.7 cm.
Receiver ⌀: 11.95 mm.

812
Tromba (D♭), Looped
Italy? late 19th century
No inscription

Painted (silver, blue) brass. Single loop.
Receiver I-slide with clamp. Decorative
pommel on bell section.

88 cm.
Bell ⌀: 17.1 cm.
Receiver ⌀: 10.2 mm.

914
Tromba (G♭), Looped
Italy? late 19th century
No inscription

Painted (black, red) brass. Single loop, curved
corpus, upturned bell. Mouthpiece soldered
to corpus.

85 cm.
Bell ⌀: 15.4 cm.

915
Tromba (B♭), Looped
Italy? late 19th century
No inscription

Brass. Single loop (I⌀: 14.5 cm.). Receiver
I-slide with clamp.

61 cm.
Bell ⌀: 12.3 cm.
Receiver ⌀: 11.5 mm.

811

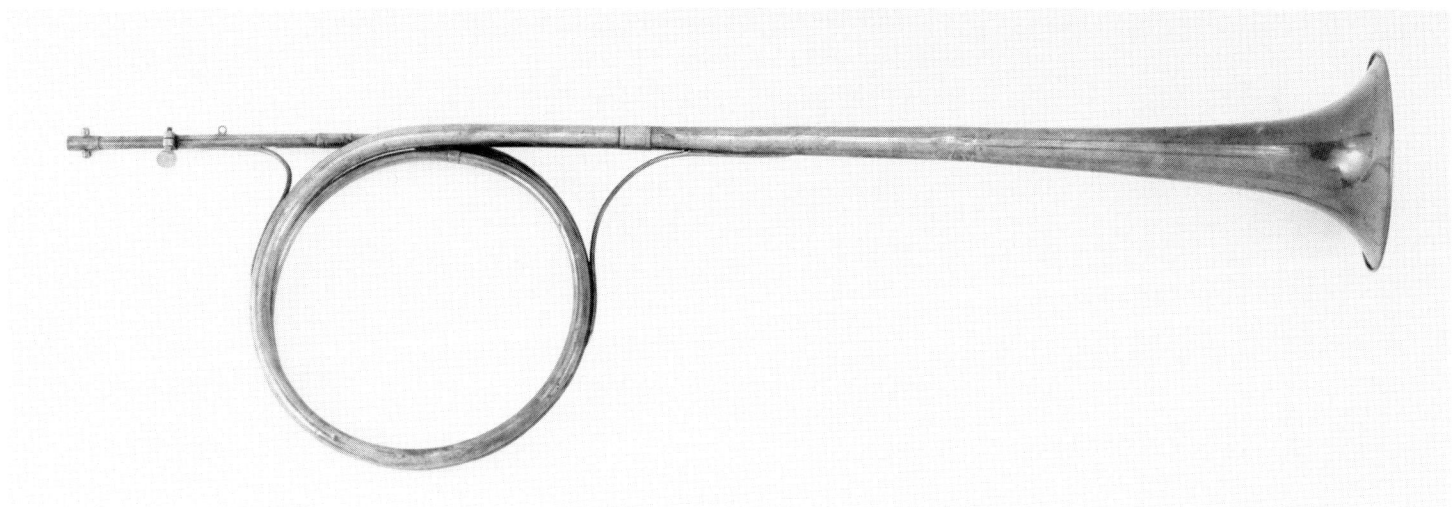

812

1361
Tromba (C), Looped
Milan, 1884
Giuseppe Pelitti (fl. ca. 1835-1893)

Painted (silver) brass. Portion of tube folded; single loop. U-slide. Ring on mouthpipe; bulbous boss on bell section.

[coat of arms] / * * / G. PELITTI. MILANO. / 1884 / BALLO METEMESICOSIS / * / DO

116 cm.
Bell ⌀: 15.3 cm.
Receiver ⌀: 10 mm.

1369
Tromba (F), Looped
Italy? late 19th century
No inscription

Painted (black, grey) brass. Single loop, two bends, second loop in bell flare.

155 cm.
Bell ⌀: 24.5 cm.

904
Tromba (B♭), Coiled
Italy? late 19th century
No inscription

Painted brass. Two loops. Large bore. Mouthpipe missing.

88.5 cm.
Bell ⌀: 22.7 cm.

922
Tromba (D♭), Coiled
Italy? late 19th century
No inscription

Painted brass. Four loops. Large bore. Mouthpipe missing. Similar to 904.

75.4 cm.
Bell ⌀: 22.8 cm.

909
Tromba (C/B♭), Coiled
Italy, late 19th century
Maker unknown

Brass; German silver fittings and brace. Three bends, two loops. Long straight telescoping tuning slide; U-slide. Shank missing.

TROMBA. BASSA. / DO. E SI B.

57.8 cm.
Bell ⌀: 15.5 cm.
Receiver ⌀: 11.7 mm.

909

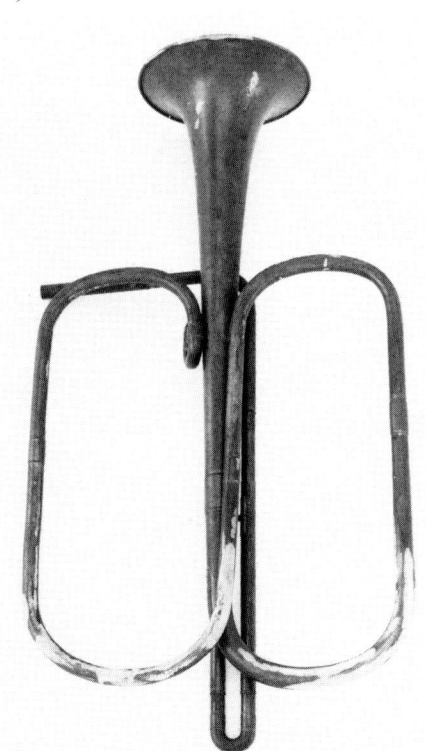

1365

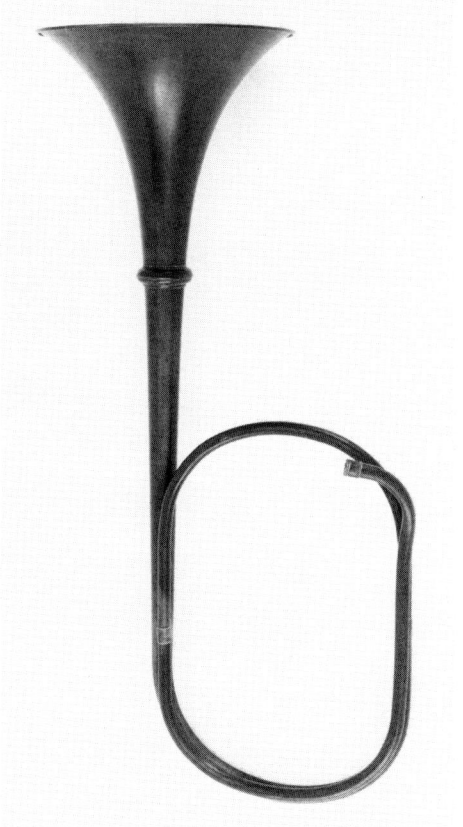

1365
Tromba (D), Coiled
Italy, late 19th century
No inscription

Brass. Single loop. Decorative pommel on bell flare. Appears to have been manufactured by the maker of 909.

71.2 cm.
Bell ⌀: 23.9 cm.
Receiver ⌀: 11.9 mm.

918
Tromba (Duplex Horn), Coiled
Italy? late 19th century
No inscription

Brass. Two conical tubes, bells of different diameters, single receiver. Exchange mechanism (missing) fits into slots on V-shaped mouthpipe.

55 cm.
Bell ⌀, left: 27.2 cm.; right: 21.2 cm.
Receiver ⌀: 14.2 mm.

876
Tromba (D), Circular
Milan, late 19th century
Giuseppe Pelitti (fl. ca. 1835-1893)

Brass. Single loop.

[coat of arms with seal of commune of Milan] / * * / G. PELITTI. MILANO. / * / 46946 / * / 68

Corpus ⌀: 40 cm. (L: 65 cm.)
Bell ⌀: 15.8 cm.
Receiver ⌀: 11.1 mm.

876

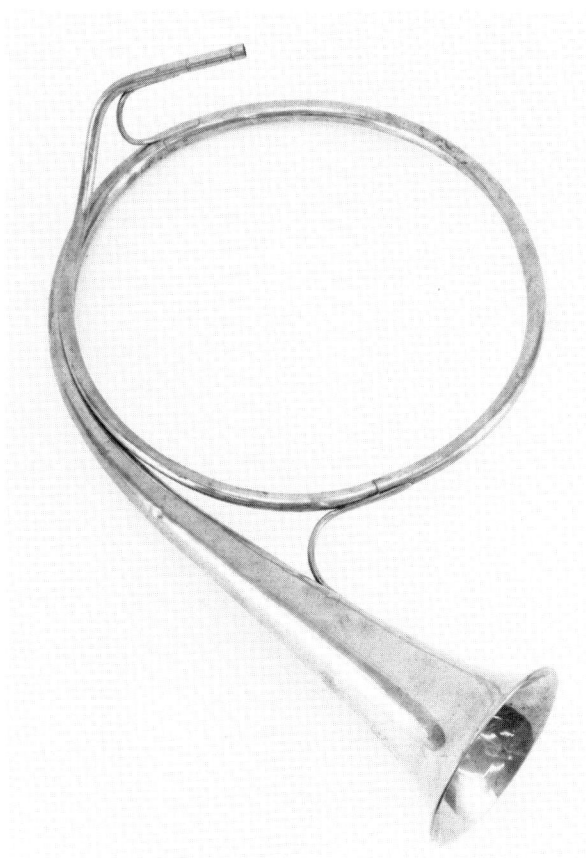

918

926

926
Tromba (B♭), Circular
Italy? late 19th century
No inscription

Brass; painted dragon's head bell. Portion of tubing twice looped, corpus with single large loop.

Corpus ⌀: 49 cm. (L: 91 cm.)
Receiver ⌀: 11.5 mm.

928
Tromba (D), Circular
Italy? late 19th century
No inscription

Brass; painted dragon's head bell. Portion of tube looped, corpus with single large loop. Large bulbous ferrule.

Corpus ⌀: 32.4 cm. (L: 71.3 cm.)

1362
Tromba (F), Circular
Milan, late 19th century
Camillo Sambruna (fl. 1886-1906)

Brass. Tube with two bends, single large loop. U-slide. Water key; ring on mouthpipe.

C. SAMBRUNA / MILANO

Corpus ⌀: 57.5 cm. (L: 111.5 cm.)
Bell ⌀: 21.3 cm.
Receiver ⌀: 13.2 mm.

1362

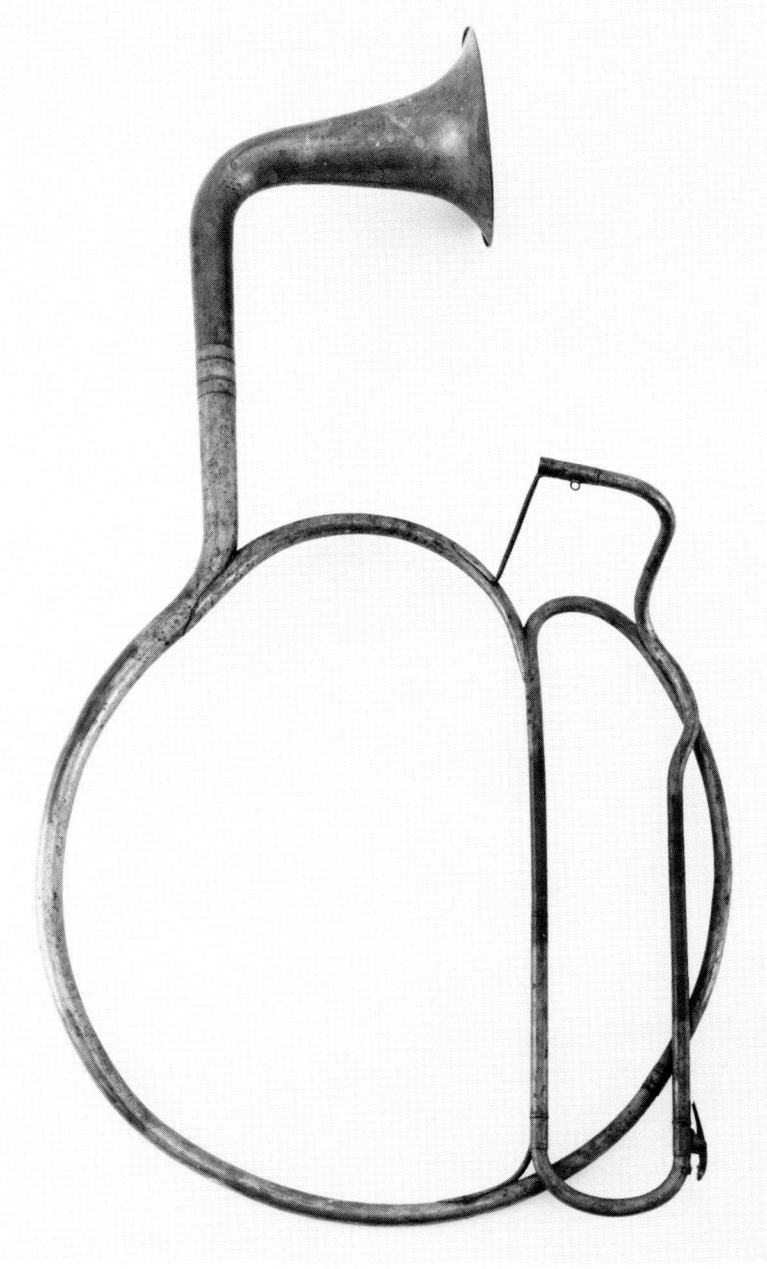

1372
Tromba (D♭), Circular
Italy? late 19th century
No inscription

Painted (black, gold) brass. Small portion of tube folded, corpus with two loops. U-slide.

Corpus ⌀: 43 x 33 cm. (L: 99 cm.)
Bell ⌀: 19.9 cm.

929
Tromba (incomplete), Circular
Italy? late 19th century
No inscription

Brass. Small portion of tubing looped. Bell section, mouthpipe missing.

Corpus ⌀: 60 cm.

1353
Tromba (A), G-shaped
Milan, late 19th century
Giuseppe Pelitti (fl. ca. 1835-1893)

Painted (gold, brown, white, red) brass. Receiver I-slide with clamp. Two transverse braces; ring on mouthpipe.

On medallion: PELITTI / [coat of arms with central crescent] / MILANO

74 cm.
Bell ⌀: 15 cm.
Receiver ⌀: 13 mm.

905
Tromba (B), Valved, G-shaped
Italy? late 19th century
No inscription

Brass. Single transverse brace. Single Périnet valve, bottom spring. Receiver I-slide with clamp, U-slide.

68.3 cm.
Bell ⌀: 15.1 cm.
Receiver ⌀: 10.4 mm.

919
Tromba (F), G-shaped
Milan, late 19th century
Giuseppe Pelitti (fl. ca. 1835-1893)

Brass. Two bends. Two transverse braces; ring on mouthpipe brace.

On medallion: G. PELITTI. MILANO. / [coat of arms with seal of commune of Milan] / PREMIATO CON 40 MEDAGLIE E 8 BREVETTI

Corpus ⌀: 62.5 cm. (L: 214 cm.)
Bell ⌀: 15 cm.
Receiver ⌀: 13 mm.

920

920
Tromba (E), Valved, G-shaped
Milan, late 19th century
Giuseppe Pelitti (fl. ca. 1835-1893)

Brass. Three Périnet valves, bottom springs. Two transverse braces; ring on mouthpipe brace.

On medallion: G. PELITTI. MILANO. / [coat of arms with seal of commune of Milan] / PREMIATO CON 40 MEDAGLIE E 8 BREVETTI

Corpus ⌀: 63.3 cm. (L: 84 cm.)
Bell ⌀: 23 cm.
Receiver ⌀: 11 mm.

906
Tromba (B♭), Valved, G-shaped
Milan, late 19th century
Giuseppe Pelitti (fl. ca. 1835-1893)

Brass. Three Périnet valves, bottom springs. Two transverse braces; ring on mouthpipe brace. Identical to 920.

On medallion: G. PELITTI. MILANO. / [coat of arms with seal of commune of Milan] / PREMIATO CON 40 MEDAGLIE E 8 BREVETTI

Corpus ⌀: 77 cm. (L: 102 cm.)
Bell ⌀: 22.5 cm.
Receiver ⌀: 11 mm.

Systems of Valves

1435
Two Vienna Valves
Maker and provenance unknown

Silver-plated brass. Piston action. Valves from alto instrument.

16 x 15 cm.

1436
Three Vienna Valves
Maker and provenance unknown

Brass; attached to wooden display mount. Piston action. Valves from baritone instrument.

22 cm.

1437
Three Périnet Valves, Cross section
Paris, early 20th century
Besson (founded ca. 1838)

Brass. Second valve casing stamped: BESSON / [crown] / BREVETE.

15.5 cm.

1438
Three Double Rotary Valves
U.S.A., late 19th century
J. S. Johnson?

Brass. Articulated crank action, flat keys. Second valve casing stamped: 41098.

9.5 x 10 cm.

1435

1438

Membranophones   *Timpani*

1466
Timpani
England? mid-19th century
No inscription

Copper bowls; iron counterhoops, painted (black) claw-shaped standards; flesh heads with metal hoops. Heads attached to bowls with ten brass lugs; tuned by floating inner hoop with semi-circular braces on screw mechanism.

⌀, Heads: 55; 58.5 cm.

1466

Tubular Drums

1468 (formerly 388 A)
Concert Snare Drum
U.S.A., mid-19th century
No inscription

Brass, shallow cylinder drum; dark stained and painted (red) wooden counterhoops; flesh heads with metal hoops. Eight braces and rods with lug tensioning; eight gut snares, brass strainer with screw mechanism.

H: 19.5 cm.
∅, Head: 40.5 cm.

388
Side Drum
Paris, late 19th century
Michel Colas & Cie

Brass, waisted tubular drum; painted (blue) wooden counterhoops; flesh heads with metal hoops. Cord rope and tug ear tensioning; two gut snares, brass strainer with screw mechanism. Serial number: 143. Two dark stained wooden sticks (388 A and B).

MICHEL COLAS & CIE / BREVETÉ RUE DU PETIT ... 32 & ... / A PARIS

H: 37 cm.
∅, Head: 39 cm.

388

386

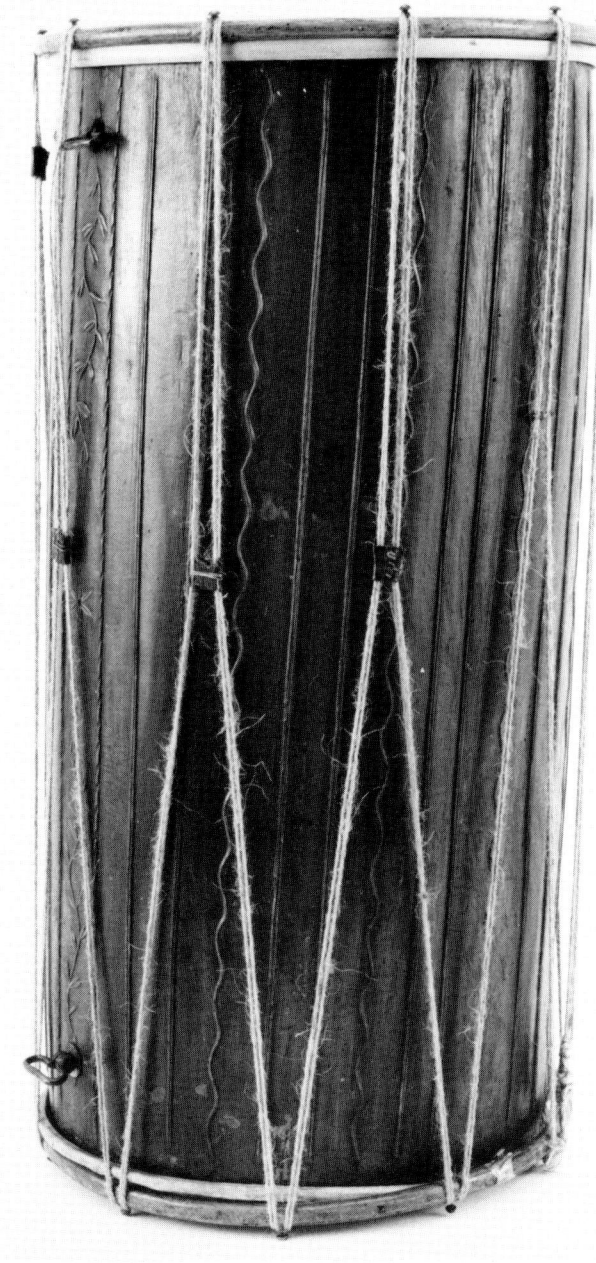

387
Side Drum (Reproduction)
Holland, late 19th century
Maker unknown

Wood, cylinder drum decorated with painted (red, blue, white) geometric designs, coat of arms (gold, red, blue) with inscription: (within unfurled banner) HAAR 1572 LEM. Cord rope and tug ear tensioning; two gut snares, brass strainer with screw mechanism (missing).

H: 34 cm.
⌀, Head: 37.5 cm.

385
Tenor Drum (Reproduction)
Switzerland? late 19th century
Maker unknown

Wood, long cylinder drum decorated with painted (red, green, yellow) geometric designs, arabesques (green, silver), three coats of arms; flesh heads with wooden hoops. Cord rope and tug ear tensioning.

H: 60 cm.
⌀, Body: 33 cm.
⌀, Head: 34.5 cm.

386
Tenor Drum
France? late 18th century?
Maker unknown

Stained and varnished wood, long cylinder drum decorated with carved geometric and vinestem designs; flesh heads and hoops (replacements); pine counterhoops with screws (replacements); two iron strap holders (later additions). Cord rope and tug ear tensioning.

H: 76.5 cm.
⌀, Body: 36 cm.
⌀, Head: 38 cm.

314
Pot Drum
France? early 20th century
Maker unknown

Painted metal (blue, red); flesh batter and snare heads separated by a narrow wooden hoop; brass counterhoop. Six braces and rods with wing nut tensioning; two gut snares, brass strainer with screw mechanism. Crude.

H: 19 cm.
⌀, Head: 24 cm.

393
Bass Drum
Italy? late 19th century
Maker unknown

Brass, shallow cylinder drum; painted (black) wooden counterhoops; one flesh head with metal hoop. Cord rope and tug ear tensioning. Shell with two holes through which a painted (black) brass pole with ornamental headpiece passes.

Depth: 21 cm.   H (pole): 195 cm.
⌀, Head: 76.5 cm.

1496
Bass Drum
Chicago, late 19th/early 20th century
The Harmony Co.

Maple, shallow cylinder drum; two flesh heads (missing). Cord rope and tug ear tensioning.

Label: HARMONY DRUM / PATENT APPLIED FOR / MANUFACTURED BY / THE HARMONY CO. / CHICAGO, ILL. U.S.A.

Depth: 30.5 cm.
⌀, Head: 73 cm.

Frame Drums

397
Tambourine, with Pole
Italy? 19th century

Upright painted (black, gold, silver) pole with shield; stained and varnished wooden tambourine (flesh head nailed to wooden hoop, five pairs of metal jingles) and bell (decoratively painted [purple] with three concentric circles) mounted on shield.

H, Pole: 206 cm.
Tambourine, ⌀: 18.5 cm.   Depth: 5 cm.
Bell, ⌀: 8 cm.

399
Tambourine
Italy, late 19th century
Maker unknown

Narrow painted (blue, red) pine; six small brass clapper bells mounted on brass wires; flesh head nailed to hoop.

⌀: 38 cm.   Depth: 9.5 cm.

400
Tambourine
Italy? 19th century

Painted (brown, beige) wood frame with vinestem decoration (in green); six pairs of brass jingles (one pair missing); flesh head tucked under wooden hoop. Six braces and rods with screw tensioning.

⌀: 41.5 cm.   Depth: 8 cm.

401
Tambourine
Italy?

Pine frame, painted (blue) counterhoop; ten pairs of brass jingles; flesh head nailed to wooden hoop. Five brass braces and rods with lug tensioning.

∅: 39.5 cm.   Depth: 8.5 cm.

404
Tambourine
France

Pine frame; nine pairs of decoratively stamped (floral designs) tin jingles; flesh head nailed to frame (top) with vinestem decoration (yellow, green), inscribed: Marie Josephe de Saxe / Dauphine de France 1767; (bottom) with a portrait of a woman reading, vinestems (gold).

∅: 44 cm.   Depth: 7 cm.

405
Tambourine
Italy, 1886

Painted (gold) and carved wooden frame; ten pairs of metal jingles (missing); flesh head nailed to frame decorated with a portrait of a peasant woman, signed: M. Belli, 1886.

∅: 45 cm.   Depth: 9.5 cm.

410
Tambourine
Valencia, 19th century

Pine frame decorated with wooden cord and thread balls; five sets of painted (yellow) jingles; flesh head nailed to frame decorated with painting of a street scene.

∅: 23 cm.   Depth: 4 cm.

411
Tambourine
U.S.A.? early 20th century

Painted (red) wooden frame; forty-nine rings (five missing) mounted on brads inside frame; flesh head glued to frame. Decorated with nickel-plated copper studs.

∅: 36 cm.   Depth: 5 cm.

412
Tambourine
U.S.A.? early 20th century

Painted (red) wooden frame with decals (floral motif); three pairs of nickel-plated metal jingles; flesh head nailed to frame.

∅: 25 cm.   Depth: 4.5 cm.

Friction Drums

420
Friction Drum
Spain?

Red clay bucket; single flesh head with a small hole pierced in the center through which passes a cane stick. The player alternately pulls up or pushes down on the stick, causing the membrane to vibrate.

H, Body: 8 cm.   ⌀, Head: 9.5 cm.

421
Friction Drum
Italy?

Sheet tin pot, soldered seam; single flesh head; cane stick.

H, Body: 19.5 cm.   ⌀, Head: 19.5 cm.

420

Singing Membranes

423
Singing Membrane ("Kazoo")
New York, early 20th century
The Kazoo Co.

Pine, side aperture; onion skin membrane; perforated nickel-plated tin band protects membrane.

11 cm.

424
Singing Membrane ("Vocophone")
U.S.A.

Two sections: pine mouthpipe (covered with gold and silver paper) with side aperture, onion skin membrane, and painted (black) mouthpiece, cardboard bell (covered with gold and silver paper).

23.4 cm.

423

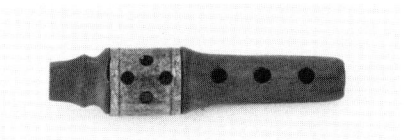

427

425
Singing Membrane, Horn-Shaped
Germany?

Two nickel-plated tin sections with soldered brass bell. Side aperture in lower section; removable top section with perforations to protect membrane (missing).

22.6 cm.

426
Singing Membrane, Horn-Shaped
Germany?

Two nickel-plated tin sections with soldered brass bell. Upper section missing. Similar to 425.

34 cm.

427
Singing Membrane, Horn-Shaped
U.S.A.?

Brass, front aperture; onion skin membrane. Walls of tube pierced with four small holes below the membrane.

28 cm.   Bell ⌀: 13.5 cm.

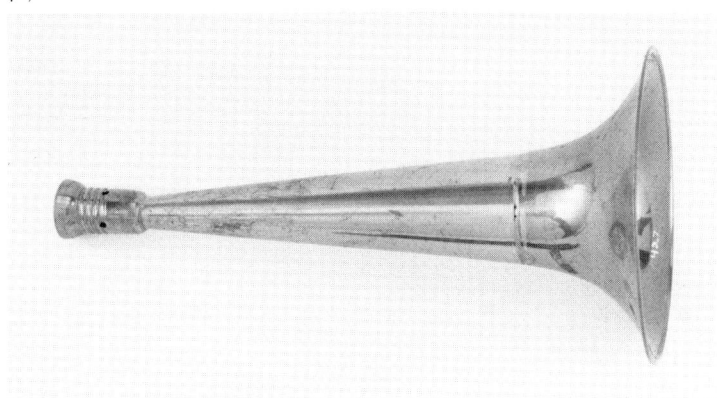

Idiophones — *Concussion Sticks, Castinets, Cymbals*

67
Concussion Sticks
Italy?

Pine. Central slat and handle with two additional slats, attached to corpus with eight brass screws. Held in one hand and struck against the palm of the other.

50.6 cm.

70
Castinets
England?

Ebony, with handle. Disk-shaped.

L: 11.1 cm.   W: 4.1 cm.

71
Castinets
England?

Boxwood, with handle. Shell-shaped.

L: 27 cm.   W: 4.7 cm.

98
Small Cymbals
Italy

Patinated bronze. Reproduction of Roman instruments.

⌀: 9 cm.   Depth: 3.5 cm.

167 and 182
Cymbals
Turkey?

Brass. Leather handles.

⌀: 35.7 cm.

67

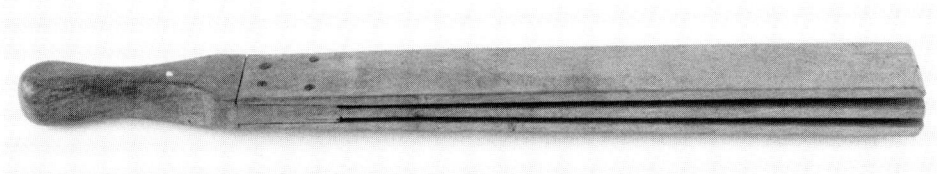

70

71

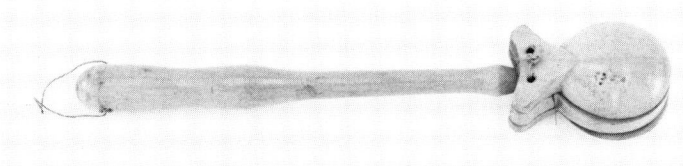

*Musical Coins,
Tuning Fork,
Xylophones,
Glockenspiels*

232-233
Musical Coins
U.S.A.

Eight flat, round, nickel-plated disks, with notched sides. Sound G major scale.

⌀: 5.7-8.3 cm.

250
Tuning Fork
Paris, 19th century
Rudolph Koenig

Steel; oak knob handle. Spruce resonator case, stamped: UT3 / RUDOLPH KOENIG / À PARIS.

UT3 / 512 VS / [monogram:] R K

21.7 cm.
Resonator: 30.7 x 11.5 x 6.5 cm.

214
Xylophone (Toy)
U.S.A.

Twenty-two painted (gold) metal bars; painted (red; silver decorative tape) pine resonator. Diatonic compass: c′-c′′′′.

66 cm.

245
Xylophone (Toy)
U.S.A., 19th century, last quarter
Schoenhut Co.

Eighteen painted (silver, gold) metal bars; varnished pine resonator, scalloped silouette. Diatonic compass: c′-f′′′. Decal (oak leaf cartouche) with manufacturer's symbol: TRADE [harlequin blowing a curved horn above a lyre] MARK.

52 cm.

232-233

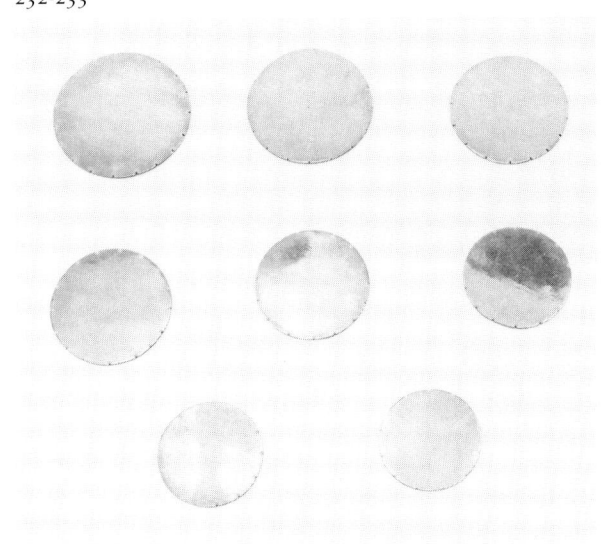

250

234 and 252
Glockenspiel, Portable (Bell Lyra)
France?

Single row of thirteen flat, rectangular steel bars, graduated in length; brass lyre-shaped tubular frame with eagle's head ornaments at finials. Compass: c′-g′′ with seven extra bars (252 A-G). Backs of bars stamped: 23.

72 x 53 cm.

249
Keyboard Glockenspiel ("Parition Mustel")
Paris, 19th century, last quarter
Victor Mustel

Twenty-four flat, rectangular metal bars, arranged in keyboard sequence. Chromatic compass: c′-b′′. Hammer action activated by boxwood button keyboard (dark stained accidentals). Felt-covered hammers strike bars from beneath. Case lid missing.

c′ Bar: V. MUSTEL / BTE. S.G.D.G.

48.5 x 33 x 10 cm.

249

Bells

173
Bell Tree
France or Germany? 19th century

Two rows of bell metal cup-shaped bells of different pitch, thirteen diatonic (one missing) and eleven chromatic (compass: b♭-b″♭), suspended on wooden rods; brass fittings; painted (gold) stand. A light metal beater (missing) is passed over the edges of the bells producing a glissando effect.

⌀, Bells: 4-8 cm.
L, Holder: 43 cm.

183
Resting Bell
Rome, 1902

Bell metal; dark stained walnut box resonator.

⌀, Bell: 9.1 cm.
Resonator: 12.9 x 9.3 x 8.3 cm.

261
Disk-Gong
Italy?

Iron. Reproduction of supposed antique instrument.

⌀: 25.5 cm.

103 to 107
Clapper Bells (Cowbells)
Switzerland?

Hammered brass sheets, bent and soldered. Quadrilateral shape.

H: 12.2; 11.4; 12.1; 12.7; 12.9 cm.

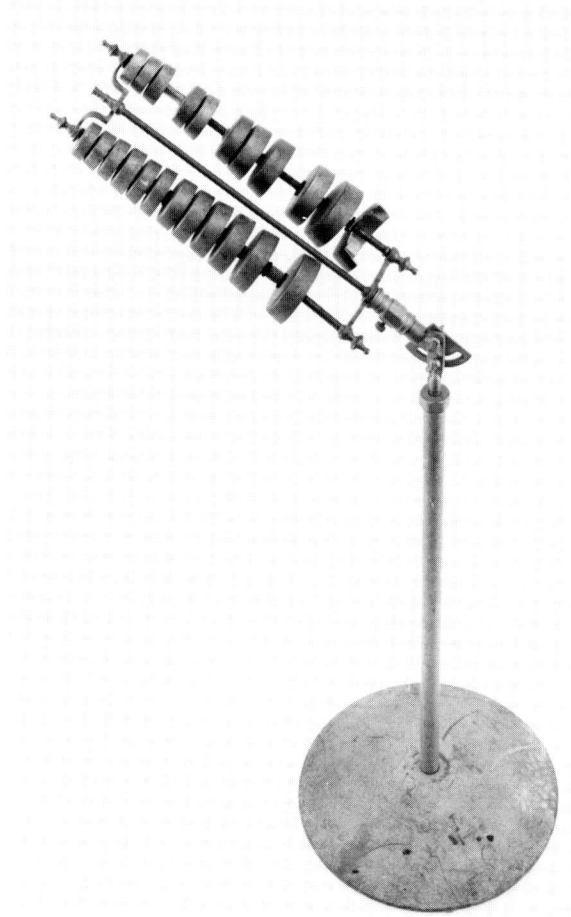

173

183

160

108
Clapper Bells
France?

Three bell metal bells; oak yoke; brass handle. Bells pitched: E♭, F, G.

⌀, Bells: 12; 12.1; 12.5 cm.
L, Yoke: 34.8 cm.

116
Clapper Bells (Communion Bells)
Germany?

Three bronze bells; cup-shaped iron holder, handle.

⌀, Holder: 10.2 cm.   H: 14.2 cm.

118
Clapper Bell (Church Bell)
Germany?

Brass, decoratively cast with vinestem decoration, symbols and names of the four evangelists: MATHEUS: JOHANNES: LUCAS: MARCUS.

⌀: 11.5 cm.   H: 15 cm.

118

126
Clapper Bell (Goat Bell)
Italy?

Brass, with decorative bands. Leather cord.

⌀: 6 cm.   H: 11.7 cm.

127
Clapper Bell (Cowbell)
Italy?

Hammered brass sheets, riveted together. Quadrilateral shape.

⌀: 8 cm.   H: 12.9 cm.

143
Clapper Bell (Library Bell)
Italy?

Three decoratively cast brass sections, threaded joints. Bell section contains a reservoire with perforated top for sand; mid-section with compartment for writing quills; handle.

⌀: 17.2 cm.   H: 15.1 cm.

143

147
Clapper Bell (Cowbell)
Switzerland?

Painted (black, blue, white) and glazed earthenware. Damaged.

⌀: 8.7 x 4.7 cm.   H: 8.9

172
Clapper Bells
France? late 19th century

Set of twenty-five bronze hand bells; brass clappers (decoratively cast) and mounts; leather and felt bushings; leather handles stamped with pitches.

⌀: 4-8 cm.

174
Clapper Bells (Clochette de Timon)
Italy?

Two nickel-plated brass bells placed edge to edge, two clappers; nickel-plated handle and mount.

⌀, Larger Bell: 7.5 cm.   H: 13.2 cm.

174

181
Clapper Bells (Communion Bells)
Germany?

Four brass bells, brass holder with four spokes and handle. Four small brass crucifix decorations.

⌀, Bells: 5.2-6.2 cm.
L, Holder: 22.4 cm.

185-202
Clapper Bells
Bradford (GB), 19th century
J. Shaw Sons & Co.

Set of eighteen bronze hand bells; brass clappers and mounts; leather and felt bushings; leather handles stamped with pitches.

J. SHAW SON & CO. / LEEDS ROAD / BRADFORD

⌀: 7.5-14.2 cm.

110
Pellet Bells
Florence, late 19th century
Leopoldo Franciolini shop

Twelve brass bells of various sizes; painted (red) wooden oval holder with handle. Damaged. (See Ripin: 39, illus. 2.)

⌀, Bells: 4-8.5 cm.
⌀, Holder: 40 x 35.3 cm.   L, Handle: 37 cm.

113
Pellet Bells, Tuned
Italy or France? 19th century

Twelve to seventeen nickel-plated brass pellet bells attached to eleven black leather straps, handles stamped with pitches: LA, LA♯, SI, DO, DO♯, RE♯, MI, FA, FA♯, SOL, SOL♯; end of each strap with decorative bell (without clapper). Boxwood beater (one side leather-covered) with cane handle.

⌀, Bells: 2.5-3.2 cm.   L, Straps: 90 cm.

164
Pellet Bell (Animal Bell)
Italy?

Decoratively cast brass.

⌀: 4.4 cm.   H: 5.8 cm.

166
Pellet Bell (Animal Bell)
Italy?

Nickle-plated brass.

⌀: 5.4 cm.   H: 12.1 cm.

181

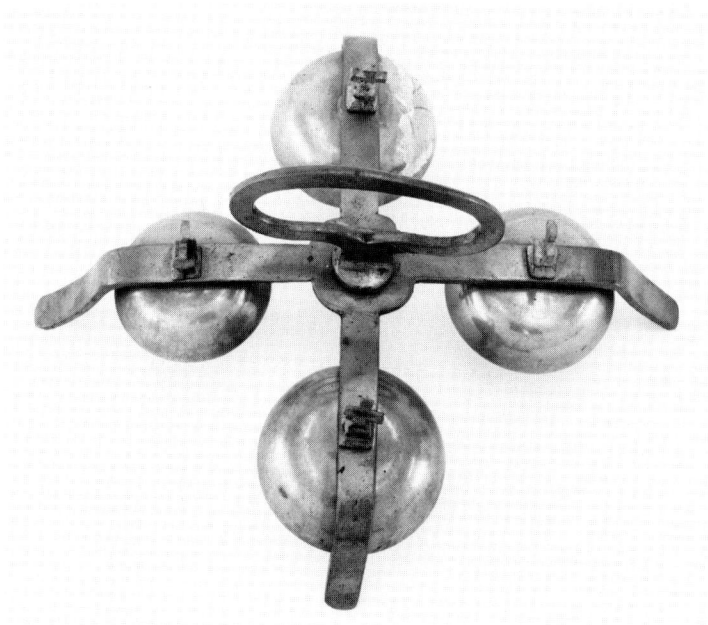

172
Pellet Bells (Harness Bells)
Italy?

Three nickel-plated brass bells; nickel-plated metal holder with three spokes; leather strap with metal buckle.

⌀: 5.5 cm. H, Holder: 12.4 cm.

176
Clapper and Pellet Bells (Harness Bells)
Italy?

Two nickel-plated clapper bells placed edge to edge, two clappers; four nickel-plated pellet bells; nickel-plated metal holder with four spokes, threaded mount at base.

⌀, Clapper Bells: 5.4 cm.
⌀, Pellet Bells: 4 cm.   W, Holder: 14.4 cm.

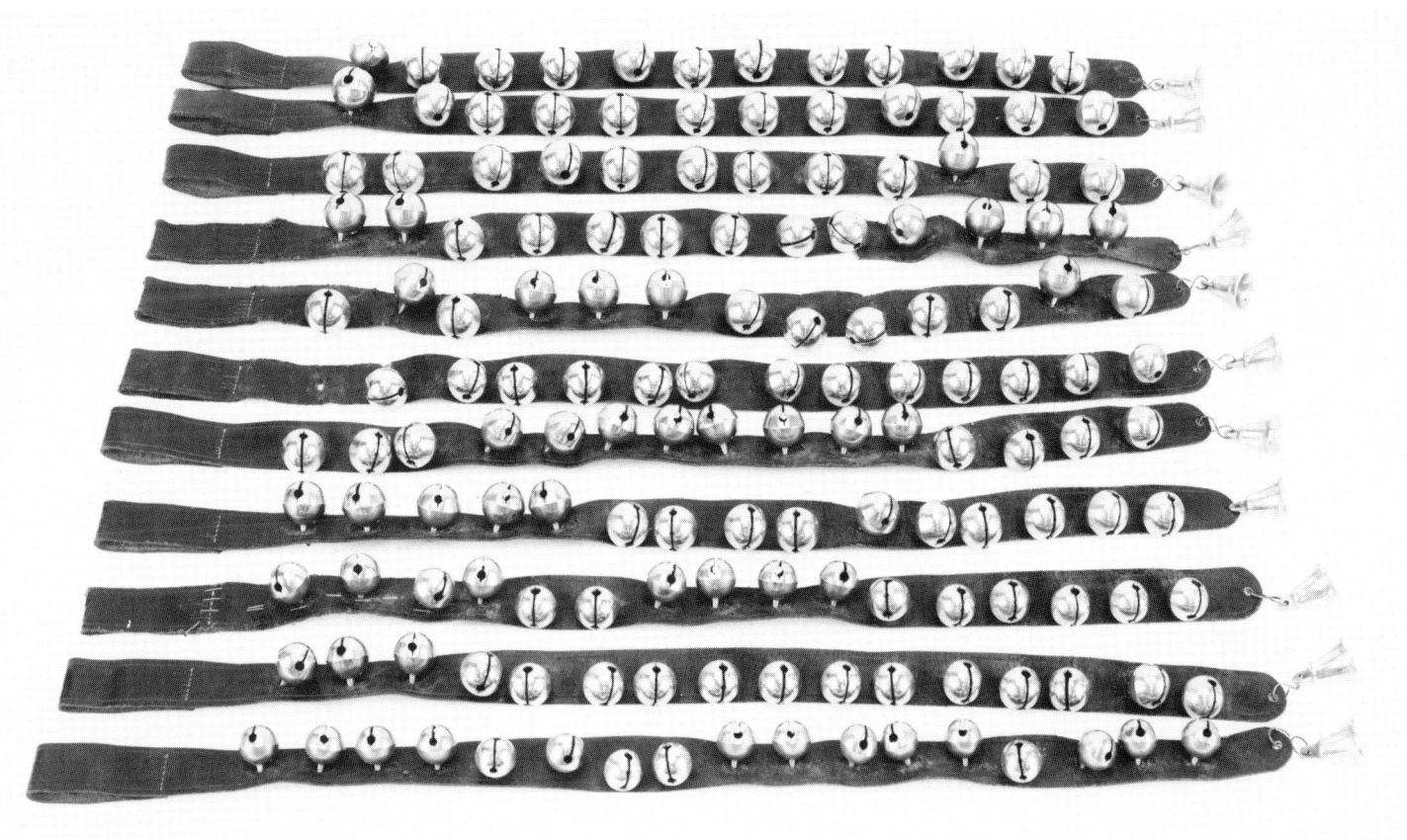

Crescents, Rattles

256
Crescent
Italy?

Upright steel pole (missing); painted (black) wooden handle; ornamental headpiece with decorative brass ball, bell-shaped ornament with four small pellet bells, tin crescent with four small pellet bells; two "horsetails."

H: 52.7 cm. (extant section)

257
Crescent
Florence, late 19th century
Leopoldo Franciolini shop

Upright painted (red) wooden pole with leather handle; ornamental headpiece with decorative brass crescent, ball, inverted cone with eight small pellet bells and eight small clapper bells (three missing), lyre with two pellet bells (one missing), large crescent with eight pellet bells (one missing) and ten clapper bells (one missing); two "horsetails." (See Ripin: 39, illus. 2.)

H: 153 cm.

259
Crescent
Italy?

Upright pole (missing); ornamental headpiece with decorative brass ball, crescent with four small clapper bells, bell-shaped ornament with four small clapper bells; two "horsetails." Similar to 256.

H: 40.3 (extant section)

257

68
Sliding Rattle (Triccaballaca)
Italy?

Three boxwood hammers on rods atttached to a frame. When shaken, outer hammers strike fixed middle hammer.

H: 33 cm.   W: 21 cm.

69
Sliding Rattle (Triccaballaca)
Italy?

Three black walnut hammers on rods attached to a frame. Similar to 68.

H: 42.4 cm.   W: 32.1 cm.

81
Scraped Stick without Resonator
Italy?

Notched oak stick, varnished handle. Thirteen sets of tin jingle nailed to the corpus; small clapper bell at top.

67.8 cm.

75
Cog Rattle (Boatswain's Rattle)
U.S.A., before 1848

Walnut cogwheel, tongue, and bulbous housing; brass mounting plates. Tongue strikes cog when crank is turned.

L: 33.5 cm.   W: 13 cm.

76
Cog Rattle (Boatswain's Rattle)
U.S.A.?

Two oak cogwheels; two painted (black) wooden tongues; painted (black) oak frame and handle with decorative turnings. Tongues strike cogs when player whirls the instrument.

33.3 cm.

77
Cog Rattle (Toy)
England?

Two pine cogwheels, two tongues, painted (red, brown) frame and handle.

19 cm.

78
Cog Rattle (Watchman's Rattle)
England?

Dark stained oak cogwheel, tongue, frame, and handle with decorative turnings.

24.4 cm.

69

76

Nail Violin,
Jew's Harp,
Blown Plaques

413
Nail Violin
Germany?

Semicircular maple resonator with two small f-holes; flat spruce top. Twelve iron nails around circumference, pitched: f′♯, g′♯, a′♯, b′, c′′♯, d′′♯, e′′, f′′♯, g′′♯, a′′♯, b′′, d′′′♯.

H, Nails: 3.5-7 cm.
Resonator: 20 x 12.5 cm.

1960
Jew's Harp
U.S.A.?

Iron.

18 cm.

428
Blown Plaques
England?

Two convex nickel-plated tin disks crimped together, small aperture. The player hums into the instrument; sympathetic vibration of disks modifies and amplifies the sound of the voice.

⌀: 7 cm.

429
Blown Plaques
France?

Two convex boxwood disks, small aperture.

⌀: 6.8 cm.

413

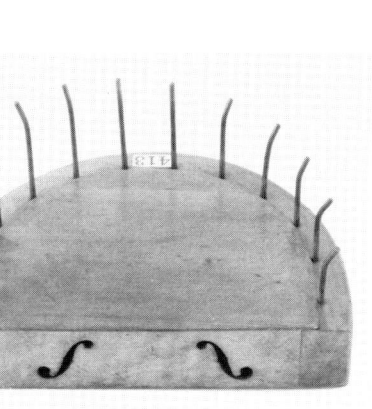

1960

429

Bibliography

Heyde 1978 — Heyde, Herbert. *Flöten. Musikinstrumenten-Museum der Karl-Marx Universität Leipzig, Katalog.* Vol. 1. Leipzig: VEB Deutscher Verlag für Musik, 1978.

Heyde 1980 — _____. *Trompeten, Posaunen, Tuben. Musikinstrumenten-Museum der Karl-Marx Universität Leipzig, Katalog.* Vol. 3. Leipzig: VEB Deutscher Verlag für Musik, 1980.

Heyde 1982 — _____. *Hörner und Zinken. Musikinstrumenten-Museum der Karl-Marx Universität Leipzig, Katalog.* Vol. 5. Leipzig: VEB Deutscher Verlag für Musik, 1982.

Langwill — Langwill, Lyndesay G. *An Index of Musical Wind-Instrument Makers.* 6th rev. ed. Edinburgh, Scotland: L. G. Langwill, 1980.

Ripin — Ripin, Edwin M. *The Instrument Catalogs of Leopoldo Franciolini.* Music Indexes and Bibliographies, no. 9. Hackensack: Joseph Boonin, 1974.

Stanley — Stanley, Albert A. *Catalogue of the Stearns Collection of Musical Instruments.* 2d ed. Ann Arbor: The University of Michigan Press, 1921.

Warner 1968 — Warner, Robert A., and von Huene, Friedrich. "A Jacob Denner Recorder in the United States of America." *Galpin Society Journal* 21 (1968): 88-85.

Warner 1970 — _____. "The Baroque Recorders in the Stearns Collection of Musical Instruments." *Galpin Society Journal* 23 (1970): 69-81.

Young — Young, Phillip T. *Twenty-Five Hundred Historical Woodwind Instruments: An Inventory of the Major Collections.* New York: Pendragon Press, 1982.

Index 1
*Maker or Dealer,
Location in Catalogue,
Accession Number*

Abbate, A., & Figlio, 106 (842), 107 (921)
Adler (shop), 58 (680)
Altrichter, (Ferdinand) Julius (Hermann), 135 (936)
Ammann, Ulrich, 40 (642)

Baack, Edward, 51 (671)
Bader, J., & Co., 139 (948)
Bainbridge, William, 13 (515)
Banks, J. & H., 56 (678)
Baudel, Maurice, 15 (587)
Bechonnet. Effiat, 67 (693)
Bernareggi, 79 (931)
Besson, 149 (1437)
Besson, Fontaine, 95 (857), 113 (840 891), 139 (940)
Besson & Co. Ltd., 110 (887), 126 (1560), 127 (1561)
Bleszner, Au., 11 (1591)
Boosey & Co., 58 (681)
Buescher Band Instrument Co., 46 (1787 1797)
Buffet, Auger, jeune, 44 (635)
Buffet, Crampon & Cie., 21 (1499), 24 (1627), 43 (631), 44 (639), 45 (638), 52 (1780)

Cahusac, Thomas, 17 (560), 49 (665)
Camp, William, 22 (1912)
Chappel, S. Arthur, 140 (949)
Christman, C. G., 33 (621)
Cloos, George, 30 (1921)
Coeffet, Jean-Baptiste, 78 (899)
Colas, Michel, & Cie., 151 (388)
Colas, Prosper, 9 (503 504)
Conn and Dupont, 122 (860)
Conn, C.G., Ltd., 37 (1798), 48 (1796)
Courtois, Antoine, 130 (869)
Courtois, Antoine-[Auguste] Mille, 88 (885), 119 (894)
Courtois Frère, 87 (882)
Couturier, père, 101 (850)

D'Almaine & Co., 13 (516)
Darche, 78 (934)
David, Louis, 79 (933)
Denner, Jacob, 10 (506)
Distin, Henry, & Co., 129 (867)
Doerfel, 72 (727)
Dubois & Couturier, 79 (902)
Dürrschmidt, C. W., 87 (883)

Dumont, Pierre, 36 (1793)

Ebblewhite, John Henry, & Son, 21 (565)
Eschenbach, Franz, 40 (822)

Fiehn, H., 10 (483)
Firth, Hall & Pond, 18 (1498), 20 (1500)
Firth, Pond & Co., 18 (1908)
Fische, N. I.(?), 10 (507)
Fischer, Carl (dealer), 35 (1739)
Franciolini, Leopoldo (dealer), 39 (628), 56 (677), 65 (661), 66 (688), 75 (829 830 832), 76 (834, 835, 836), 77 (903), 78 (923), 111 (889), 162 (110), 164 (257)

Gautrot, Pierre Louis, 62 (686), 134 (944)
Geipel, Christoph, 61 (684)
Graves & Co., 94 (855)
Grenser, (Johann) Heinrich, 32 (615), 42 (633)
Gretch Co., 15 (1822)
Günter, 73 (735)
Gunkel, Henry, 32 (618), 120 (853)

Halary, Jules-Léon Antoine, 43 (630)
Hall and Quinby, 121 (856)
Harmony Co., 153 (1496)
Hawkes, William Henry, & Sons, 24 (1652)
Haynes, The William S., Co., 38 (1848, 1849)
Heckel, Wilhelm H., 52 (1654)
Heckel (shop), 60 (683 1744)
Henderson, Peter, 68 (696)
Hesse, Wilhelm, 41 (634)
Higham, Joseph, 128 (1904)
Holly, Anton, 101 (865)
Holton, Frank, & Co., 46 (1795, 1799), 48 (1791)
Humphrey, Guy, Paris: 36 (1794)

Jehring, Julius, 59 (1558)
Johnson, J. S., 149 (1438)

Kazoo Co., 156 (423)
Keat, Henry and Sons, 91 (852), 116 (892)
Kersten, Johann Gottfried, 84 (847)
Key, Thomas, 34 (617), 57 (679)
Klemm & Bro. (dealer), 18 (1911)
Klüh, 92 (848)
Koch, Stephen, 51 (669), 53 (672)
Kodisch, Johann Carl, 99 (825)
Koenig, Rudolph, 158 (250)

Köhler (Kohler), John Augustus, 123 (863)
Kohlert, Vincent, Söhn, 23 (1650), 36 (1593)
Kruspe, Franz Carl, 11 (508)
Kruspe, Johann Eduard, 114 (893), 119 (895)
Kruspe, Carl, 45 (636)

Labbaye, Jacques Christophe, fils, 100 (884)
Langhamer, C. Anton, 138 (945)
Laurent, Claude, 18 (571)
Lawson, Joseph, 17 (561)
Lecomte, Arsène-Zoé, & Cie., 58 (682)
Leriche, A., 84 (875)
Lindenberg, C. F., 91 (823)
Löhner, J. A., 19 (1928)
Loomis, Allen, 47 (1596)
Lyon and Healy (dealer), 18 (1910)

Mahillon, B., jeune, 92 (847)
Mahillon, Charles, & Cie., 46 (640), 62 (685), 116 (1363)
Mangeant, 54 (675)
Martin Frères, 32 (1493, formerly 616 A), 35 (1556)
Mathieu, Charles, 14 (512 575), 40 (643)
Mazzetti, A. E., 16 (484)
Meinhold, Gebr., 73 (731)
Messner, Ch., & Cie., 73 (730)
Metzler, Valentin, 31 (616)
Meyer, Heinrich Friedrich, 23 (569)
Michaud, Nic.-Firmin, 131 (871)
Mignolet, Jean, 26 (1653)
Mollenhauer, Johann, 34 (622)
Monzani, Tebaldo, 20 (562 563)
Müller, Louis, 92 (845)
Müster, 72 (728)
Mustel, Victor, 159 (249)

Palanca, Carlo, 17 (558)
Parsons, Chas. H., & Co. (dealer), 115 (1962)
Payne, G. C., 23 (567)
Pelitti, Giuseppe, 11 (502), 64 (599, 656), 82 (782), 96 (803, 805, 819, 820, 898, 1368), 102 (817), 103 (910), 109 (924, 925, 1354, 1357), 119 (1356), 140 (913), 141 (1358, 1360), 142 (809, 916), 144 (1361), 145 (876), 147 (1353), 148 (919, 920)
Peloubet, C., 22 (573)
Penzel & Müller, 38 (1788, 1789, 1790)
Périnet, Etienne Francois, 82 (810)
Petrus Asina Longa, 98 (804)

Potter, Henry, & Co., 132 (939)
Potter, Richard, 21 (564)
Potter, William Henry, 23 (566)
Proser, 17 (561)

Raoux, Marcel-Auguste, 86 (880)
Riley, Edward, 32 (1555)
Riva, Giacinto, 51 (668)
Riviére & Hawkes, 129 (868)
Roedel, Johann Josef, 25 (568)
Rossano Fratelli, 104 (1359)
Roth, Charles, 45 (637)
Rottenburgh, Jean-Hyacinth-Joseph, 51 (667)

Sambruna, Camillo, 105 (840), 142 (811), 146 (1362)
Sattler, Johann Cornelius, 9 (505)
Sauerhering, H., 37 (625)
Saurle, Michael, 100 (821)
Savary, Jean-Nicolas, jeune, 57 (1743)
Sax, Adolphe (Antoine Joseph), 45 (637), 47 (641), 89 (937), 94 (844), 116 (896), 132 (900)
Sax, Henri, 62 (687)
Schadenberg, Franz, 58 (1742)
Schilke Co., 99 (1759)
Schmidt, Johann Gottlob, 111 (888)
Schmittschneider, André Antony, 115 (897)
Schoelnast, F., 42 (632)
Schoenhut Co., 158 (245)
Schreiber Cornet Mfg. Co., 129 (1494, formerly 586 A)
Seidel, Joseph, 39 (629)
Selmer, Henrit et Cie., 37 (1739)
Selmer Co., 46 (1792)
Shaw, J., & Co., 162 (185-202)
Souvé, 11 (576)
Stowasser, Ignaz, 123 (866)

Tabard, F., 12 (509)
Teschner, R., : 16 (482)
Thibouville-Buffet, 25 (570)
Thibouville-Lamy, (Louis-Emile) Jerôme, 35 (1557, formerly 629 A)
Triébert, père, Guillaume, 54 (674, 676)
Tourraine et Cie., 102 (1741)

Uhlmann, Leopold, 102 (841)
Uhlmann, Leopold, & Sohn, 136 (947)

Walch, Paul, 29 (581)
Wallis, Joseph, & Sons Ltd., 138 (946)
White, N. H., & Co., 139 (1934)
Whitney, C. J., & Co. (dealer), 123 (864)
Willame, 34 (620)
Wilson, Harry (dealer), 130 (870)
Wright, Elbridge G., 138 (1784)
Wurlitzer, Rudolph, and Bro., 121 (858)

York, J. W., and Sons, 113 (1968)

Zencker, J. G., 31 (614)

Index 2
Stearns Collection Accession Number : Page Number in Catalogue

67: 157	198: 162	468: 14	574: 27	652: 64
68: 165	199: 162	469: 14	575: 14	653: 64
69: 165		470: 14	576: 11	654: 64
70: 157	200: 162	471: 14	578: 28	655: 64
71: 157	201: 162	473: 15	579: 28	656: 64
75: 165	202: 162	474: 15	580: 29	657: 65
76: 165	214: 158	480: see 474	581: 29	658: 65
77: 165	232: 158	481: 15	582: 30	659: 65
78: 165	233: 158	482: 16	583: 26	660: 65
81: 165	234: 159	483: 16	585: 26	661: 65
98: 157	245: 158	484: 16	586: 27	665: 49
	249: 159	485: 16	587: 15	666: 51
103: 160	250: 158	486: 13	594: 48	667: 51
104: 160	252: 159	486 A: see 1471	595: 48	668: 51
105: 160	256: 164	487: 13	596: 48	669: 51
106: 160	257: 164	489: 14	597: 48	670: 52
107: 160	259: 164	493: 11	598: 49	671: 51
108: 161	261: 160		599: 64	672: 53
110: 162		502: 11		673: 54
113: 162	314: 153	503: 9	613: 71	674: 54
116: 161	385: 152	504: 9	614: 31	675: 55
118: 161	386: 152	505: 9	615: 32	676: 55
122: see 113	387: 152	506: 10	616: 31	677: 56
126: 161	388: 151	507: 10	616 A: see 1493	678: 56
127: 161	388 A: see 1468	508: 11	617: 34	679: 57
143: 161	393: 153	509: 12	618: 32	680: 58
147: 161	397: 153	510 A: see 1472	620: 34	681: 58
164: 162	399: 153	511: 12	621: 33	682: 58
166: 162		512: 14	622: 34	683: 60
167: 157	400: 153	513: 11	623: 34	684: 61
172: 163	401: 154	513 A: see 1591	624: 36	685: 62
173: 161	404: 154	515: 13	625: 37	686: 62
174: 161	405: 154	516: 13	626: 33	687: 62
176: 163	410: 154	558: 17	628: 39	688: 66
181: 162	411: 154	559: 26	629: 39	691: 66
182: 157	412: 154	560: 17	629 A: see 1557	692: 67
183: 160	413: 166	561: 17	630: 43	693: 67
185: 162	420: 155	561 A: see 1473	631: 43	694: 67
186: 162	421: 155	562: 20	632: 42	695: 68
187: 162	423: 156	563: 20	633: 42	696: 68
188: 162	424: 156	564: 21	634: 41	697: 68
189: 162	425: 156	565: 21	635: 44	698: see 697
190: 162	426: 156	566: 23	636: 45	699: 70
191: 162	427: 156	567: 23	637: 45	
192: 162	428: 166	568: 25	638: 45	700: 71
193: 162	429: 166	569: 23	639: 44	712: 49
194: 162	446: 28	570: 25	640: 46	713: 73
195: 162	452: 14	571: 18	641: 47	719: 74
196: 162	466: 14	572: 18	642: 40	726: 72
197: 162	467: 14	573: 22	643: 40	727: 72

728: 72	838: 102	887: 110	937: 89	1494: 124	1789: 38
729: 72	839: 102	887 A: see 1478	939: 133	1496: 153	1790: 38
730: 73	840: 105	888: 111	940: 136	1498: 18	1791: 48
731: 73	841: 102	889: 111	941: 136	1499: 21	1792: 46
732: 73	842: 106	890: 112	942: 133		1793: 36
733: 74	844: 94	891: 113	943: 136	1500: 20	1794: 36
734: 74	845: 92	892: 116	944: 134	1507: 14	1795: 46
735: 73	846: 92	893: 114	945: 138	1552: 29	1796: 48
736: 74	847: 93	894: 119	946: 138	1554: 27	1797: 46
768: 81	848: 93	895: 119	947: 136	1555: 32	1798: 37
773: 81	849: 94	896: 116	948: 139	1556: 35	1799: 46
777: 81	850: 101	897: 115	949: 140	1557: 35	
779: 81	851: 83	898: 96		1558: 59	1822: 15
780: 82	852: 91	899: 78	1352: 147	1559: 125	1847: 33
781: 82	853: 120		1353: 147	1560: 126	1848: 38
782: 82	854: 120	900: 132	1354: 109	1561: 127	1849: 38
791: 80	855: 94	901: 132	1355: 97	1591: 11	
792: 80	856: 121	902: 79	1356: 119	1592: 17	1904: 128
	857: 95	903: 77	1357: 109	1593: 36	1905: 22
803: 96	858: 121	904: 144	1358: 141	1596: 47	1906: 22
804: 98	859: 121	905: 148	1359: 104		1907: 22
805: 96	860: 122	906: 148	1360: 141	1616: 19	1908: 18
807: 82	861: 122	908: 142	1361: 144	1626: 25	1909: 18
808: 82	862: 122	909: 144	1362: 146	1627: 24	1910: 18
809: 142	863: 123	910: 103	1363: 116	1628: 24	1911: 18
810: 82	863 A: see 1559	911: 105	1364: 96	1648: 14	1912: 22
811: 142	864: 123	912: 142	1365: 145	1650: 23	1913: 22
812: 143	864 A: see 1560	913: 140	1366: 142	1651: 22	1914: 24
813: 83	865: 101	914: 143	1365: 145	1652: 24	1915: 29
814: 83	866: 123	915: 143	1366: 142	1653: 26	1916: 30
816: 83	867: 129	916: 142	1367: 142	1654: 52	1917: 29
817: 102	868: 129	917: 142	1368: 142	1665: 35	1918: 30
818: 83	869: 130	918: 145	1369: 144		1919: 30
819: 96	870: 130	919: 148	1370: 138	1721: 19	1920: 30
820: 96	871: 131	920: 148	1371: 97	1737: 37	1921: 30
821: 100	872: 131	921: 107	1372: 147	1738: 35	1922: 30
822: 90	873: 131	922: 144	1373: 80	1739: 35	1923: 30
823: 91	874: 84	923: 78		1740: 127	1928: 19
825: 99	875: 84	924: 109	1435: 149	1741: 102	1934: 139
827: 100	876: 145	925: 109	1436: 149	1742: 58	1960: 166
828: 103	877: 104	926: 146	1437: 149	1743: 57	1962: 115
829: 75	878: 84	928: 146	1438: 149	1744: 60	1968: 113
830: 75	879: 86	929: 147	1466: 150	1759: 99	1971: 105
831: 75	880: 86	930: 141	1468: 151	1780: 52	1993: 31
832: 75	881: 86	931: 79	1471: 13	1782: 52	1994: 80
833: 76	882: 87	932: 132	1472: 27	1783: 39	
834: 76	883: 87	933: 79	1473: 18	1784: 138	
835: 76	884: 100	934: 78	1475: 26	1785: 95	
836: 76	885: 88	935: 77	1478: 111	1787: 46	
837: 102	886: 88	936: 135	1493: 32	1788: 38	